THE **BOOK** OF

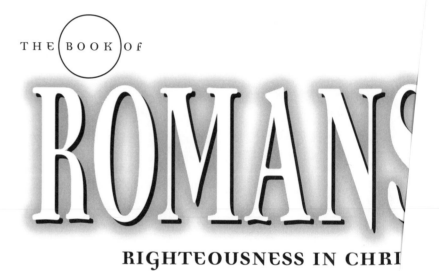

ROMANS

RIGHTEOUSNESS IN CHRI

AMG *Publishers*

CHATTANOOGA, TENNESSEE

TWENTY-FIRST CENTURY
BIBLICAL COMMENTARY SERIES

THE BOOK OF

ROMANS

RIGHTEOUSNESS IN CHRIST

WOODROW
KROLL

GENERAL EDITORS

MAL COUCH & ED HINDSON

Unless otherwise noted, Scripture quotes are taken from the NEW AMERICAN STANDARD BIBLE, Copyright © 1960, 1962, 1963, 1968, 1971, 1972, 1973, 1975, 1977, by the Lockman Foundation. Used by permission. (www.Lockman.org)
Scriptures marked KJV are from the King James Version of the Bible.
Scriptures marked NIV are from the HOLY BIBLE, NEW INTERNATIONAL VERSION®. NIV®. Copyright © 1973, 1978, 1984 by International Bible Society. Used by permission of Zondervan. All rights reserved.

ISBN 0-89957-814-4

Cover Design by Phillip Rodgers
Editing and Text Design by Warren Baker
Editorial assistance provided by Weller Editorial Services, Chippewa Lake, MI

Printed in the United States of America
19 18 17 16 15 –R– 10 9 8 7 6 5

*To all followers of Christ today who,
like the Roman believers of Paul's day,
face persecution, famine, and even death
just because they are Christians*

Twenty-First Century Biblical Commentary Series

Mal Couch, Th.D., and Ed Hindson, D.Phil.

The New Testament has guided the Christian Church for over two thousand years. This one testament is made up of twenty-seven books, penned by godly men through the inspiration of the Holy Spirit. It tells us of the life of Jesus Christ, His atoning death for our sins, His miraculous resurrection, His ascension back to heaven, and the promise of His second coming. It also tells the story of the birth and growth of the Church and the people and principles that shaped it in its earliest days. The New Testament concludes with the book of Revelation pointing ahead to the glorious return of Jesus Christ.

Without the New Testament, the message of the Bible would be incomplete. The Old Testament emphasizes the promise of a coming Messiah. It constantly points us ahead to the One who is coming to be the King of Israel and the Savior of the world. But the Old Testament ends with this event still unfulfilled. All of its ceremonies, pictures, types, and prophecies are left awaiting the arrival of the "Lamb of God who takes away the sin of the world!" (John 1:29).

The message of the New Testament represents the timeless truth of God. As each generation seeks to apply that truth to its specific context, an up-to-date commentary needs to be created just for them. The editors and authors of the Twenty-First Century Biblical Commentary Series have endeavored to do just that. This team of scholars represents conservative, evangelical, and dispensational scholarship at its best. The individual authors may differ on minor points of interpretation, but all are convinced that the Old and New Testaments teach a dispensational framework for biblical history. They also hold to a pretribulational and premillennial understanding of biblical prophecy.

The French scholar René Pache reminded each succeeding generation, "If the power of the Holy Spirit is to be made manifest anew among us, it is of primary importance that His message should regain its due place. Then we shall be able to put the enemy to flight by the sword of the Spirit which is the Word of God."

The epistle to the Romans has long been recognized as the greatest of Paul's letters. It provides the clearest and most succinct statement on the doctrine of salvation in all the New Testament. William Tyndale's prologue to this epistle calls the book of Romans the "most excellent part of the New Testament, and the most pure gospel . . . in the whole scripture."

No book of Scripture has played a more significant role in the history of the Church. Such notables as Augustine, Martin Luther, John Bunyan, and John Wesley all referred to the impact of Romans as a significant factor in their conversion experiences. Countless others have shared similar testimonies of its influence on their personal living and their ministries.

John Murray, in the preface to his commentary on Romans, writes, "Its theme is the gospel of his grace, and the gospel bespeaks the marvels of his condescension and love. If we are not overwhelmed by the glory of that gospel and ushered into the holy of holies of God's presence, we have missed the grand purpose of this sacred deposit." This is a letter like no other letter in the New Testament. May the magnitude of its truth challenge your mind, and may the depth of its riches stir your soul.

Contents

Introduction   xi

I. Prologue: The Biblical Definition of Righteousness

1. Greetings to the Roman Christians   3
   Romans 1:1–7
2. Paul's Desire to Visit Rome   7
   Romans 1:8–16
3. The Righteous Shall Live by Faith   13
   Romans 1:17

II. Condemnation: The Human Need for Righteousness

4. Immoral People Are Condemned   21
   Romans 1:18–32
5. Moral People Are Condemned   29
   Romans 2:1–16
6. Jewish People Are Condemned   33
   Romans 2:17 — 3:8
7. All People Are Condemned   39
   Romans 3:9–20

III. Justification: The Divine Provision of Righteousness

8. Justification by Faith Explained   47
   Romans 3:21–31
9. Justification by Faith Illustrated   55
   Romans 4:1–25
10. Justification by Faith Experienced   63
    Romans 5:1–11
11. Justification by Faith Imputed   75
    Romans 5:12–21

IV. Sanctification: The Christian's Need for Holiness

12. Sanctification Explained in Principle   89
    Romans 6:1–14

13. Sanctification Explained in Practice   97
    Romans 6:15–23
14. Sanctification and the Demands of the Law   105
    Romans 7:1–6
15. Sanctification and the Battle Within   111
    Romans 7:7–25
16. Sanctification and Freedom from Sin's Power   121
    Romans 8:1–13
17. Sanctification and the Benefits of Sonship   127
    Romans 8:14–17
18. Sanctification and the Prospects for the Future 135
    Romans 8:18–30
19. Sanctification and the Power of God   145
    Romans 8:31–39

V. Redemption: The Divine Purpose for Israel

20. The Sovereignty of God and Israel's Past   153
    Romans 9:1–33
21. Human Responsibility and Israel's Present   165
    Romans 10:1–21
22. The Purpose of God and Israel's Future   175
    Romans 11:1–36

VI. Application: The Christian's Need for Biblical Living

23. Living a Life of Sacrifice   189
    Romans 12:1–8
24. Living a Life of Service   197
    Romans 12:9–21
25. Living a Life of Submission   207
    Romans 13:1–14
26. Living a Life of Sensitivity   217
    Romans 14:1 — 15:13
27. Paul's Future Plans   231
    Romans 15:14–33
28. Paul's Personal Greetings   237
    Romans 16:1–24
29. Doxology   245
    Romans 16:25–27

    Appendix: Letter Writing in the Bible   249
    Bibliography   253
    Notes   255

Introduction

No other book of the Bible more completely sets forth the great doctrines of the Christian faith than Paul's epistle to the Romans. No other writing has more powerfully confronted the human mind with the mind of God. No other book so systematically destroys human alibis, pretenses, and attempts at self-justification. In Romans, Paul's magnum opus, he thoroughly demolishes with unanswerable logic every argument a person can muster against the claims of God.

Romans has rightly been called "the Constitution of Christianity." Some refer to it as "the Christian Manifesto," and still others have dubbed it "the Cathedral of the Christian Faith." Search wherever you wish, you will find nowhere a more complete compendium of Christian doctrine. In this one letter are recorded the doctrines of justification, sanctification, divine condemnation, divine election, the perseverance of the saints, total depravity, the last judgment, the fall of man, the revelation of God in nature, the final restoration of the Jews, and so much more. This epistle stands at the head of Paul's epistles as the brazen altar did before the Holy Place. You'll remember that no one could enter the Tabernacle until having passed the brazen altar. Likewise, no one can enter the great doctrinal epistles of the New Testament without first passing Romans, for it is the gateway to New Testament truth.

Let's begin our study of this essential epistle with some questions that will aid us in understanding how it came to be written and why it fits so squarely in the middle of New Testament truth.

Who Founded the Church at Rome?

As the capital of the empire, Rome was the largest, most important city in the first-century world. Located about fifteen miles from the Mediterranean Sea, Rome was a teeming metropolis. In 1941 an inscription was discovered at Ostia that indicated that in A.D. 14 the city had a population of 4,100,000.[1]

One of the most troublesome questions about the church at Rome is its origin. Who founded it and when? Catholics the world over venerate Peter as the first pope, the founder of the church at Rome. But is that true? Can it be historically proven that Peter founded the Roman church? Some evangelical Christians lean more toward Paul as the man used by God to plant this church. But can that be proven? Actually, it is impossible to determine with great certainty who founded the church in this great metropolis. We can, however, with some degree of certainty, rule out both Peter and Paul. Here's why.

It is evident that Paul did not establish the Roman church, because in his letter to the Romans (1:10–11, 13, 15) he makes frequent reference to the fact that at the time of writing he had never been to Rome. If the apostle had not yet set foot in the great city, we can dismiss quickly any thought that he founded the church. He would have had to visit Rome, preach the gospel, lead some people to Christ, and begin a fledgling church if he was indeed the founder. But that never happened.

So what about Peter? The Catholic view, which adamantly holds to Petrine founding of the church at Rome, is based on a statement of Eusebius in his *Ecclesiastical History*, book 11, chapter 14. Today, however, it is believed that Eusebius's statement is inaccurate.

This church historian recorded that Peter went to Rome during the second year of the reign of the Roman Emperor Claudius to encounter the impostor Simon Magus, the sorcerer who tried to buy the power of the Holy Spirit (see Acts 8:18–19). The second year of the reign of Claudius was A.D. 42. We know what Eusebius said, but what does the Bible say?

In A.D. 42 Peter was still in Jerusalem, not Rome. The Bible calls him a pillar in the church of Jerusalem but never in the church in Rome (Gal. 2:9). The Bible frequently mentions him as being active in Jerusalem (see Acts 9) but never in Rome. The Bible records that he was certainly in Jerusalem up until and during the Council of Jerusalem (Acts 15). Since the Council of Jerusalem can be dated A.D. 49, the Bible places Peter squarely in the thick of things at Jerusalem, and thus it would have been highly unlikely for Peter to have been in residence in Rome earlier than that.

But there's more. In the salutation of the last chapter of Romans, Paul greets twenty-seven individuals living in Rome by name. But where is Peter's name? If Peter was bishop of the church by that time, why did Paul not greet him as well? It would have been an apostolic faux pas to greet so many people individually by name and forget to mention Peter, especially if he was the head of the church. It doesn't seem likely Paul would make such a mistake. It is more likely that Peter was not in Rome even when Paul penned his epistle to the Romans.

Still, the Bible says more. Luke has been demonstrated to be the most accurate historian of the first century A.D.[2] If Peter, as prominent as he was, had founded the church at Rome, how could Luke have overlooked such an important fact in recording the history of the early church in Acts? Would such an oversight be possible? Or is it more likely that Luke didn't record it because it didn't happen?

In addition, there's that pesky statement of Paul recorded in Romans 15:20: "I aspired to preach the gospel, not where Christ was already named, that I might not build upon another man's foundation." Set aside any biases or preconceived notions. If Peter had founded the church at Rome, why was Paul so eager to preach there (Rom. 1:15)? Why would he want to go to a city where the gospel had already taken root? That was clearly contrary to his stated objectives. The only answer is to accept what the Bible implies: Neither Peter nor Paul established the Roman church.

Then who did? We don't know, but two possibilities should at least be considered. First, it is possible that those who founded the Roman church were just simple believers who were present on the Day of Pentecost. Acts 2:9–11 mentions that among those in Jerusalem on that eventful day were "visitors from Rome, both Jews and proselytes" (v. 10). Perhaps those believing Jews and proselytes carried their new faith back to the imperial city and started the church there. Even if it's not as romantic, at least this explanation has solid biblical possibilities.

Second, it may be that families from churches Paul or others planted in Asia Minor migrated west and settled in Rome. Discovering the faith of one another (as Christians often do), they may have gathered together to worship independent of the Jewish synagogues and thus started the first church at Rome. This, too, has solid biblical possibilities.

The church at Rome apparently owed its origin to the migration of Christians from the eastern part of the empire who were converted through their contact with the gospel there. It is generally accepted that when Paul wrote Romans there was a church of considerable size at Rome.

Was the Roman Church Jewish?

The contents of this epistle make it evident that the Roman church was composed of both Jews and Gentiles. There was a Jewish community in Rome as early as the second century B.C. It was greatly enlarged by Pompey's conquest of Judea in 63 B.C. when Jewish prisoners of war were marched into Rome in his grand procession. Cicero makes reference to the size and influence of the Jewish colony in Rome in 59 B.C. (*Pro Flacco* 66). In A.D.19 the Jews of Rome were expelled from the city by a decree of Emperor Tiberius. Another mass expulsion took place during the reign of Emperor Claudius (A.D.41–54). It was by this edict that Aquila and Priscilla were forced to migrate to Corinth where they encountered Paul (Acts 18:2). But the effects of this expulsion order were temporary. Less than three years after the death of Claudius, Paul wrote to the Jewish Christians in Rome, speaking of their faith as a matter of common knowledge. The original nucleus of the church must have been Jewish.

Some scholars argue that the composition of the Roman church remained Jewish throughout its early years. Notably, Theodor Zahn maintains that "in Rome the Gentile Christians constituted a comparatively small minority."[3] However, the Bible hints that the Gentile element in the Roman church was predominant at the time of Paul's writing. Even though he addressed the Jews in 4:1 when he spoke of Abraham as "our forefather according to the flesh," there are many direct references to the Gentiles in the letter. In Paul's introduction, he spoke of the "obedience of faith among all the Gentiles" (1:5). He desired fruit among the Romans, "even as among the rest of the Gentiles" (1:13). After reviewing God's dealings with Israel in chapters 9—11, it is to the Gentiles that Paul gives concluding admonitions: "But I am speaking to you who are Gentiles" (11:13). Later when he wrote to the Philippians from Rome, Paul intimated that it was among the Gentiles that the gospel had chiefly taken hold in Rome (Phil. 1:13; 4:22). By the time he wrote this epistle, the church that had begun in Jewish hearts had taken on a decidedly Gentile tone, and Paul, as the apostle to the Gentiles, had to be pleased.

Where Was Paul When He Wrote the Letter?

The contents of the epistle to the Romans indicate that it was written from Corinth on Paul's third missionary journey. Again, ask yourself, "What does the Bible say?" The events of this epistle fit perfectly into the chronology of Acts 20:1–5. Paul's eastern journeys were over; his face was set toward the West (Acts 19:21; Rom. 15:23–24). At this time, Paul was heading to Jerusalem with the collection for the poor (Rom. 15:24–27) after his three-month visit to Corinth (Acts 24:17). The apostle emphasized this collection in his letters to the Corinthian Christians (see 1 Cor. 6:1–4; 2 Cor. 8:9). "The reference to Cenchrea (Rom. 16:1), the port of Corinth, and the recommendation of Phoebe, a servant of the church there, who apparently was about to depart for Rome (and apparently carried the letter with her), are further indications of the apostle's whereabouts when he wrote the letter."[4]

We conclude, then, that Romans must have been written only a bit later than the Corinthian epistles. When Paul wrote the letter, he mentioned that

Timothy, Sosipater, Gaius, and Erastus were with him (Rom. 16:21–23). Timothy, Sosipater (Sopater is the shortened form), and Gaius were all mentioned as being with Paul in Corinth during his three-month visit: "And he was accompanied by Sopater of Berea, the son of Pyrrhus; and by Aristarchus and Secundus of the Thessalonians; and Gaius of Derbe, and Timothy; and Tychicus and Trophimus of Asia" (Acts 20:4). By cross-referencing these passages, we can see that the men mentioned in Romans were the same men who were with Paul at Corinth. His journeys put him at Corinth, and his companions put him at Corinth, so we must conclude that it was from there that he wrote the epistle to the Romans.

When Did Paul Write the Letter?

It may be possible to pinpoint the date of writing even further. Acts 20:1–3 mentions that after Paul's life was threatened by the mob in the great theater of the Ephesians, "he came to Greece. And there he spent three months, and when a plot was formed against him by the Jews as he was about to set sail for Syria, he determined to return through Macedonia." Luke, the author of the book of Acts, mentioned that they "sailed from Philippi after the days of Unleavened Bread" and arrived at Troas in five days (Acts 20:5–6). The Feast of Unleavened Bread began with Passover on the fourteenth day of the first month (Abib) in the Jewish calendar. This would mean that Paul left Corinth not later than March of that year.

It seems likely that when Paul finished his letter to the Romans, Phoebe, a Christian woman who was headed to the imperial city on business, either volunteered or was asked by Paul to carry the letter personally. She was a trustworthy woman, and she did have Rome as her destination (16:1). Phoebe was a deaconess at the church of Cenchrea, which was the eastern seaport city for Corinth on the Aegean Sea. Since all navigation on the Mediterranean stopped in the middle of November out of safety concerns for winter sailing and did not resume until the middle of March, plans for Phoebe to travel to Rome would hardly have been made before the spring. Thus, it seems the letter was written toward the end of Paul's three-month stay in Corinth, late March of A.D. 57, although some estimate the year was perhaps A.D. 58.

Why Did Paul Write the Letter?

During the decade A.D. 47 to 57, Paul had spent most of his time intensively evangelizing the territories that border the Aegean Sea and planting churches throughout Asia Minor and Greece. His eastern campaign was now concluded, but his apostolic task was by no means complete. During the winter of A.D. 56–57, which he spent at the house of his Corinthian friend Gaius (16:23), he apprehensively looked forward to an immediate journey to Jerusalem, where he hoped the gift he bore from the Gentile churches to the poor Jewish saints there would help salve the wounds of controversy and strengthen the bonds between the mother church and the churches of the Gentiles. Once this mission was complete, Paul could continue his dream to labor where no man had labored and build where no man had built. His choice was Spain, the oldest Roman colony in the West. But a journey to Spain would afford opportunity to realize another lifelong ambition, to visit Rome and spend some time with the believers there.

The purpose of Paul's letter to these Romans believers can be summarized as follows:

1. To enlist the cooperation and support of the church at Rome for the inauguration of his missionary campaign in the West. Paul realized the strategic and political importance of this city. He needed the assistance of the believers at Rome to launch him into missionary activity in the West as the church at Antioch had done in the East.

2. Paul also wanted to enlist the prayer support of the Roman Christians for his forthcoming venture at Jerusalem (15:30–33). He was concerned about the outcome of his journey there and rightly so.

3. Paul was emphatic in his claim to be the apostle to the Gentiles. Since Rome was the capital of the Gentile world, it was entirely appropriate that he visit the church there.

4. Paul knew that the Roman church had come into existence without the authoritative leadership of an apostle of the Lord. Thus, Paul wanted to add validity to their existence by instructing them in the faith through his epistle.

5. Paul desired to deposit a compendium of theological truth, and the capital city of the empire was the natural place for him to do so. Besides, Paul was apprehensive about the immediate trip to Jerusalem, and perhaps his letter to the Romans would be his final opportunity to draft a theology of the Christian faith in a written, changeless form. As Adam W. Miller says, "He bequeaths to them in the form of the Epistle the gospel that he would preach to them, should he be permitted to reach there, and if not, they have his letter to read and refer to again and again."[5] Paul certainly fulfilled these purposes. This epistle has proved to be one of the bulwarks of evangelical Christianity.

Are We Sure Paul Was the Author?

That Paul was the author of the epistle to the Romans is indisputable and universally acknowledged. On internal grounds, Paul claims to be the author: "Paul, a bond-servant of Christ Jesus . . . to all who are beloved of God in Rome, called as saints" (1:1, 7). The writer makes personal references that can apply only to Paul (cf. 11:13; 15:15–20). The style, argument, and theology are all Pauline. If you ask what the Bible says, the Bible says the apostle Paul wrote Romans.

But there are also external grounds for believing Paul was the author. Outside of the Bible, quotations from this epistle are found in Clement of Rome, Ignatius, Justin Martyr, Polycarp, Hippolytus, Marcion, the Muratorian canon, and the Old Latin and Syriac versions. All of them ascribe the authorship of Romans to the apostle. That's strong external proof. Romans has been recognized as written by Paul and a part of the canon of Scripture since the time of Irenaeus, A.D. 130–202. That's significant, because it places evidence for a solid belief in Paul's authorship of Romans in the next generation or two after him.

Why Is Romans So Important?

I don't believe the importance of the Epistle to the Romans can be overstated. In the summer of A.D. 386, Aurelius Augustinus, a native of Tagaste in North Africa and professor of rhetoric at Milan, was on the brink of beginning a new life. Taking up his scroll, he read, "Not in carousing and drunkenness, not in sexual promiscuity and sensuality, not in strife and jealousy. But put on the Lord Jesus Christ, and make no provision for the flesh, in regard to its lusts" (Rom. 13:13–14). "No further would I read," he said, "nor had I any need; instantly, at the end of this sentence, a clear light flooded my heart and all the darkness of doubt vanished away."[6] Such was the conversion experience of Augustine.

In November 1515, an Augustinian monk and professor of sacred theology at the University of Wittenberg, Germany, began to expound this epistle to his students. As he prepared his lectures, he became more and more convinced that "the just shall live by faith." "I greatly longed to understand Paul's Epistle to the Romans," he wrote, "and nothing stood in the way but that one expression, 'the righteousness of God.' . . . Night and day I pondered until . . . . I grasped the truth that the righteousness of God is that righteousness whereby, through grace and sheer mercy, he justifies us by faith. Thereupon I felt myself to be reborn. . . ."[7] Through the reading of this epistle, Martin Luther was born into the family of God.

On the evening of May 24, 1738, John Wesley unwillingly attended a society meeting at Aldersgate Street where someone was reading Luther's *Preface to the Epistle to the Romans.* Wesley wrote in his journal, "About a quarter before nine, while he was describing the change which God works in the heart through faith in Christ, I felt my heart strangely warmed. I felt I did trust in Christ, Christ alone, for my salvation; and an assurance was given me that he had taken my sins away, even mine; and saved me from the law of sin and death."[8] This event, more than any other, launched the evangelical revival of the eighteenth century.

The great Swiss Reformer John Calvin said of this epistle, "When anyone understands this Epistle, he has a passage opened to him to the understanding of the whole Scriptures." Twentieth-century theologian James I. Packer comments that, "There is one book in the New Testament which links up with almost everything that the Bible contains: that is the Epistle to the Romans. . . . From the vantage point given by Romans, the whole landscape of the Bible is open to view, and the broad relation of the parts to the whole becomes plain. The study of Romans is the fittest starting point for biblical interpretation and theology."[9]

Overestimating the importance of this singular letter by the apostle Paul would be difficult. And it can have the same effect on you as it has had on other readers if your heart is prepared for change.

Challenge:

To read it + be open
to change instead
of reading it in a
spirit of complacency.

The Biblical Definition of Righteousness

Romans 1:1–17

Frederic Godet observed, "The Reformation was undoubtedly the work of the Epistle to the Romans, as well as of that to the Galatians; and the probability is that every great spiritual revival in the church will be connected as effect and cause with a deeper understanding of this book."[1] Be prepared. Before you read Paul's epistle to the Romans, make sure you are ready for the result. You cannot say what might happen if you undertake an intensive study of this epistle. What happened to Augustine, Luther, Calvin, and Wesley, who left a mark on the world, could happen to you today. So let the reader beware. This letter is like spiritual napalm, burning away the stains of sin in your life. It's like genetic engineering, rearranging your priorities to fit those of your Creator. It's the literary equivalent of the Declaration of Independence and the Magna Charta blended into one. Do not begin a serious study of this epistle unless you are willing to bear the consequences. Reading through Romans repeatedly results in revival.

CHAPTER 1

Greetings to the Roman Christians
Romans 1:1–7

Preview:

Paul proclaims himself an apostle of the Lord and one who has specifically been set aside for the gospel of God. Salvation was promised by the prophets, and it has to do with God's Son, Jesus Christ. Jesus' resurrection from the dead declared Him the Son of God with power. For His name's sake, Paul and the other apostles are to bring about "the obedience of faith" to the Gentiles.

All the elements of first-century letter writing (see Appendix: Letter Writing in the Bible, p. 249) are evident in the first seven verses of Paul's epistle to the Romans. You will notice several of these elements as you read Paul's epistolary introduction.

Bond-Slave and "Called" Apostle (1:1–2)

As in each of the recognized Pauline epistles, Paul begins this letter with his name, according to first-century style: "Paul, a bond-servant of Christ Jesus, called as an apostle" (v. 1). Paul calls himself a bond-servant (Greek, *doulos*, bond-slave) of Jesus Christ. In his mind, since a Roman slave was answerable only to his master, Paul was not just servant to the Lord but slave as well and answerable only to Him (1 Cor. 4:1–4). In addition, he was a "called" apostle. Paul claimed apostleship on at least four grounds: (1) he was a chosen vessel of God (Acts 9:15); (2) he was personally commissioned by Christ (Acts 9:6); (3) he had actually seen the risen Lord (1 Cor. 9:1); and (4) he was the recipient of divine revelation (Gal. 1:10–12, 16–17).

In addition, Paul was "set apart for the gospel of God" (v. 1). The apostle was separated by God for the ministry of the gospel long before his Damascus Road experience. Paul says that God "set me apart, even from my mother's womb, and called me through His grace" (Gal. 1:15). With Paul's pedigree (Phil. 3:5–6), he would have made an excellent servant of God to his own people, the Jews. But in the providence of the Almighty, Paul was set apart to the gospel of God as an apostle to the Gentiles (Acts 9:15). Thus, a disastrous schism between the Jewish and Gentile segments of the early church was avoided through the unique ministry of Paul.

Who Is the Gospel? (1:3–4)

With the mention of the "gospel" (Greek, *euangelion*) of God in verse 1, the apostle begins an explanation of the person of that gospel, Jesus Christ. In most modern translations of the Bible, the first sentence of Romans contains in excess of 125 words and encompasses seven verses. We can proceed directly from verse 1 to verse 7 without losing Paul's train of thought. But the mere mention of the gospel of God prompts him to include the interlude of verses 2 through 6, in which he describes this gospel as that "which He promised beforehand through His prophets in the holy Scriptures" (v. 2). The gospel was not an innovation of the messianic Jews or the newly formed band of Christians. It had been preannounced by the Old Testament prophets from Genesis 3:15 to Malachi 4:2. By quoting sixty-one times from the Old Testament, Paul indicated to the Jews that their scriptures were, in reality, speaking of Jesus Christ just as much as the followers of the Nazarene were. The gospel concerns God's Son, the Lord Jesus (v. 3). The gospel is not about Jesus Christ; the gospel *is* Jesus Christ. And what do we know about Jesus? He "was born of a descendant of David according to the flesh" (v. 3). The Davidic descent of Jesus Christ was the fulfillment of the promise that one from the chosen line would sit on the throne of David forever (2 Sam. 7:13; Jer. 33:17).

But there's more, and this is very important. Notice that although Jesus Christ was born of the seed of David according to the flesh, He was not born the Son of God. He was "declared the Son of God with power" (v. 4). The word rendered "declared" (Greek, *horizō*) has the meaning of "appointed" or "marked out by unmistakable signs." It is used in Acts 10:42 and 17:31 of Christ's appointment as Judge. There was a time when Jesus Christ was not yet born of the family of David, but there was never a time when He was not the

X was appointed as the Son of ☉ by the HS

Son of God. Christ was not *born* but eternally *is* God the Son. You do not have to make someone something he already is. You simply have to declare him to be who he is. The fact that Jesus is God the Son graphically and unmistakably was revealed to the world "by the resurrection from the dead, according to the spirit of holiness" (v. 4). There is an obvious antithesis between according to the flesh and according to the Spirit. Here is a distinction between the two states of Christ's humiliation and His exaltation. His humiliation came when He voluntarily was made in the likeness of men (Phil. 2:7), but His exaltation came when He was resurrected by the Holy Spirit of God.

Grace and Apostleship (1:5–7)

Probably better translated "grace of apostleship," Paul regards his apostolic calling as a heavenly gift. It was the grace given to him by God. He didn't seek this calling, he didn't pray for it, but once he received it, he used it to the fullest. The purpose of his apostleship was "to bring about the obedience of faith among all the Gentiles, for His name's sake" (v. 5). Paul wanted to bring the Gentile nations of the world into obedience to the faith (i.e., the body of doctrine he taught). This would include the Gentiles of the capital of the Roman Empire "among whom you also are the called of Jesus Christ" (v. 6). The expression "the called" is a favorite of the apostle to indicate a very particular group—those who have trusted the Lord Jesus as Savior (cf. 8:28). Thus, in writing to the Roman church, Paul was not stepping outside of his apostolic authority but merely acting within it. He wanted to instruct "all who are beloved of God in Rome, called as saints" (v. 7) in those things that make for good doctrine and godly living.

What does Paul mean when he addresses the believers in Rome as "saints" (v. 7)? Sainthood is not to be identified with the practice of canonization that later arose in the Roman church. A saint is one called of God and "holy" (Greek, *hagios*), that is, set apart to God for specific service. The saints of Rome were beloved of God, which marks them out as the undeserving yet grateful recipients of God's love. Yet they also were set apart from the world by God to engage in specific forms of service to Him. Those who enjoy God's love must always take seriously the responsibilities of that love. Love and service, being loved and being set apart as saints, always go hand in hand.

One of the interesting features of the Pauline style is that in every one of his epistles these two words appear together. "Grace and peace" are never separated by Paul (cf. Rom. 1:7; 1 Cor. 1:3; 2 Cor. 1:2; Gal. 1:3; Eph. 1:2; Phil. 1:2; Col. 1:2; 1 Thess. 1:1; 2 Thess. 1:2; 1 Tim. 1:2; 2 Tim. 1:2; Titus 1:4; Philem. 1:3). "The words 'grace and peace,' so common in Paul's salutations, probably

saints = those called to be his holy people"

unite the Greek and Jewish modes of greeting. The Greek says *Chaire!* which literally means 'Rejoice!' The Jew says *Shalom!* meaning 'Peace!' Only, in uniting these two modes of greeting, Paul changes *chaire* to the similarly-sounding and more distinctively Christian word *charis*, 'grace.'"[1] Paul, a Hebrew of the Hebrews but the apostle to the Gentiles, was the bridge between the Jews and Gentiles of the first-century church. When he said hello to the churches, it was always with the double greeting "Grace and peace," demonstrating that God's unmerited favor and love are available to all people through Jesus Christ.

Paul addressed many congregations during his days as an apostle, some of them on multiple occasions. But he never wrote a letter so packed with theological teaching and practical application as he did the saints who were called of God at Rome. Little wonder this letter has been dubbed "the Constitution of Christianity."

Study Questions

1. What does Paul mean by "bond-servant"?

    Paul answers to God alone — G is in charge — above even Paul himself

2. Why does Paul refer to Christ as a descendant of David "according to the flesh"?

3. List the ways God used to bring Paul to his position as an apostle.

4. What was behind Paul's writing this letter to the Roman Christians? (See the introduction.)

CHAPTER 2

Paul's Desire to Visit Rome
Romans 1:8-16

Preview:
Paul commends the Roman church for their faith being proclaimed every-where. The apostle had a great desire to visit this outstanding assembly. He wanted to encourage them, further "establish" them in their faith, and bring about additional "fruit" among them. The gospel is the power of God for everyone, beginning with the Jews, and then for Greeks and all Gentiles.

Paul wanted badly to visit the believers in Rome. After all, their "faith [was] being proclaimed throughout the whole world" (v. 8). Is this apostolic hyperbole? No, so strong was the faith of these Roman believers that, like the church of the Thessalonians (1 Thess. 1:8), Paul speaks of it in worldwide terms. The expression "throughout the whole world" is common for every-where. Paul couldn't travel anywhere in the Roman Empire without encoun-tering Christians who were talking about what God was doing in Rome.

Paul as Prayer Warrior (1:9-10)

The apostle's claim in verses 9 and 10 is strong. "For God, whom I serve in my spirit in the preaching of the gospel of His Son, is my witness as to how unceas-ingly I make mention of you, always in my prayers." Paul's prayer life is inter-twined with his life of service. The word the apostle uses for service (Greek, *latreuō*) is that of the function of a priest in the temple and is very frequently used by Paul to mean worship (cf. Phil. 3:3; 2 Tim. 1:3). A great deal of Paul's priestly service to the Lord was his regular pattern of intercessory prayer on the behalf of other believers (cf. Eph. 1:16; Phil. 1:3; Col. 1:3; 1 Thess. 1:2; 2 Tim. 1:3; Philem. 1:4). For every busy pastor who has mistakenly come to believe that preaching is his business and prayer is the business of a few elders (or more likely, a few widows in the church), we have only to notice what the apostle had to say to the Roman church at the very beginning of his letter to them. He prays for them, unceasingly, as a priestly function of his office as an apostle and bond-servant of Jesus Christ. Any pastor struggling with the reality that his number one duty to his people is to pray for them needs only to see what the apostles did for the church. When the complaint arose in the Jerusalem church that the Hellenistic widows were being overlooked, the Twelve selected deacons to be in charge of the daily tasks of the church and then said, "But we will devote ourselves to prayer, and to the ministry of the word" (Acts 6:4). Prayer first, preaching second. The chief prayer warrior of the local church is to be the pastor.

We can learn much from Paul's life as a prayer warrior. Notice these seven characteristics of Paul's prayers.

Prayer should be thankful (v. 8). The apostle said, "First, I thank my God through Jesus Christ for you all." In Paul's unceasing prayers, he was first of all thankful. It appears he never entered God's presence in prayer without a time of thanksgiving and adoration.

Prayer should be personal (v. 9). Paul prayed for particular churches and for particular people. In fact, he told the Romans, ". . . unceasingly I make mention of you." That's personal. He didn't pray for all the Christians in the world, or even for all the churches in his sphere of influence; rather, he prayed for the Roman, Ephesian, and Philippian Christians.

Prayer should be continual (v. 9). Paul uses two adverbs in verses 9 and 10 that indicate he was consistent in his prayers for the believers at Rome— "unceasingly" and "always." Paul never stopped praying for the Romans. Prayer was his priestly service to God in behalf of other believers; he would not stop, nor would he be interrupted.

Prayer should be sincere (v. 9). Paul's prayers were not filled with platitudes, clichés or well-worn phrases. They were genuine, absolutely sincere. He knew what he was saying was true, and the Romans would know it too, because Paul could say, "For God . . . is my witness" (v. 9).

Prayer should be flexible (v. 10). The apostle did not demand to know how God would get him to Rome, what ship he would take, what cabin he would have on board, or even when the journey would be made. He simply prayed "if perhaps now" (KJV says "if by any means") God would permit him to come to Rome.

*When Paul prayed, the purpose of his requests would have been for God's Glory— Not his own gain —Submissive to God's will

Prayer should be submissive (v. 10). When we are not certain of God's will, we must do as Paul did and be submissive to God's will. That's why James said, "You ought to say, 'If the Lord wills, we shall live and also do this or that'" (James 4:15). Paul's prayer for the Romans demonstrated this kind of submission when he said, "If perhaps now at last by the will of God I may succeed in coming to you" (v. 10).

Prayer should be specific (vv. 11–12). Paul prayed for the specific reasons he wanted to come to Rome (vv. 11–12), he thanked God in his prayer for the specific faith of the Romans known throughout the world (v. 8), and he even prayed that he would "succeed in coming" to visit the Roman believers. That's getting to the heart of the matter when you pray.

Paul as Homesick Friend (1:11)

Paul now states his purpose in wanting to come to Rome. He says, "For I long to see you" (in current idiom, "I am homesick for you"). Paul gives three reasons for this deep longing to be with the Roman believers. First, Paul wanted "to impart some spiritual gift" to them. Paul wanted to be more than a blessing to them; he wanted to build them up in the most holy faith and explain to them more fully what it meant to be "in Christ Jesus." Knowing that this local church had not had the apostolic stamp of approval placed on it, Paul wished to visit them to do so. Second, Paul desired the Romans to reciprocate, that he "may be encouraged together" with them. The apostle had a lifelong desire to preach the gospel in Spain where no one had laid a foundation. Rome was to be a stopover for that journey. Paul would need lodging, food, and Christian fellowship. He wanted the Roman believers to provide these for him. Finally, verse 13 indicates that Paul's desire was not only to evangelize Spain but also Rome, the capital of the Gentile world. He says, "that I might obtain some fruit among you also." Ever the evangelist at heart, Paul did not look to Rome simply as a launching pad for further evangelistic effort but as a needy field itself.

Paul may never have been to the city of Rome, but he certainly was homesick for the fellowship of the believers there. Christians have a bond that transcends family and friendship. Paul had that bond with the Christians in Rome. He was homesick to see them, and minister to them, and be ministered to by them.

Paul as Debtor (1:14)

Paul viewed himself as a debtor to the whole world. He said, "I am under obligation both to Greeks and to barbarians, both to the wise and to the foolish"

(v. 14). This indebtedness was not something the apostle prayed for or sought. It was laid upon him, as it is on every believer. Paul had been placed in debt by the love of Jesus Christ (2 Cor. 5:14). The Pauline concept of Christian service is that each believer is deeply in debt. Isaac Watts was inspired by this concept to pen the words of the hymn "At the Cross," "But drops of grief can ne'er repay the debt of love I owe. Here, Lord, I give myself away, 'tis all that I can do." Paul felt he had a responsibility to give nothing less than himself to the propagation of the gospel by which he was saved.

But why did the apostle mention the Greeks and the barbarians? In the Jewish mind, there were only two kinds of people—Jews and everybody else, the Gentiles. In the Greek mind there were only two kinds of people—Greeks and everybody else, barbarians. And in God's mind there are only two kinds of people—the saved and the lost (1 John 5:12). From the golden age of Athens under Pericles in the fifth century B.C. until the decline of that empire, Greece was more highly civilized and educated than any other society of its time. However, when Paul contrasted the Greek with the barbarian, it is evident that he included the Romans with the Greeks.[1]

Paul as Eager Servant (1:15)

The expression "I am eager to preach the gospel" appears in the middle of a trilogy of first person statements concerning Paul's preaching of the gospel of Christ. The first is "I am under obligation" (v. 14). The third is "I am not ashamed" (v. 16). The core statement is, "I am eager" (v. 15). Isn't that the way it should be with all of us who are in debt to the love of God?

All of us should be unashamed of the gospel of Christ (v. 16). But not all are ready to preach the gospel. Paul was not only able and willing, but he was ready to preach as well. He was a clean vessel, not just a chosen vessel. He was ready to be used of God. Paul was like the old country preacher who, when asked how he prepared his Sunday sermon, said, "I read myself full, think myself clear, pray myself hot, and let myself go." Many believers are not ready to be let go because they are not read full of God's Word, clear-minded about Christian doctrine, or prayed up. Paul was ready to be "let go" and sent to Rome by any means.

We are under obligation and we are not ashamed; therefore, as debtors to Christ, we should be eager to preach the gospel as well. If we aren't, if there is something wrong with the middle statement in this trilogy, perhaps the other two are not true either.

Paul as Unashamed Preacher (1:16)

In stating the theme of the gospel as the good news that Christ died for our sins, Paul makes a bold claim that he is not ashamed of that news. He may have had our Lord's warning in the back of his mind (Luke 9:26). Regardless, Paul is quick to point out, "I am not ashamed of the gospel"

We might well ask why Paul would have been ashamed of the gospel. After all, it was "the power of God for salvation." But perhaps he would have been ashamed to spread the gospel because of the fierce persecution for those who had come to believe in this message. As a Jew, Paul could have been ashamed of the gospel because the Jews abhorred it as subverting the law. As an educated man, he might have been ashamed because to the wise Greek the gospel was sheer foolishness. He might have been ashamed of the gospel because, according to the pagans, Christians were branded as atheists, a brand no Pharisee could tolerate. This atheism was not a theoretical denial of the existence of the gods but was a practical refusal to recognize pagan deities as truly God. For those whom the Romans considered to be "Christian atheists," the consequences were severe, perhaps forced labor in mines or even capital punishment.

Although for these and other reasons Paul could have been ashamed of the gospel of Christ, there is never a hint in the Pauline corpus that he ever was ashamed (quite the contrary, see Rom. 9:33; 10:11; 2 Tim. 1:8, 11–12, 16). Paul now gives the reason why he is not ashamed of the gospel of Christ. "It is the power of God," the great and admirable mystery hidden with God from before the foundation of the world. The gospel, through the Holy Spirit of God, does what no amount of mere human reasoning or argumentation can do. It compels people to face the reality of their own sin and guilt, the inevitability of divine judgment, and the need for a perfect substitute to make atonement for sin if they are to survive at all. The gospel is the dynamite (Greek, *dunamis*) that blasts away self-complacency, self-delusion, and sinful self-reliance. Nothing else can do this, for nothing else is "the power of God for salvation to everyone who believes."

Paul the Jewish Evangelist (1:17)

Paul deliberately proclaimed that the gospel is for everyone. He did so because there were many Jewish believers who thought the gospel was not for the Gentile. The gospel is for all; it is the power of God for salvation to everyone, without distinction of age, sex, race, or physical disability. But faith is the key to receiving the gospel, and the gospel is to be proclaimed first to the Jew.

From the days of Abraham, the Jews have always been divinely distinguished from all the rest of the world in many and great privileges. They are the royal family of the human race. They are the rightful heirs to the Promised Land. They are the chosen nation of God. They were given the oracles of God. They had a covenant with Jehovah God. It was through the Jews that Christ Jesus came. Originally the preaching of the gospel was addressed to them exclusively (Matt. 10:5–6). During His ministry on earth, Jesus Christ was a minister to those of the circumcision only (Rom. 15:8). The spread of the gospel was to begin in Jerusalem, the center of Judaism (Acts 1:8). Paul did not forget that the gospel was to be first directed toward God's chosen nation, Israel, but the words "and also to the Greek" indicate that Paul was well aware that the message of the gospel is a universal message, for everyone needs it. It is not for just the Jew or the Roman citizen, it is not just for the wise, but it is for the Gentile and the Roman slave as well.

Although the gospel is for everyone, there is a restriction placed on that universality. That restriction is faith. The gospel is "the power of God for salvation to *every one who believes*." To the Jew first, as was done in the first century, to the rest of the world, as has been the case in each subsequent century, is the pattern for preaching. But no amount of skill, no degree of charisma, no slick presentation of the gospel to Jew or Gentile is sufficient to force the efficacy of the gospel on an unwilling hearer. The gospel is God's power that brings salvation to all who hear and believe. It is dynamite. But those who do not believe simply get blown apart by the gospel; they are not saved by it. For this dynamite we call the gospel to be efficacious, it must be believed. That was true in the first century; it is true in the twenty-first century. Faith is the key to salvation in every generation.

Study Questions

1. What does Paul mean by writing that the Romans' faith was proclaimed "throughout the whole world"?

2. From verse 9, how does Paul say he was serving God? What did he mean by "spirit"?

3. From verses 10–13, list the reasons why Paul says he desired to visit the church at Rome.

4. In terms of his preaching the gospel, to whom does the apostle feel obligated? Why?

5. What is the gospel able to do for individuals?

CHAPTER 3

The Righteous Shall Live by Faith
Romans 1:17

Preview:
God will grant salvation by imparting His righteousness to those who believe. God's imparted righteousness through Christ Jesus is at the heart of the gospel message. Righteousness comes by faith and is to be lived out by faith in the life of the believer.

Do you remember when your mother asked you, "How many times do I have to tell you to clean up your room?" Most of us do. It seems that in a perfect "mother world," once should be enough. If Mom says, "Do it," we should do it, or suffer the horrendous consequences. That's the feeling you get with the just living by faith. Romans 1:17 is not the first time God's Word has informed us on this principle. In fact, Paul is quoting the prophet Habakkuk.

Habakkuk 2:4

In the dark days of Jehoiakim's reign, just before the men and women of Judah were carried off into Babylonian captivity, the prophet Habakkuk was used of God to pen a most unusual message. The book of Habakkuk is filled with woes pronounced on Babylon, an unrelenting condemnation of the evil empire. And yet, in the midst of all this gloom and discouragement, there is a message of courage and hope. It is recorded in Habakkuk 2:4. It's like finding an emerald in a bowl of pea soup. God said, "Behold, as for the proud one, His soul is not right within him; but the righteous will live by his faith." In contrast with the self-reliant, proud, boastful Babylon, the people of God would find their righteousness by being reliant on God and living faithfully for Him.

Romans 1:17

Habakkuk 2:4 counts as once. Like your mother's admonition to clean up your room, once should have been enough. But here Paul says it again. He has just told us that the gospel is "dynamite," and now he tells us that through the gospel the righteousness of God is revealed. "For in it [the gospel] the righteousness of God is revealed from faith to faith; as it is written, 'But the righteous man shall live by faith'" (v. 17). The theme of this epistle is that we cannot live *joyfully* before God and others unless we live *righteously* before God and others. We've now been told twice.

Galatians 3:11

But Paul says it again in Galatians 3:11. "Now that no one is justified by the Law before God is evident; for, 'The righteous man shall live by faith.'" Paul was demonstrating to the Galatian believers the difference between the works of the Law and faith in God. He used Abraham as an example, as he will in our study in Romans (chap. 4). A theme is developing around this concept of righteous people living by faith: We are saved, not by our works, but by faith in Jesus Christ. Therefore, we should continue to live by faith, just as we were saved. That's what it means to be just or righteous. This makes three times.

Hebrews 10:38

There's one more. This time the admonishment is from the writer of Hebrews (10:36–38):

> For you have need of endurance, so that when you have done the will of God, you may receive what was promised.
> For yet in a very little while,
> He who is coming will come, and will not delay.
> But My righteous one shall live by faith;
> And if he shrinks back, My soul has no pleasure in him.

It is a different author, but the same theme. That's four times. How many times does God have to tell us in His Word that He expects us to live a faithful life? How many times will people look for righteousness in keeping statutes rather than in faithful living? If you want to be righteous, live the way you were saved. The just shall live by faith.

Romans 1:17 begins with "For" as a connective to verse 16. In fact, you cannot make sense of verse 17 without verse 16, because Paul uses the pronoun "it" without an antecedent in the verse. The pronoun "it" refers back to the gospel of verse 16. So we may read Romans 1:17, "For in the gospel the righteousness of God is revealed." Remember that the gospel is not about Jesus Christ; the gospel *is* Jesus Christ. God's righteousness is revealed, not through the law, but in the person and work of Jesus.

Questions about Righteousness

Righteousness is that aspect of God's holiness that is seen in His treatment of His creatures. Simply put, righteousness represents how God treats us. Jesus Christ is our righteousness. He is how God treats us. We are unrighteous, unholy, and unlovely, yet Christ died for our sins (1 Cor. 15:3).

How is righteousness obtained? "From faith to faith." Righteousness is received by faith in Christ Jesus and is in turn revealed in faithful living. Thus, in answer to the question, "How are the righteous to live?" Paul quotes Habakkuk 2:4, "The righteous shall live by his faith." This faith implies more than mere acceptance of Christ's righteousness for salvation; it implies a lifestyle that is characterized by faith and righteous living. It was this truth that excited Martin Luther and ignited the Protestant Reformation.

Here is how Luther explained the passage that began his walk of faith with God:

> The righteousness of God comes altogether from faith, but in such a way that there appear constant growth and constant greater clarity, as it is written in 2 Corinthians 3:18; "We . . . are changed into the same image from glory to glory." The words "from faith to faith" therefore signify that the believer grows in faith more and more, so that he who is justified becomes more and more righteous (in his life). This he adds in order that no one might think that he has already apprehended (Phil. 3:13) and so ceases to make progress (in sanctification); for that indeed means that he begins to fall behind.[1]

Unmerited Righteousness

Paul's letter to the Romans is all about righteousness, God's righteousness—how we need it, how we obtain it, and how we live by it. In the introductory comments of his letter, he prepares his readers to know that there is no righteousness without the gospel, and there is no gospel without Jesus. So anyone who reads his letter, whether in the first or twenty-first century, must know that there is nothing we can do to obtain this righteousness. It is God's gift to us through the person of Jesus, the gospel of God.

When Augustus Toplady took refuge during a storm in a large fissure of a huge rock near Burrington Coombe, England, that place of refuge caused him to reflect on Jesus Christ as his rock of refuge. He also recognized how Jesus as his rock of refuge was available to him and penned these lines in the hymn "Rock of Ages":

> Could my tears forever flow, could my zeal no languor know.
> These for sin could not atone; Thou must save, and thou alone.
> In my hand no price I bring, simply to Thy cross I cling.

Augustus Toplady had it right. Martin Luther had it right. The apostle Paul had it right. The gospel is the power of God for salvation to everyone who believes in Jesus Christ as Savior. For by the gospel the righteousness of God is revealed, and we receive it by faith and live in it by faith.

What Is Righteousness?

Since righteousness is the key word in Paul's epistle to the Romans and since the righteous living by faith is the key concept of the epistle, it must be important in Paul's thinking. But what righteousness is Paul talking about? Is it God's righteousness, His personal attribute of being righteous?

The righteousness Paul talks about in Romans is not God's attribute. When we become righteous, we do not become God. The subjective genitive used in Romans 1:17 (righteousness "of God") implies that this righteousness is the way God treats us as a result of our response in faith to the gospel (cf. 3:22). When we trust Jesus Christ as our Savior, God responds by imputing righteousness to our spiritual account, which before had only sin imputed to it. To be justified by God means to be declared righteous. As John Witmer points out,

> "Righteousness" and "justify," though seemingly unrelated in English, are related in Greek. "Righteousness" is *dikaiosunē*, and "justify" is *dikaioō*. Paul used the noun many times in his epistles, including twenty-eight times in Romans (1:17; 3:21–22, 25–26; 4:3, 5–6, 9, 11, 13, 22; 5:17, 21; 6:13, 16, 18–20; 8:10; 9:30; 10:3–6 [twice in v. 3], 10; 14:17). And Paul used the Greek verb fifteen times in Romans (2:13; 3:4, 20, 24, 26, 28, 30; 4:2, 5; 5:1, 9; 6:7; 8:30 [twice], 33). To justify a person is to declare him forensically (legally) righteous.[2]

Being declared righteous doesn't mean you never sin. It simply means you legally stand forgiven because someone—Jesus Christ—has paid the debt for your sin. And anyone who is truly justified by faith in Jesus Christ is going to live in the spirit of that justification. Hence, the just shall live by faith. Our journey into eternal life started with saving faith, it continues with sanctifying faith, and one day it will be complete in glorifying faith. For now, enjoy the fact that God is willing to declare you righteous and treat you as if you are righteous all because of what Jesus did for you at Calvary.

Since God gives us His righteousness in salvation, what does this have to do with the way we live out our Christian life? By quoting Habakkuk 2:4, Paul gives us a hint. Habakkuk says of the person who walks around with pride, "His soul is not right within him; *but the righteous [one] will live by his faith*" (italics mine). In other words, we are saved by faith, and we walk by faith, not by works or self-effort. Faith and imparted righteousness for salvation have to do with what is called *positional truth*, that is, our position as a believer in Christ. Faith and living righteously have to do with *experiential truth*, that is, how we live out our experience as Christians on a daily basis. By saving faith, we receive the righteousness of Christ; by experiential sanctifying faith, we live out the Christian life. In that life we "walk by faith, not by sight" (2 Cor. 5:7).

On righteousness living, Ryrie writes, our "sanctification is the present experiential or progressive work of continuing to be set apart during the whole of our Christian life."[3]

Study Questions

1. Define righteousness.
2. What is meant by Paul's statement that it is "revealed from faith to faith"?
3. What does the apostle have in mind by quoting Habakkuk 2:4?

SECTION II: CONDEMNATION

The Human Need for Righteousness

Romans 1:18—3:20

The apostle Paul was a rabbi trained at the feet of the great Gamaliel in Jerusalem. He was a strategic thinker; he had a logical mind. He would have made a great engineer had God not called him to be a missionary and church planter. His arguments in this letter to the Romans build one on the other in flawless logic. He begins by proving that the entire world is condemned before God because the entire world has sinned and deserves that condemnation. Were it not for God's grace, we all would be eternally separated from God.

CHAPTER 4

Immoral People Are Condemned
Romans 1:18–32

Preview:

Paul says the wrath of God hangs over the heads of all who are ungodly. People are without excuse for denying God, because they have the witness of creation about His unseen attributes, eternal power, and divine nature. They go on in their excuses, claiming to be wise and attributing to God likenesses of corruptible man and animals. God has given people over to a depraved mind, whereby they act out all sorts of evil and wholeheartedly join others who practice evil.

With the introduction complete, thanksgiving made, and the theme of his epistle stated, Paul now turns to the heart of the doctrinal teaching in Romans. Paul has both good news and bad news for the world. The good news, which will shortly follow, is that God has provided atonement for our sins. The bad news, which he explores first, is that all people need atonement for their sins. Before you can appreciate the good news, you must know that there is bad news. Before Paul tells us that the gift of God is eternal life, he tells us that the wages of sin is death. Verse 18 begins the groundwork Paul lays for his case against humankind's self-righteousness. His aim is to show that the whole world is morally bankrupt, unable to receive a favorable verdict at the judgment bar of God, and desperately in need of divine mercy and pardon.

Immoral People Have Clearly Known the Truth (1:18–20)

God's attitude toward the sin of humankind is not one of tolerance. He does not simply hold people accountable for what may be reasonably expected of them in view of their nature as sinners. If God did, His holiness and purity would be soiled by complicity with our guilt. God hates sin. His wrath is a holy aversion to all that is evil, and thus verse 18 declares, "For the wrath of God is revealed from heaven." Wrath is as essential to divine righteousness as love and mercy are. God could not be free from wrath unless He were also free from all concern about His moral universe. Thus, like it or not, wrath against sin is as much a part of the divine nature as love for this sinful world.

God's wrath is revealed from heaven "against all ungodliness and unrighteousness of men." Ungodliness has to do with religion, our relation to a sovereign God. Unrighteousness has to do with morality, our relation to others. Ungodliness is sin against the being of God. Unrighteousness is sin against the will of God. Humans are both religious sinners (they are ungodly) and moral sinners (they are unrighteous). The unrighteous live as if God's will has not been revealed. The ungodly live as if there is no God. God's wrath is against both, because unrighteous and ungodly people "suppress the truth in unrighteousness" (v. 18). The word *suppress* (Greek, *katechō*), carries the meaning of "hold down," "keep back," hence suppress. Those who are unrighteous and ungodly restrain the truth of God's righteousness. The meaning of this word is clearly seen in the way it is used in Luke 4:42, "And when day came, He [Jesus] departed and went to a lonely place; and the multitudes were searching for Him, and came to Him, and tried to keep Him from going away from them." The people suppressed Jesus, or attempted to keep him from leaving them. Paul contends that the unsaved have had the righteousness of God revealed to them. They have known the truth about God's existence and moral requirements, yet they have continually suppressed the truth of His righteousness because it is the nature of humanity to be ungodly and unrighteous.

Are the Gentiles Lost? (1:19–20)

The apostle now anticipates the question "If these ungodly people do not have full knowledge of God, are they really lost?" The key word in Paul's answer is the first word of verse 19, "Because." Paul now presents two lines of argument that prove that the condemnation of sinners does not rest on the depth of their knowledge of God but on what use they make of that knowledge.

Paul first advances that the reason the Gentiles (or anyone who willingly suppresses the knowledge of God) are lost is because of the revelation of God in nature. All people have sufficient knowledge of God to make them responsible to God. That knowledge arises from the fact that "since the creation of the world His invisible attributes, His eternal power and divine nature, have been clearly seen, being understood through what has been made" (v. 20). For further evidence, see David's comments in Psalm 19:1. People's minds are capable of drawing obvious conclusions from effect to cause. To the animals below us, the phenomena of nature may just be a spectacle before their eyes, making no impression on their minds. But to humans, they have a language, a communication. They awake wonder, awe, a basic idea of God and His right-eousness. Even God's eternal power and something of His divine nature are demonstrated. Nature does not simply give the impression that God is an abstract principle or a distant deity. Nature and the world in which we live give us clues that God is a real person, the Supreme Person, transcendent above His creation and not part of it. The testimony of nature alone is sufficient to lead humans to an understanding of the personal, righteous character of God. Thus, Paul concludes that if people would just stop suppressing the truth of God revealed to them in nature, they would come to understand and worship God. But they choose not to cease and desist; they continue to suppress the truth they have, and thus they are without excuse. Their suppression of innate knowl-edge that there must be a divine Creator has made people culpable for their own sin. They have no excuse for the judgment they bring on themselves. They are guilty because they have suppressed the truth.

Immoral People Have Clearly Rejected God (1:21–23)

The problem with immoral people is not that they are uneducated or unso-phisticated as much as it is that they hate God. They hate what God stands for, and they hate His intrusion into their lives. They hate the twinge of guilt they get when they first do what they know is wrong, and then they keep on hat-ing Him long after they have lost those feelings of guilt and have simply aban-doned themselves to the consequences of their sin.

Paul's second line of argument is that the Gentiles are lost because of the revelation of God to the conscience. As if the natural world around us isn't enough, God has planted in the heart of every man and woman the knowledge that there is a righteous God. "For even though they [the Gentiles] knew God" (v. 21) and knew that He deserved to be glorified, they willfully chose not to glorify Him as God. They did not ascribe to His person the holiness, perfection, and sovereignty that are His alone. They chose to worship other things, not God. To add injury to insult, the Gentiles accepted the good things of nature from the hand of God but were not thankful for them. And what happened as a result? "They became futile in their speculations, and their foolish heart was darkened" (v. 21). In order to suppress the witness of the ordered structure of the universe and the innate testimony of the conscience, fallen people had to develop a reasoning process that conjured up human solutions that the Bible calls "futile speculations." God must consider many of the explanations given to students in university classrooms around the world today "futile speculations." This reasoning is described by God as vain or futile, because the whole structure of man-made philosophy is devoid of divine truth and therefore intrinsically invalid. "The fear of the LORD is the beginning of wisdom, and the knowledge of the Holy One is understanding" (Prov. 9:10). Without these necessary components, education becomes a futile search for the truth that ends in the sanitary landfill of human reasoning.

Thus, by suppressing the truth of God and believing their man-made falsehoods, the pagans plunged their foolish hearts deeper into darkness. When they exalted their human reasoning and paraded their wisdom before their peers, they acted as fools. The foolish heart is not one simply deficient in intelligence; it is a heart deficient in the moral understanding of who God is and therefore incapable of righteousness and godliness, let alone understanding and intelligence. Laboring under the self-imposed handicap of this extreme deficiency, the pagans "exchanged the glory of the incorruptible God for an image in the form of corruptible man and of birds and four-footed animals and crawling creatures" (v. 23). By creating their own gods, gods suitable to their own fallen conception of deity, the unsaved have violated the first commandment (Ex. 20:3). They have devised their own concept of deity and placed it above the one true God. More than just conceptualizing what they thought God ought to be, the pagans actually created animal-like images of their concept of God. In so doing, they violated the second commandment (Ex. 20:4).

People do the same today. They don't like to believe there is a God, and when they are repeatedly told in their education they don't need a god, those who could be the enlightened have their foolish hearts darkened and become pagan in the biblical sense of the word. They don't always make images (although some worship their car, their job, their portfolio, their girlfriend or boyfriend, or something else), but they always deny the rightful place of God over His creation. In so doing, without even realizing it, twenty-first-century people became guilty of the same futile imagination of which the nations of the world are guilty. The result is the same, as the judgment is the same.

The apostle has thus given two reasons why men and women without God are lost and deserving of condemnation: (1) because of the revelation of God in nature (vv. 19–20), and (2) because of the revelation of God in their conscience (vv. 21–23). The wrath of God is revealed from heaven against anyone who suppresses the truth of these two witnesses. Men and women are still suppressing them today in the classroom, on the job, and in life. As long as people suppress the truth, they will never experience the truth (John 14:6). To the unbeliever who does not suppress this fundamental light, the Lord

Jehovah grants additional enlightenment of His person. God makes sure a Bible, a gospel tract, a missionary, or someone or something crosses the unbeliever's path and leads that person to additional truth and eventually to salvation. Those who are guilty of suppressing the available truth they have about God, however, do not receive additional light that leads to salvation. Instead, they receive the just condemnation of God—His wrath revealed from heaven against all ungodliness and unrighteousness.

Immoral People Have Clearly Become Degenerate (1:24–31)

Ungodliness and unrighteousness have a mutual terminal point. The destination of ungodly or unrighteous behavior is always idolatry. The word "Therefore" indicates that the retribution to follow finds its ground in the antecedent sins and is therefore justifiable. Because the nations participated in idolatry, God gave them up to impure passions. As seen by Paul's use of the term elsewhere (cf. 2 Cor. 12:21; Gal. 5:19; Eph. 5:3; Col. 3:5; 1 Thess. 4:7), "impurity" (v. 24) means sexual aberration by which they would dishonor their own bodies between themselves. Somehow, some way, ungodliness and unrighteousness always lead to sexual impurity, whether heterosexual or homosexual. It just seems that humans cannot deny God's existence and influence in their lives and stay out of the gutter of their own lust.

Suppression of the truth that God revealed to the nations became the basis for their idolatry and consequently, they foolishly began to believe their own lies about origins and ends.[1] Paul acknowledges that they "worshiped and served the creature rather than the Creator" (v. 25). This is the double whammy of sin. People degraded themselves in what they worshiped and at the same time exalted those things that were created by God to a position higher than the One who created them. The nations clearly become degenerate and must suffer the consequences if they do not turn to God in faith.

The results of choosing disobedience over obedience to God are immediately and forever devastating as we find stated three times in these verses (vv. 24, 26, 28): "Therefore God gave them over in the lusts of their hearts to impurity, that their bodies might be dishonored among them" (v. 24). Since they suppressed the truth, God gave them what they wanted, to dishonor their bodies with impure lusts. In addition, verse 26 says, "For this reason God gave them over to degrading passions." The degrading passions" spoken of here (Greek, *pathē atimias*) were passions of infamy or vile passions. God takes a dim view of these kinds of passion. The passionate expressions of the nations simply degraded them, made them less than human. The apostle goes on to explain that women who suppressed the truth about God "exchanged the natural function for that which is unnatural" (v. 26). And men who suppressed the truth did the same. "The men abandoned the natural function of the woman and burned in their desire toward one another, men with men committing indecent acts and receiving in their own persons the due penalty of their error" (v. 27).[2]

And there is one more "God gave them over" statement. When people engage in disgusting and despicable behavior, it warps their mind. They begin to believe that what they are doing is not so bad; in fact, it's their chosen lifestyle, and God ought to leave them alone. That's why verse 28 says God gave them over to a depraved mind. The word *depraved* means "unapproving" or "undiscerning." They are simply too sinful to know what sinful is. People of undiscerning minds join Act Up; they march in gay pride parades; they accuse moral people of being intolerant and using hate speech. Condemning homosexuality and illicit heterosexuality is not hate speech; it is love talk. It is the kind of talk that comes from a heart of love toward those who are undiscerning because their minds are warped from suppressing the truth. People who love those who hate God speak out because they believe that judgment awaits adulterers and the homosexuals, and they are not so callous as to remain quiet. They won't let their friends and family go to hell without a fight. These people are only hatemongers in the minds of those who no longer possess the ability to discern right from wrong. If we read the Bible, we understand that.

And what is the final description of those who suppress the truth God reveals to them? Paul says they are filled with all unrighteousness, wickedness, greed, and so on (vv. 29–31). "Being filled" expresses (by the Greek perfect tense) that the nations are not simply tainted by the catalogue of sins that follow, but are, in fact, saturated with them. Thus, the ugly character traits listed as the result of abandonment by God include

> being filled with all unrighteousness [Greek, *adikia*]; [sexual] wickedness [Greek, *ponēria*], greed [Greek, *pleonexia*, grasping for more than is needed], evil; full of envy, murder, strife, deceit, malice [Greek, *kakia*, intending evil toward others], they are gossips, slanderers, haters of God, insolent, arrogant, boastful, inventors of evil [thinking up new ways to offend God and feed their lust], disobedient to parents, without [spiritual or moral] understanding, untrustworthy, unloving, unmerciful. (vv. 29–31)

This gallery of iniquity was not only true of the first-century world, but reads much like our newspapers today.

Paul's Conclusion (1:32)

"Although they know the ordinance of God, that those who practice such things are worthy of death, they not only do the same, but also give hearty approval to those who practice them" (v. 32). The pagan world is not unaware of God's displeasure with these activities. Homosexuals, adulterers, greedy people, slanderers are not happy little sinners. Their conscience may be seared, but it still pricks them occasionally. They know what God's Word says, because preachers, radio Bible teachers, and Christian writers won't let them forget it. Therefore, fully cognizant of the consequences of their sin, they continue to defy the Lord God of heaven and take great pleasure in keeping company with those who do the same.

Paul's inescapable conclusion is that the nations are never without a witness to the presence and personality of God. They have the witness of nature and the witness of their own conscience. Nevertheless, they have deliberately suppressed these witnesses to the truth and have consistently opted for a lie in place of the truth. They have chosen the course of idolatry, which is always accompanied by debauchery. Thus, God has revealed His wrath from heaven against all ungodliness and unrighteousness of people who suppress the truth of God. In addition, God has given them over to their idolatry, to their infamous passions, and to an undiscerning and unapproving mind, a mind that knows God's law but cannot bring the flesh to abide by it.

Are the Gentiles lost? Yes. Those in far-off lands living under the plague of ignorance, with no Bible and no one to tell them of God's love are lost because they have suppressed God's truth and acted in ways they know are contrary to nature. Likewise, unbelievers who live in modern urban settings are lost. They are living under a chosen plague of ignorance, with a Bible at every turn and people constantly telling them of God's love and the need to repent. They have suppressed God's truth and have acted in ways they know are contrary to God and nature. All who suppress the truth are lost, deserving of God's wrath, and destined for eternal punishment because of their sin. It is the just compensation for disregarding God's truth. The entire unbelieving world is lost, desperately wicked, desiring evil, and deserving condemnation. If they do not repent and turn to God, one day they will no longer suppress the truth but be judged by it. Then, however, it will be too late.

Study Questions

1. How can the wrath of God be defined?
2. What can people see about God in nature?

3. From verses 21–23, list what Paul says people do in their denial of God.

4. What is Paul alluding to in verses 26–27?

5. What would cause people to go on in their sin and not turn away from death?

CHAPTER 5

Moral People Are Condemned
Romans 2:1-16

Preview:
The apostle is more specific here about those who practice sin and yet feel that they somehow can escape judgment. They make light of God's kindness and refuse to come to repentance and a change of heart. Such people fail to obey the truth but instead obey unrighteousness. Keeping the Law is not the answer for salvation, nor is it enough to allow a sinner to escape judgment. People's secret sins will be judged by the gospel.

In chapter 1, Paul painted a picture of the deplorable condition of the nations. The apostle knew, however, that there would be a whole class of people who would say "amen" to what he had said about the nations. These were the self-righteous moralists. So Paul expanded his argument to show that "all ungodliness and unrighteousness of men" includes the moralist as well as the debauched pagan. Moralists are inexcusable when they judge others for sin but are blind to their own sin. They only condemn themselves when they condemn others. "For in that you judge another, you condemn yourself; for you who judge practice the same things" (v. 1). It is obvious that these moral people were not involved in the sexual deviations of the Gentiles, else Paul could not have called them moral. There is no morality in debauchery. But inwardly they were living in an identical manner to what others were living outwardly. Perhaps these moral people did not commit adultery, but did they lust? Our Lord put them in the same category (Matt. 5:27–28). Maybe these moral people did not steal, but did they covet? Stealing and covetousness are listed together in Mark 7:21–22. Perchance these moral people did not commit murder, but did they

for what sins do I judge others while having inner struggle w/ the same principle?

hate? The Bible says that if you hate your brother, you are guilty of murder (1 John 3:15). Only a fool would judge another while he or she is doing the same thing, because that person would be condemned by his own judgment.

Moral People Are Condemned According to the Truth (2:2–5)

When God judges, it is always according to truth, in full accordance with the facts. Moralists may attempt to hide the facts, but God always exposes them. God's searching eye always ferrets out the truth. So Paul challenges those who appear to live morally on the outside but live immorally on the inside. "And do you suppose this, O man, when you pass judgment upon those who practice such things and do the same yourself, that you will escape the judgment of God?" (v. 3). Since the judgment of God is according to truth, it is foolhardy for moralists to believe that God will judge others and not them. Since they do in their hearts what others do in their lives, moralists must withstand the same judgment as the ones they condemn. To put ourselves in the position of the moralist would mean to despise God's kindness (Greek, *khrēstotēs*), forbearance (Greek, *anochē*, the willingness to tolerate the intolerance of others), and patience (Greek, *makrothumia*, patience that forgives until there is no more hope of repentance). The goodness of God leads us to repentance. In judging others, moralists have completely missed the purpose of God's goodness. It never occurs to moralists that they personally need the goodness of God just as blatant sinners do. They are unaware of their need for repentance.

After years of glossing over personal sin and guilt, the pride of moralists will not allow them to have a change of mind (Greek, *metanoia*), which is repentance (v. 5). Thus their pride and sinful hearts stockpile the wrath of God so that in the day of wrath, the day of God's righteous judgment, the Lord God will deal as justly with moral people as He does with the immoral ones.

Moral People Are Condemned According to Their Works (2:6–10)

When the unsaved appear before the final judgment bar of God, the Great White Throne Judgment, salvation will not be the issue there. This is a judgment to determine the degree of punishment (Rev. 20:11–15). Thus God will mete out punishment in relation to the evil deeds of the individual. By the same token, at the Judgment Seat of Christ, where only believers appear, God will reward us according to our deeds (2 Cor. 5:10). Paul's comment about perseverance in doing good has caused some to question Paul's commitment to salvation by faith alone. But we need not worry. Perseverance in doing good does not mean that we are saved by doing good. Paul is expressing an eternal truth. Obedience to God does well in every dispensation. When Cain brought his fruit as an offering and God rejected it, God said, "If you do well, will not your countenance be lifted up?" (Gen. 4:7). Cain did not bring his offering in faith, and thus it was not accepted (Heb. 11:4). Obedience to God in bringing the proper sacrifice in faith would have been doing well. Today, in the age of grace, the perfect sacrifice has already been made for us. We need bring nothing. To do well, we must only place our faith in Christ Jesus as Savior. Thus faith in Christ is perseverance in doing good in this age. This is what will bring "glory and honor and immortality," that is, eternal life.

The moralist is likened to "those who are of selfishly ambitious" (v. 8). This formula is similar to other such expressions as those who are "of the circumcision" (4:12; Tit. 1:10); "those who are of faith" (Gal. 3:7); "those who are of the Law" (4:14). Those who create a spirit of rivalry or factionalism have promised to them wrath (Greek, *thumos*, "a sudden outburst of anger"), indignation (Greek, *orgē*, "angry agitation of the soul"), tribulation (Greek, *thlipsis*, "affliction"), and distress (Greek, *stenochōria*, "dire calamity"). Opposed to the reward of the unrighteous, Paul now indicates that the reward of the righteous is glory, honor, and instead of immortality as in verse 7, peace. The formula of impartiality is then the same. As the gospel was promised to the Jew first and also to the Greek, so likewise the fruit of unrighteousness is of the Jew first and also of the Gentile.

Moral People Are Condemned Without Regard to Who They Are (2:11–16)

An eternal truth is that God deals in condemnation without favoritism just as He deals in salvation without favoritism. Respect of persons (Greek, *prosōpolēmpsia*, literally "lifting the face") simply means partiality (cf. Deut. 10:17; 2 Chr. 19:7; Acts 10:34; Gal. 2:6; Eph. 6:9; Col. 3:25; 1 Pet. 1:17). God is impartial in that He does not change His pattern "to the Jew first," whether righteousness or unrighteousness is involved. Here's how the principle of divine impartiality is applied: "For all who have sinned without the Law will also perish without the Law; and all who have sinned under the Law will be judged by the Law" (v. 12). Unchecked and unatoned for sin leads to perdition whether we are Jewish and living under the Law or are Gentile and living apart from the Law. If the moralist is to live by the Law, then the hearers of the Law are not just before God; only the doers of the Law are justified. The antithesis between merely hearing the Law and doing it is elaborated in James 1:22–25.

"The doers of the law" is an expression also found in the literature of the Dead Sea Scrolls. The moralist (now identified with the Jews beginning at verse 9) is no better off than the Gentiles if the moralist has the Law but does not keep it. The reason follows in the next verses.

"For when Gentiles who do not have the Law do instinctively the things of the Law, these, not having the Law, are a law unto themselves" (v. 14). Although the Gentiles do not possess the Old Testament Law, nevertheless, they intuitively do those things that are contained in the Law. Why? The Gentiles manifested a moral principle at work in their hearts that the Jews did not. When they broke their own ethical code, their conscience (Greek, *suneidēsis*) would prick them and cause them to feel guilty. "The etymology of the word, both in Greek and in English (from Latin) implies, conscience is a knowledge along with (or shared with) the person. It is the individual's inner sense of right and wrong; his (to a certain extent divinely imparted) moral consciousness viewed in the act of pronouncing judgment upon himself, that is, upon his thoughts, attitudes, words, and deeds, whether past, present or contemplated."[1] The result of the Gentiles' guilt, however, was that they would excuse themselves by making a defense for their actions. But Jew and Gentile alike must one day face the judgment of God when peoples' secrets (Greek, *ta krupta*) are judged by the Lord Jesus Christ according to the truth.

Being moral is insufficient to be righteous. These are not synonymous concepts. Moral people may possess a heightened conscience and live in light of it, but God demands righteousness, not just morality. Since no one innately possesses such righteousness, God deals with the moral and the immoral in the same way. Both fall short of God's glory (Rom. 3:23). While moralists may be better citizens, they are not better candidates for heaven. The human need for righteousness permeates both blatant sinners and moralists.

Study Questions

1. Is Paul saying that people sin because of their ignorance or that they practice evil deeds fully aware of what they are doing? Explain.

2. Specifically, how does God demonstrate the riches of His kindness, forbearance, and patience to the lost world?

3. In this section of verses, how does Paul describe the heart, the attitudes, and the motives of those who are lost?

4. Are human beings still sinners if they "sinned without the Law"?

5. What is the purpose of the Law?

6. How is the "work of the Law" shown in the heart?

CHAPTER 6

Jewish People Are Condemned Romans 2:17–3:8

Preview:
Paul now addresses the problem of sin, the Law, and Jews who "boast in God."
The Jews often claimed a certain purity but still went on in their sinning. Doing
something externally, like trying to keep the Law, does not make one a child of
God. Being Jews who knew the oracles of God had advantages, but they still
must be justified before the Lord in their hearts in order to be called believers
and God's own!

Israelites who remained in Palestine or returned to it after the Babylonian captivity were designated as "Jews," even though tribes other than Judah were included. Paul calls himself a "Jew" in Acts 21:39 but an "Israelite" in Romans 11:1 and "a Hebrew" in Philippians 3:5. All three names refer to the same people; but in a technical sense, "Hebrew" is the racial name, "Israel" is the national name, and "Jew" is the religious name of the sons of Jacob.

Jewish Law Cannot Make a Jew Righteous (2:17–24)

The Jews rested in the Law because it was described as "your wisdom and your understanding in the sight of the peoples" (Deut. 4:6). Jews did not have to travel around the world to study in a distant university. They did not have to rely on the philosophy of the Gentiles. Jews trusted the Law to be all that they needed and the best education they could get (v. 17). Thus they boasted in the God who gave that Law. But Jews had more on their minds. They claimed to "know His will, and approve the things that are essential, being instructed out of the Law" (v. 18). Because they had received catechetical training in the Law as youths, and rabbinical teaching as men, Jews felt confident that they could prove (Greek, *dokimazō*) or discern those things that are more essential for life. Confident that they would be saved by their Law, Jews were convinced that they had been made righteous and therefore were able to assume four roles: guide for the blind (the blind being Gentiles in their un-Jewish darkness); light for those in darkness (Gentiles needed to be enlightened by Jews who were enlightened by the Law); corrector of the foolish (because they did not know the Law, Gentiles were fools); teacher of the immature (Gentiles were spiritually or religiously immature, objects of Jewish disgust).

Paul uses a touch of sarcasm in his question: "You, therefore, who teach another, do you not teach yourself?" (v. 21). The Jews were prepared to teach the Gentiles the commandments of the Law but were themselves breaking those commandments. Paul notes in verse 21, "You who preach that one should not steal, do you steal?" (the eighth commandment). And in verse 22, "You who say that one should not commit adultery, do you commit adultery?" (the seventh commandment). Again in verse 22, "You who abhor idols, do you rob temples?" (the second commandment). The Jews were ready to preach morality, but their lives did not back up their message. They were stealing from one another, perhaps by collecting extreme interest; they were committing adultery; and they were profaning the house of God by commercialism. Therefore Paul asked the biting question, "You who boast in the Law, through your breaking the Law, do you dishonor God?" (v. 23). Transgression of the Law brings dishonor to God. The Jews claimed to have known the Law but were unable to claim they kept it.

What was the result of Jewish hypocrisy? "For 'the name of God is blasphemed among the Gentiles because of you' " (v. 24). Paul's quotation from Isaiah 52:5 confirms that the inadequacies in the lifestyles of the Jews caused the Gentiles to speak lightly of the God of Israel. The Word of God was actually being blasphemed among the Gentiles because of the inconsistency of the Jews. Much the same thing could be said today about hearers of the Word but not doers in the evangelical church.

Jewish Circumcision Cannot Make a Jew Righteous (2:25–27)

The Jews were still looking for righteousness through their vaulted position before God. If their Law could not make them righteous because they didn't keep it, perhaps the rite of circumcision could do the job. Maybe they could claim salvation through circumcision. Paul hits the issue head-on. "For indeed circumcision is of value, if you practice the Law" (v. 25). Notice that the apostle did not say, "Indeed circumcision justifies." That has never been true. But circumcision is not a meaningless rite if it aids in keeping the Law. However, when the Jew does not keep the Law, his circumcision has become the same as uncircumcision. If the Jew trusts in his circumcision for salvation and does not keep the Law, his circumcision is meaningless.

"If therefore the uncircumcised man [the Gentile] keeps the requirements of the Law," Paul asks, "will not his uncircumcision be regarded as circumcision?" (v. 26). Now the tables are turned completely. If an uncircumcised Gentile gives his heart to God and lives in a righteous relationship to the Jewish Law, he is more pleasing to God than the circumcised Jew who does not. As bad as that is for the Jewish ego, there's more. "And will not he who is physically uncircumcised, if he keeps the Law, will he not judge you who though having the letter of the Law and circumcision are a transgressor of the Law?" (v. 27). Remember, the Jew prided himself on being a guide to the blind, a light to those in darkness, a corrector of the foolish, and a teacher of the immature (vv. 19–20). The sin of the circumcised but unworthy Jew will be graphically demonstrated by the example of the Gentile who, though uncircumcised, nevertheless pleases God. Lack of circumcision would not condemn a Gentile, just as being circumcised would not save a Jew. The key is the Law. If the Law was broken, the Jew became as helpless as the Gentile. Therefore, the circumcised Jew is in the same pitiful state as the uncircumcised Gentiles if the Jew has broken the Law. Since all the Jews have broken the Law, Paul's conclusion is that his circumcision cannot save the Jew, for he has broken the Law.

Jewish Birth Cannot Make a Jew Righteous (2:28–29)

Paul just keeps moving through Jewish objections like Sherman through Atlanta. If the Law cannot make a Jew righteous and his circumcision cannot, what about his birthright? Surely that has to count for something. Paul jumps right in. "For he is not a Jew who is one outwardly. . . . But he is a Jew who is one inwardly" (vv. 28–29). Here we see the double sense in which the term *Jew* is used. Frequently people use *Christian* as a term in opposition to *heathen*. In another sense, true believers in the Lord are called Christians. Paul is making the case that not all who are called Jews are truly Jewish. Possessing the Law does not make one Jewish. Circumcision does not make one Jewish. Even birth in a Jewish family does not make one Jewish. As strange as that seems, Paul is using the term *Jew* in a specific sense. He says that two things are necessary to be truly Jewish: (1) to be born of Abraham through Isaac (that circumcision that is outward in the flesh); and (2) to be spiritually in tune with

Abraham's God (that circumcision that is inward in the heart or spirit). As the apostle Paul is using the word, no one can claim to be Jewish who is not born of Abraham through his son Isaac. But to the requirement of outward circumcision (ancestry from Abraham), Paul adds the requirement of the circumcision of the heart. This spiritual or ethical circumcision is seen throughout the Scriptures (e.g., uncircumcised lips in Exodus 6:12; uncircumcised ears in Jeremiah 6:10; and uncircumcised hearts in Leviticus 26:41). Jews who are born after the seed of Abraham through Isaac but do not have their hearts circumcised in the way that Abraham did, that is, "to love the LORD your God with all your heart" (Deut. 30:6; see also Jer. 4:4), are not truly Jews. They are Jews outwardly but not inwardly. They are born of Abraham but not born again by the Spirit of God. The only true Jew is one who is a Jew by race and a believer by God's grace. Thus Paul concludes that mere physical birth alone cannot make a Jew righteous.

Jewish Arguments Cannot Make a Jew Righteous (3:1–8)

At the beginning of chapter 3, Paul anticipates various arguments from the Jews in rebuttal to his conclusion that Israel's Law, their circumcision, and their birth could not save them. These theoretical objections are stated in the even numbered verses, and Paul's answer to each objection is stated in the odd numbered verses.

Question: "Then what advantage has the Jew?" (v. 1). If the Jews are condemned along with the Gentiles, what advantage is there in being the chosen people of God? An attendant question: "Or what is the benefit of circumcision?" Since circumcision is the sign of Israel's covenant relationship with God, what advantage is that relationship if being Jewish will not save?

Answer: "Great in every respect" (v. 2). Paul contends that there are many privileges that God has granted to Israel. A list of them is given in chapter 11; it is not necessary for Paul to enumerate them here. Rather, he simply points out one as an example of the others. The Jews were entrusted with the oracles of God. One of the chief ancestral privileges of Israel was that they were the custodians of God's words. Acts 7:38 and Hebrews 5:12 mention these oracles, the Old Testament Scriptures. It was a great advantage to the Jew to be singled out by God and entrusted with the reception, inscription, and transmission of the Old Testament Scriptures. That was true of no one else. The Jews should be proud. But having the Word of God does little good if you don't read and obey it.[1]

Question: "If some did not believe, their unbelief will not nullify the faithfulness of God, will it?" (v. 3). As keepers of the Old Testament, the Jews had in fact failed to comprehend the message of the Old Testament, especially the prophetic and messianic passages. The unbelief of the Jews is seen in their rejection of Jesus as Messiah, and consequently they did not believe the oracles of God they so carefully guarded. The question is, "Will Jewish unbelief negate the faithfulness of God?" Paul's answer is a classic.

Answer: "May it never be!" This expression (Greek, *mē genoito*) corresponds to the Hebrew *chalilah*, which is translated the same in the KJV of Genesis 44:17; Joshua 22:29; 24:16; and 1 Kings 21:3 among others. It is an expression that indicates a recoiling abhorrence, utter shock, and disgust. It has been variously translated "good heavens," "no way," "may it not prove to be so," "perish the thought," "God forbid," and so on.

"Let God be found true, though every man be found a liar" establishes a principle that is found throughout this epistle. God does not purpose or will according to extraneous influences but according to what He Himself is. If men prove unfaithful to God's oracles, He is nevertheless faithful in His promises to them. Why? He is God. He cannot be unfaithful to Himself. The quotation that follows is from Psalm 51:4, "So that Thou art justified when Thou dost speak and blameless when Thou dost judge." This is from the lips of King David who had broken the covenant of God and had found in himself no righteousness or integrity of any kind. Paul quotes this verse that his readers may clearly see the difference between the faithfulness and integrity of God and the lack of the same in man.

Question: A third objection is now theoretically advanced. "But if our unrighteousness demonstrates the righteousness of God, what shall we say?" (v. 5). This is a clever but illogical argument. It is twisting Scripture to make what is inherently evil appear to be ultimately good. Paul anticipates someone saying, "If my unfaithfulness causes God's faithfulness to be set in boldface type, is not my sin by contrast enhancing the world's concept of the absolute holiness and faithfulness of God?" What do you say? And then there is a second question: "The God who inflicts wrath is not unrighteous, is He?" Would it not be unjust of God to punish you for contributing to a more pristine picture of His true character?

The expression "I am speaking in human terms" should not be understood as an absence of divine inspiration in recording these questions, but rather that Paul is using the form of human reasoning to express this inspired truth about God. Since God's justice is not something that may be called into question, Paul indicates that only foolish human reasoning would attempt to do so.

Answer: The answer to these questions is an emphatic "May it never be!" The consequence of this line of reasoning would be to deny God the divine right to judge any person. If God cannot judge people, then who can?

"But if through my lie the truth of God abounded to His glory, why am I also still being judged as a sinner?" (v. 7). Paul had been slandered by the Jews for teaching salvation by grace apart from works. He therefore uses that situation to theorize a final argument from the Jews. If the doctrine of salvation Paul preaches is a lie, and the truth is seen in contrast to Paul's teaching, then why is Paul also judged as a sinner? Shouldn't he be considered a saint if his alleged false doctrine more clearly indicated what was true? Paul has turned the tables on the Jews by using their own logic and putting them in an untenable situation. They could not admit that Paul's teachings were true. But if they claimed them to be false, by their own logic, they would have to say that divine good arose out of Paul's doctrine.

The Jew's argued that Paul was teaching the lie, "Let us do evil that good may come" (v. 8). For those who regarded the practice of religion as merely a matter of keeping the Law, Paul's emphasis on justification by faith indeed seemed to make the Law and its keeping superfluous. But justification by faith never meant believers could blatantly disregard the precepts of the Law. If they did, their condemnation is just. Condemnation is executed on all those who, in light of their unfaithfulness, turn God's faithfulness into an opportunity for personal lasciviousness and license. This Antinomian philosophy is further condemned in Romans 6.

God loves the Jewish people. He isn't finished with them (see Rom. 11). But God is just in condemning the Jews, for they have sinned against Him; and that their sin enhances His own righteousness is but a diversion from their own culpability as sinners. The justified man, whether pagan, moralist, or Jew, is not free to do evil. Arguments to the contrary can never save anyone.

Study Questions

1. Summarize the problems the Jews had in trying to please God.

2. Could it be said that the Jews were trying to please God by their position, heritage, and good works? Explain.

3. What was so important about circumcision?

4. List ways the Jews had "an advantage."

5. If the Jews were not righteous by faith before God, could they still claim in a personal sense to be children of God?

CHAPTER 7

All People Are Condemned
Romans 3:9-20

Preview:
God's judgment and condemnation come against everyone, both Jew and Gentile. No one seeks God or can be called righteous. To sin is the natural tendency of all human beings. "No fear of God" may be the root cause of all rebellion. God's righteous demands, as reflected in the Law, condemn everyone and make him or her accountable to God. No one can be justified before the Lord by the works of Law-keeping.

Paul has shown that the Gentiles are lost because, even though they had the witness of both nature and conscience, they suppressed God's truth to them. He has shown also that moral people are lost because, even though they outwardly put on a facade to judge the blatantly immoral, inwardly they are guilty of the same sins. Likewise, the Jews are lost because they have not kept the Law, and their circumcision, ancestry, and arguments cannot save them from the condemnation of disobedience. Now Paul wraps up his argument using the courtroom terminology.

The Whole World Is Charged with the Guilt That Accompanies Sin (3:9)

The Jews enjoyed certain privileges as the elect nation of God, but these privileges did not include special treatment at the judgment bar of God. So, to the question, "Are we better than they?" Paul's answer is no, no way. His reason is simple: "For we have already charged that both Jews and Greeks are all under sin" (v. 9).

Adopting the terminology of the courtroom, Paul now takes us through the judicial procedure to determine guilt or innocence. The first step in the judicial procedure is to make an accusation or charge against the offenders. This Paul does when he says they are all under sin. The Greek word *proaitiaomai* ("charge") is a combination of the words, *pro*, meaning "before," and *altiaomai*, meaning "to bring an accusation against" or "press formal charges." Paul has charged the entire world with being innately sinful. If the evidence is sufficient and the charge can be proved, the whole world will be judged guilty before God. Notice that Paul does not say all have sinned but that all are "under sin." This means they all are under the penalty as well as the power of sin. The apostle has in mind here a very definite contrast between being "under sin" and being "under grace." Romans 6:14–15 speaks of being "under grace" with our sins pardoned and ourselves justified.

The Whole World Is Indicted Because of Sin (3:10–18)

Next in the judicial procedure is an indictment. Webster defines indictment as "a formal written statement framed by a prosecuting authority and found by a jury charging a person with an offense.[1] An indictment, then, is a formal, written charge, and every indictment must have at least one count, one specific charge. The more serious the crime, the more counts to the indictment. Paul immediately follows this pattern by quoting from a series of Old Testament passages that demonstrate, in no less than fourteen counts, the total depravity of the entire world (3:10–18).

Count 1. "There is none righteous, not even one" (v. 10). This same theme is seen throughout the Old Testament and is summarized in Psalm 14:1–3. *Righteousness* is not only the key word in this epistle, it is also the criterion by which sin is judged. The bad news is, men and women lack the righteousness necessary to live with God in His heavenly home.

Count 2. "There is none who understands" (v. 11). Not a verbatim quote, this charge is derived from Psalm 14:2 and 53:2. Here understanding is not mental but spiritual. The world is totally lacking in spiritual discernment (Eph. 4:17–18). The natural man may not be mentally deranged, but he is certainly spiritually deranged and incapable of spiritual understanding (1 Cor. 2:14).

Count 3. "There is none who seeks for God" (v. 11). In Psalm 53:2–3 David remarks that there is no one who innately seeks after God, because people by nature are sinful and want nothing to do with God. It is only when sinners are drawn by God to Himself that they seek the Lord Jesus Christ in repentance and confession (John 6:44). Because they naturally do not seek the Lord, people give evidence of being guilty of unrighteousness.

Count 4. "All have turned aside" (v. 12). People have not only "missed the mark," they have also "perverted their path." In this quote from the LXX of Psalm 14:3 and 53:4, the picture is of a camel caravan crossing the desert that has strayed from the route and cannot return to the proper path. Likewise, human beings have lost their way by deviating from God's prescribed route of righteousness.

Count 5. "They have become useless" (v. 12). People are not useful, of no benefit. Like salt that has lost its savor or fruit that has become rotten, so all people are viewed as useless, rotten, corrupted when compared to the righteousness of Christ. Of course, this does not mean that human beings are useless in this world. It means men and women can do nothing useful to contribute to their salvation. Human beings are totally unprofitable when it comes to producing that which pleases God.

Count 6. "There is none who does good, there is not even one" (v. 12). Again the written indictment comes from Psalm 14. It doesn't mean that we cannot be of benefit to society; it means that no one can do anything of spiritual or eternal value. No matter what humankind does, as far as righteousness is concerned, it is nothing but filthy rags (Is. 64:6).

Count 7. "Their throat is an open grave" (v. 13). This seventh count of the indictment is the first one that is specific. Paul addresses the chief outlets through which we can display our sin. He will speak to the sinners' throats, tongues, lips, and mouths. Paul shows his familiarity with the Old Testament by drawing on King David's prayer for protection in Psalm 5.

Nothing is more abominable than the stench rising from an open sepulcher or burial vault. The apostle graphically portrays the conversation of the wicked by likening the filth that arises from their mouths with the stench of the open sepulcher. Watched any TV or videos lately? Have you seen those warnings about language? You know what Paul is talking about.

Count 8. "With their tongues they keep deceiving" (v. 13). The sugared tongue, which is used to butter up the boss, is next listed by Paul as characteristic of sinful people. The apostle indicts the world for the Madison Avenue approach to life, which makes something out of nothing and promises what cannot be performed. Deceit, even in simple advertising or in making personal claims, is deceit nonetheless, and it is evidence of humankind's unrighteousness.

Count 9. "The poison of asps is under their lips" (v. 13). This ninth indictment is reminiscent of the final speech of Zophar, one of Job's critical friends (Job 20:14–16). The poison of the asp is stored in a bag under the "lips" of the serpent. When Paul spoke of this deadly poison, he probably had in mind the Egyptian cobra, the reptile used by Pharaoh Tutankhamen as his imperial symbol. Of the evil and violent man, David says, "They sharpen their tongues as a serpent; poison of a viper is under their lips" (Ps. 140:3). The natural man's human speech is likened to this poison.

Count 10. "Whose mouth is full of cursing and bitterness" (v. 14). Psalm 10:7 indicates that man's mouth, which was created to speak the truth of God and praise Him continually, has been perverted to speaking the lies of Satan through cursing and bitterness. You do not have to teach a person to curse; it is the common expression of the bitterness within, rooted in personal sin.

Count 11. "Their feet are swift to shed blood" (v. 15). Paul now turns his attention, not to people's words, but to their deeds. Quoting from Isaiah 59:7–8, the feet which were created to carry the gospel to the ends of the earth have in every era of history readily carried people to commit violent injustice and war against their fellow humans (see Prov. 1:8–19). Such is the result of human depravity.

Count 12. "Destruction and misery are in their paths" (v. 16). This twelfth charge in the apostle's indictment lists not only what people are seeking but also what they shall certainly receive if they continue in their unrighteous path. Calamity and misery are not only soul mates, but they always follow the sinner's futile search for happiness apart from Jesus Christ (cf. James 4:2).

Count 13. "And the path of peace they have not known" (v. 17). Unregenerate men and women can never find peace with others until they have made peace with their Creator. The United Nations and other peace-oriented agencies are doomed to failure, because humankind is a ferocious animal. Rarely will the most savage of animals destroy its own species to appease its hunger, but humans destroy fellow humans for much less. The world is filled with animosity, hatred, terrorists, and murderers. Humans will never be at peace with one another until they are at peace with God (Is. 59:8).

Count 14. "There is no fear of God before their eyes" (v. 18). Quoted from Psalm 36:1, this final charge is the fountain from which all the others spring. All the characteristics of humans, their lack of understanding, their unprofitableness, their lack of peace, and so on, stem from the fact that they do not fear God (Ps. 36:1). Since people have no spiritual understanding, and the fear of the Lord is the beginning of wisdom, humans are caught in a vicious circle. Only the external force of the Holy Spirit of God can break the circle of humankind's ignorance, arrogance, and guilt. Paul presents these fourteen specific, written counts in his indictment against the whole world.

The Whole World Prepares Its Best Defense (3:19a)

Having charged the whole world with being under sin, and having listed fourteen counts to his indictment, Paul now moves in the judicial procedure to the defense on behalf of the world. He quickly anticipates the line of argument the Jews will use in their defense. They will say that Paul's description of humankind in the preceding verses does not describe them but the Gentiles. So Paul makes it clear that whatever a law says, it says to those living under the authority of the statutes of that law. Using "Law" in reference to the entire Old Testament Scriptures, the apostle presses that he was in fact speaking of Jews as well as the Gentiles, for they had received the oracles of God and were bound by them.

Ordinarily in a civil court the time of the defense is usually given to flowery speeches, insinuation, discrediting of witnesses, muddling of the issues, and so on. But this will not be the case at the judgment bar of God. When the evidence against the universal sinfulness and guilt of humankind is presented and the opportunity for defense comes, there will be no defense. "That every mouth may be closed" is indicative of how little will be said in our defense. The mouth of the immoral person will be closed. The mouth of the moral person and religious person will also be shut. Even the mouth of the cursing and bitter person will be stopped. The figure used is dramatic, fear-inspiring, unforgettable. Everybody is standing in front of God, the Judge. The records are read, and as it were one by one the accused are given an opportunity to answer the charges made against them. However, their guilt having been exposed, they have no answer. Their mouths are silenced, stopped."[2] A silent world will stand in judgment before the holy and sovereign God, and clever lawyers, plea bargaining, offering bribes to the judge, and impassioned appeals will not help to get the sinner off. The infamous French infidel Jean Jacques Rousseau, who refused to marry and sent his illegitimate children to an orphanage, once exclaimed: "I will stand before God and defend my conduct!" Bad news for Rousseau: No one will utter a word in his defense, for no one will have a defense before the righteous God.

The Verdict Is in for the Whole World (3:19b–20)

All that remains in the judicial process is to render a verdict. The charge has been made, the indictment read. No defense can be made, for there is no supporting case for humankind. The verdict is inevitable and is now ready to he heard. "All the world may become accountable to God" (v. 19). The verdict is guilty, the only thing it can be. The word *guilty* (Greek, *hupodikos*) means to come under judgment. It does not presuppose guilt, but denotes the state of a person who has been justly charged with a crime and is both legally responsible for it and worthy of blame. The first word of verse 20 is "because." Paul is now coming to the summation of his argument and is about to make an application and draw a conclusion. He began back in chapter 1, verse 18, by proposing that "the wrath of God is revealed from heaven against all ungodliness and unrighteousness of men." He has shown that the righteousness of God is sadly needed in the world. It is needed by the pagan, the moralist, and the Jew. In fact, the righteousness of God is needed by the whole world.

Having given his proposition and the facts assembled from the Old Testament and present experience, Paul is now ready to draw a conclusion: "By the works of the Law no flesh will be justified in His sight" (v. 20). Exclamation point! Case closed. This free rendering of Psalm 143:2 (cf. Gal. 2:16; 3:11) does not have the definite article "the" before Law in the original language, and thus Paul concludes that there is no law anywhere in the world that can justify any person. The law of the Gentiles, the law of nature, the law of morality, the law of conscience, the Law of Moses—none can justify a person and make him or her righteous in the sight of God. Even the law of Christ, laid down in the Sermon on the Mount, cannot justify anyone. It is by the Law that the knowledge of sin comes, a point expanded in 5:20; 7:7–13, but no law can save a man. The Law can convict men and women of sin, and it can define sin, but it cannot emancipate them from sin. Only the grace of God can do that. The whole world is sinful and desperately in need of the righteousness of God. But if that righteousness is to come to any individual, including you and me, it must come through the agency of grace, God's grace, sovereign grace.

Study Questions

1. When the apostle Paul writes about the Gentiles, he often uses the term *Greek* (1:16; 3:9). What does this description mean in his thinking?

2. In verses 9–12, what is common in Paul's description about people and about human nature?

3. In verses 10–18, is the apostle saying that everyone is committing all of these sins all of the time? Explain.

4. In verse 19, is Paul saying all people everywhere are under the condemnation of the Law?

5. In verse 20, what does Paul say is the main purpose of the Law?

SECTION III: JUSTIFICATION

The Divine Provision
of Righteousness

Romans 3:21 – 5:21

Having clearly established that the righteousness of God is needed by men and women everywhere, Paul now proceeds to demonstrate that the righteousness of God is provided by God. Thus, the second major division of the epistle to the Romans begins at 3:21 with reference to divine provision for human need. Thank God that Paul's letter to the Romans didn't end at Romans 3:20.

CHAPTER 8

Justification by Faith Explained Romans 3:21-31

Preview:

Paul gets to the message of his epistle to the Romans: The only way one can be justified before God is by faith through Christ. The righteousness of God is imparted because of faith; justification is a gift through the grace of God. No one can boast of salvation by human works or by law-keeping. God can and will justify everyone who trusts in Him by faith apart from works.

The apostle begins this section with the Greek phrase *nuni de*, which is usually translated "but now." This phrase is used in the Pauline epistles eighteen times and twice in Hebrews. It does not occur anywhere else in the New Testament. *Nuni de* is an adverb of time. It is an expression Paul uses when transitioning from a dark, gloomy picture to something wonderful that God does for us. We humans have dug ourselves in so deep that only God can get us out. God must enter our world or else we will never enter God's world. In establishing guidelines for writers of tragedies, the Roman poet Horace in his *Ars Poetica* (191) said, "Do not bring a god onto the stage, unless the problem is one that deserves a god to solve it." The human predicament is not one that even Horace's gods can solve; only Abraham's God can solve humanity's predicament.

Two very important words pervade this passage—*righteousness* and *justify*. Although quite different in English, these two words are practically identical in Greek (*dikaios*, "to be righteous"; *dikaioō*, "to justify"). Justification is a legal declaration issued by God in which He pronounces

a person free from any fault or guilt and acceptable in His sight. "To justify means 'to pronounce and treat as righteous.' It is vastly more than being
pardoned; it is a thousand times more than forgiveness. You may wrong me
and then come to me; and I may say, I forgive you. But I have not justified
you. I cannot justify you. But when God justifies a man, He says, 'I pronounce you a righteous man. Henceforth I am going to treat you as if you
never committed any sin' "[1]

Justification Is Apart from the Law (3:21)

The righteousness of God is neither an attribute of God nor the changed
character of the believer. As defined in Romans 1:17, the righteousness of
God is Christ Himself, who met every demand of the Law for us in our place,
and who "became to us wisdom from God, and righteousness and sanctification, and redemption" (1 Cor. 1:30). God's righteousness is demonstrated
and communicated to us through the cross.

One thing is certain: "Apart from the Law the righteousness of God has
been manifested" (v. 21). This tandem (Greek, *chōris nomou*) is a strong
expression categorically stating that righteousness is totally apart from any
law. See the same use of this word in Hebrews 4:15, where the Lord Jesus was
tempted in all points as we are "yet without sin." Just as sin and Jesus Christ
have nothing in common, so, too, righteousness and the Law have nothing
in common. Righteousness was not demonstrated in keeping the Law, but it
was demonstrated at Calvary's cross when "He [God the Father] made Him
[God the Son] who knew no sin to be sin on our behalf, that we might
become the righteousness of God in Him" (2 Cor. 5:21).

Every time a man took his sacrifice to the temple for a sin offering, confessed his sin, and killed the animal, he was testifying that he had faith in a
righteousness that was not his own. Thus the Law bears witness to an external righteousness that God provides but the Law itself cannot provide (v. 21).
Likewise the prophets also witness to this righteousness (see Is. 53:6; the
same thought that is expressed in 2 Cor. 5:21 and in 1 Pet. 2:21–24). Paul further explains, "The righteousness of God [comes] through faith in Jesus
Christ." The righteousness of God does not come to one who simply has
faith in God. Being a deist is not the same as being righteous. Believing in a
god named Allah or Buddha or anyone else is insufficient to receive the righteousness of God. Those who want the righteousness of God you must find it
"through faith in Jesus Christ" (v. 22; see also 2 Tim. 3:15).

Righteousness Requires Faith in Christ (3:22)

Now Paul makes a critical distinction. "The righteousness of God through faith in Jesus Christ for all those who believe." The New International Version similarly says, "This righteousness from God comes through faith in Jesus Christ to all who believe." The King James Version, using a different manuscript family, says, "Even the righteousness of God which is by faith of Jesus Christ unto all and upon all them that believe." The words "upon all" are not included in some manuscripts (S, A, B, D, and some other versions), which is why they are not included in the New International Version or the New American Standard Bible. Nevertheless, the meaning is the same. God's righteousness is provided for all people. Therefore Christians are to go into the entire world and preach the gospel to every creature (Mark 16:15). However, even though this righteousness is provided for all, it is applied only to those who believe in Jesus Christ as Savior. The only conditional element of the gospel is faith in Jesus Christ. This righteousness is placed upon us as a cloak when by faith we receive Jesus Christ as Savior. Righteousness is from God, through Jesus Christ, to all who believe that what Jesus did at Calvary is all God requires as payment of the penalty for our sin. Martin Luther said this is the very center and kernel of the epistle and of all Scripture, and indeed it is.

This phrase "no distinction" occurs in only one other place in the epistle to the Romans. In this verse there is no distinction between the need of the Jew and the Gentile. That need is explained in the expression "for all have sinned" (v. 23). But just as there is no distinction in human need, likewise there is no distinction in divine provision (Rom. 10:12–13), the other place the expression occurs. Karl Barth says:

> The reality of the righteousness of God is attested by its universality. It is not irrelevant that it is precisely Paul, who, daring, in Jesus, to put his trust boldly in grace alone, is able, in Jesus, also to perceive the divine breaking down of all human distinctions. Indeed, Paul's courage proceeds from his insight. Because he is the Apostle of the Gentiles, he is the Prophet of the Kingdom of God. Once this interdependence was obscured, there came into being what was afterwards known as "missionary work." But this is something quite different from the mission of Paul. His mission did not erect barriers; it tore them down.[2]

The Glory of God (3:23)

Here is another mountain of a verse in chapter 3. The brief but all-encompassing statement that "all have sinned" is further enhanced by the fact that both

Jew and Gentile "fall short of the glory of God." What is the glory of God? The Bible frequently speaks of the glory of God appearing in the pillar of the cloud leading Israel (Ex. 16:10), the tabernacle of the congregation at Kadesh (Num. 14:10), the temple of Solomon (1 Kin. 8:11), the Mount of Olives at Jerusalem (Ezek. 11:23), and other places. The glory of God now, however, resides in the person of Jesus Christ (John 1:14). The glory of God is Jesus Christ.

When Stephen was stoned, he looked steadfastly to heaven and saw the glory of God and (or even) Jesus standing at the right hand of God (Acts 7:55). The knowledge of the glory of God is said to be in the face of Jesus Christ (2 Cor. 4:6). When Paul says that we have come short of the glory of God, he means that we do not measure up to the sinlessness of Jesus Christ. The Mosaic Law served as God's standard of righteousness until the coming of Christ. But when the Lord Jesus was made a curse for us, He redeemed us from the curse of the Law (Gal. 3:13; Rom. 10:4). Thus the standard of God's holiness today is not the Old Testament Law but the person of Jesus Christ. If we don't measure up to His perfect righteousness, we simply don't measure up. That's why we need the righteousness of Christ.

Three Observations (3:24)

Paul makes three observations about the righteousness of God that brings justification: The righteous man is justified freely (as a gift), and this justification is by His grace and provided through the redemption that is in Christ Jesus. Being justified as a gift means being justified without any prior conditions being met. In the Greek, "being justified" by God's grace is in the dative of means or instrumental case. This indicates that not only is our justification without prior conditions being met, but, on the other hand, it is graciously given. We do not merit justification, but we do enjoy it. One cannot have both merit and grace. Our justification was by the grace of God. Beyond this, it was through the redemption that is in Christ Jesus. Since the word *redemption* signifies a buying back, it must have been accomplished by the payment of a price. The price of our redemption was the blood of Jesus Christ (Matt. 20:28; 1 Cor. 6:20; 1 Pet. 1:18–19). Therefore, we are justified in the sight of God when the righteousness of Christ is placed upon us by the grace of God, freely and without any cause from within us. Only then does God view us as ransomed by the blood of Christ.

In summary, the main points Paul makes are these: (1) God presented Jesus Christ as an atoning sacrifice, a propitiation; (2) this sacrifice was Christ's blood; (3) it is appropriated to the sinner by faith; (4) the sacrifice was necessary because in the past God had not fully punished sin; (5) it was also necessary to validate the justice of God; and (6) this sacrifice demonstrated that it is God who justifies those who have faith in Jesus Christ.

בַ יֵ

What the New Testament Says about Saving Faith

Faith has to be in Christ (Acts 24:24).

Justification comes by faith in Christ (Gal. 2:16).

The justified person must live by faith (Rom. 1:17).

Jesus Christ becomes a place of mercy (a propitiation) through faith (Rom. 3:25).

Faith brings salvation (Eph. 2:8).

↳to appease an offended party

Righteousness comes by faith (Heb. 11:7).

Faith comes by hearing the Word of God (Rom. 10:17).

People become the children of God by faith (Gal. 3:24).

The nations must come to Christ through the obedience of faith (Rom. 16:26).

Salvation comes by believing the truth (2 Thess. 2:13).

Jesus is the finisher of (One who completes) our faith (Heb. 12:2).

Christ the Mercy Seat (3:25–26)

The Bible is filled with types, which foreshadow future persons or events, and antitypes, which are the real person or events foreshadowed. The type is the arrow; the antitype is the target. One of the most unique types in the Old Testament is the mercy seat. This was the lid on the Ark of the Covenant and was covered with gold. At each end was a golden cherub, whose wings stretched toward the center of the lid. The ark was the meeting place between God and man. Among other items of interest to Israel during their wilderness wanderings, it contained the tablets of the Mosaic Law (Ex. 25:17–22). Therefore, the mercy seat was that which covered the Law of God.

Interesting Mercy Seat an Ark of Covenant

When the translation of the Hebrew Old Testament was made into Greek (called the Septuagint) the Greek word chosen to translate "mercy seat" (Hebrew, *kaphorah*) was *hilastērion*, which means "the place of propitiation." To propitiate means to appease an offended party, and the *hilastērion* ("mercy seat") was the place where the blood was applied to appease the wrath of God against the sins of Israel. It is certainly no coincidence that the word Paul used here to describe Jesus Christ is the same word used for "mercy seat." Jesus Christ is our mercy seat, our *hilastērion*. He is the person by whom our penalty was paid and the offended party appeased. Jesus Christ is where God meets humans.

What the New Testament Says about Living Faith

Faith purifies the heart (Acts 15:9).   *sanctifying*

Believers walk by faith (2 Cor. 5:7).

Children of God stand firm in their faith (2 Cor. 1:24).

The Christian life is established by faith (Col. 2:7).

There is a "work" of faith that helps others (1 Thess. 1:3).

The Christian is protected by the breastplate of faith (1 Thess. 5:8).

Faith can grow exceedingly (2 Thess. 1:3).

Believers can be bold in faith (1 Tim. 3:13).

Believers should live sound (healthy) in the faith (Titus 2:2).

Believers should fight the good fight of faith (1 Tim. 6:12).

Faith produces good works (James 2:18).

Prayer enhances faith (James 5:15).

Faith is often tried by adversity (1 Pet. 1:7).

Believers are to be steadfast in faith (1 Pet. 5:9).

The believer's faith can overcome the world (1 John 5:4).

The believer's faith is said to be holy (Jude 1:20).

Christian faith toward God is to be seen by others (1 Thess. 1:8).

Why did Jesus Christ become our propitiation? Paul gives the answer in verse 26: "the demonstration . . . of His righteousness." When Jesus Christ died, He paid the penalty for our sin and for all the sins prior to Calvary that were not permanently dealt with (Ps. 50:16–23; Acts 17:30). God made His statement about sin at the cross. He not only *said* something about it, He *did* something about it. The righteousness of God is declared by atoning for present and future sins as well as past sins. Therefore God is the justifier of any man or woman—past, present, or future—who places his or her faith in the blood of Jesus Christ.

Final Questions (3:27–31)

The final verses of Romans 3 are the apostle's preemptive strike against our unquenchable thirst for self-aggrandizement. First: "Where then is boasting?" (v. 27). In view of the fact that it is God who justifies us by providing Christ Jesus as our propitiation, what does this do to our ability to boast of our righteousness? Paul's answer: "It is excluded." Boasting is shut out; there is no room for our boasting in the plan of God. So forget about it. As John Calvin said,

> The Apostle, after having, with reasons abundantly strong, cast down men from their confidence in works, now triumphs over their folly: and this exulting conclusion was necessary; for on this subject, to teach us would not have been enough; it was necessary that the Holy Spirit should loudly thunder, in order to lay prostrate our loftiness. But he says that glorying is beyond all doubt excluded, for we cannot adduce anything of our own, which is worthy of being approved or commended by God.[3]

"By what kind of law? Of works?" What is it that caused boasting to be inappropriate? Is it the law of works? Paul's answer, "No, but by a law of faith" (v. 27). If people could work to be justified, then they would have reason to boast. But we are saved by God's grace through faith, not of works. And why? "That no one should boast" (Eph. 2:9).

Relationships Formed in Faith
- *Christians are the household of faith (Gal. 6:10).*
- *Paul considers Timothy his son in the faith (1 Tim. 1:2).*
- *Christians can together be nourished on the words of faith (1 Tim. 4:6).*
- *Faith can be communicated (Philem. 1:5).*

Paul now comes to a teaching that is central to his theology: People are justified by faith without the deeds of the Law. This thought also came to the heart of Martin Luther and spawned the Protestant Reformation. When this concept grasps our hearts, we too come to the conclusion that salvation is *sola gratia, sola fide, soli Deo gloria* (by grace alone, through faith alone; to God alone be the glory).

More final questions: "Is God the God of Jews only? Is He not the God of Gentiles also?" (v. 29). These questions naturally arise in the Jewish mind, which still cannot conceive of the Gentiles being loved and justified by faith alone. Paul answers: "Yes, of Gentiles also" (v. 29). There is not one god of the Jews and another god of the Gentiles. There is but one God of Jews and Gentiles. Paul is not simply teaching monotheism as opposed to pagan polytheism. As a

Jew, a Hebrew of the Hebrews, but the called apostle to the Gentiles, Paul is the bridge between the Jews and Gentiles. Christ made the two one in Him (Gal. 3:28) and made the law of faith the universal law of God's salvation.

One last question: "Do we then nullify the Law through faith?" Because God saves through faith and not the deeds of the Law, does this make the Law useless? Again we are greeted with Paul's characteristic answer: "May it never be!" (v. 31). Faith in Christ is the only proper response to the Law, for what the Law could not do, Christ alone can do. The teaching that justification is by faith alone does not destroy the Law. In fact, it completes the Law, fulfills it, gives it meaning. Justification by faith alone honors the Law, because prior to Jesus Christ no one ever honored the Law by perfectly keeping it. Since the Lord Jesus did, faith in the finished work of Christ on Calvary brings the ultimate respect to the Law.

Study Questions

1. What does Paul mean when he writes that the righteousness of God "has been manifested, being witnessed by the Law and the Prophets"?

2. Define and explain *redemption*.

3. Define and explain *propitiation*.

4. How does God remain just in the way He has planned out salvation in Christ?

5. How do we establish the Law by our faith in Christ?

CHAPTER 9

Justification by Faith Illustrated
Romans 4:1–25

Preview:

Abraham becomes the example of one who was justified for salvation through his faith. By his trust in the Lord, his faith was reckoned (accounted) to him as righteousness. The promises of God came to Abraham not through circumcision or law-keeping, but totally through his trust. The story of Abraham's faith in God was recorded for our benefit today. Jesus died for our transgressions and was raised from the dead that we might be justified.

Paul has just firmly established that the righteousness of God is apart from the Law (3:21) and that people are justified by faith apart from the deeds of the Law (3:28). He is aware, however, that Jews will offer the case of Abraham as a rebuttal to his teaching. The apostle's own people were still engrossed with the idea that being Jewish ought to afford them certain judicial privileges in the eyes of God. Thus, in this chapter, Paul introduces "Abraham, our forefather according to the flesh" (v. 1). Paul's use of the possessive pronoun "our" and the qualifying phrase "according to the flesh" indicates that he is identifying himself with his people, the Jews. The question is, was Abraham saved by his acts of good works and obedience, or was he saved by the faith of which Paul spoke in the preceding chapter? Here's Paul's proposition: "For if Abraham was justified by works, he has something to boast about; but not before God" (v. 2).

Faith Credited as Righteousness (4:3–5)

As a Hebrew, a rabbi, a member of the Sanhedrin, and a Pharisee, Paul knew exactly how to settle a Jewish argument. He could have debated the point, but instead he says, "For what does the Scripture say?" (v. 3). This is a lesson we all should learn well. Whenever we are asked for a moral, ethical, or eternal answer, we should ask ourselves, "What does the Scripture say?" The apostle answers his own question by quoting what Moses records in Genesis 15:6: "And Abraham believed God, and it was reckoned to him as righteousness" (v. 3). What do we mean when we say that faith was credited to Abraham for righteousness? The word translated "reckoned" (Greek, *logizomai*) is a commercial term used with regard to credits and debits. It means to set to one's credit or lay to one's charge. If you authorize your lawyer to write checks on your bank account, and he does so, although the check is written by him and the money is received by him, the amount of the check is charged to you. This one word, *logizomai*, occurs eleven times in this chapter and means "to count," "to reckon," or "to impute." Abraham was not righteous. Justification never means to make a person righteous. It only means that God reckons and treats a person as if he or she were righteous.

Paul further reasons that justification by works requires the principle that people may earn their salvation by doing good. If this principle were true, good people would be saved by their good works, and salvation would not be a gift at all. But justification by faith rests on the principle that God imputes righteousness to the ungodly as a free gift. Salvation is not earned by sinners, but is freely given when they put their faith in the substitutionary death of Jesus Christ.

The Testimony of a King (4:6–8)

Paul has made a case for Abraham's justification apart from works; now he strengthens that case with another Old Testament illustration. The purpose of introducing David's testimony is twofold: (1) It meets the requirements of the Jews' Law regarding two witnesses (see Deut. 19:15, referred to by Jesus in Matt. 18:16 and by Paul in 2 Cor. 13:1 and 1 Tim. 5:19). David corroborated what was said about Abraham and further illustrated salvation apart from works. (2) David gave witness that the same principle of justification was operative even for those living under the Mosaic Law.

"Just as David also speaks of the blessing upon the man to whom God reckons righteousness apart from works" (v. 6). Even King David, the type of the messianic king, knew the truth of the words he penned in Psalm 32:1–2, which Paul quotes in verses 7 and 8. As believers, our iniquities are forgiven and our sins are covered. The reason believers' sins are not reckoned to them is that their sins have been imputed to Christ Jesus in their place (see Is. 53, cf. 1 Pet. 2:24–25).

The Role of Circumcision (4:9–12)

Paul has well argued that justification is by faith alone. He has illustrated, by the lives of Abraham and David that God has never worked on a principle of justification by works. Yet it is difficult for the Jews, the sons of Abraham, to accept that they may be justified in exactly the same way as the Gentiles. Thus, these verses introduce another potential argument against justification by faith.

It is true that both pre-law Abraham and under-law David received righteousness. But, the Jews would argue, both of them were also circumcised. Since circumcision is the sign of the covenant between God and His chosen people (Gen. 17:9–14), is it not possible that circumcision was the ground of their justification? "Is this blessing then upon the circumcised, or upon the uncircumcised also?" (v. 9). This immediately prompts the question as to the timing of the reckoning of righteousness. When was righteousness reckoned to Abraham? Was it after he was circumcised or before? The answer is clear. Faith was credited to Abraham while he was yet uncircumcised (v. 10).

The facts are these. (1) Genesis 15:6 records the event of Abraham receiving righteousness from God. (2) Sometime after that, Abraham had a son by Hagar when he was eighty-six years old (Gen. 16:16–17). (3) At least one year had to elapse between the Genesis 15:6 and the conception and birth of Hagar's son so that at the outside Abraham was eighty-five years old when righteousness was imputed to him. (4) Ishmael was thirteen years old when both he and Abraham were circumcised (Gen. 17:25–26). (5) Abraham had righteousness imputed to him at least fourteen years before he was circumcised. Paul concludes that circumcision had nothing whatever to do with the imputation of righteousness to Abraham.

This does not mean that circumcision was unimportant. Abraham "received the sign of circumcision, a seal of the righteousness of the faith" (v. 11). Circumcision did not bring righteousness but was the visible sign to Abraham's descendants of the righteousness that was imputed to him by faith. Also, circumcision was God's seal of righteousness. The same is true of Christian baptism. It does not bring about salvation but is an outward sign declaring salvation and is God's seal of approval on the finished work of Christ in behalf of the believer. Abraham received righteousness before he was circumcised that he might be the father of all who believe, whether circumcised or not. Abraham, therefore, not only bears a physical relationship with the nation Israel, but also bears a spiritual relationship with all who believe by faith, whether Jew or Gentile.

Abraham's Inheritance (4:13–16)

Each of Abraham's descendants expected to receive the inheritance of Abraham. That inheritance was no less than the world (v. 13). Although not directly stated, this promise is drawn from Genesis 12:3 and the correlative promises given in Genesis 18:18; 22:18; and elsewhere. Abraham's heritage was limited in geographical terms to the land between Egypt and the Euphrates (Gen. 15:18; cf. 13:14–15). "For the promise to Abraham or to his descendants that he would be heir of the world was not through the Law, but through the righteousness of faith" (v. 13). After Abraham's aborted attempt to slay his son Isaac on Mount Moriah, God said to his faithful follower, "In your seed all the nations of the earth shall be blessed, because you have obeyed My voice" (Gen. 22:18). The word translated "seed" here (Hebrew, *zerah*) is one of those collective nouns that can mean a large number of descendants (as in Gen. 13:16) or at other times a single, unique descendant (Jer. 41:8).

With these variations in mind, how are we to interpret the promise that "all the nations of the earth shall be blessed" through Abraham? Some today would claim that the outstanding contributions of the Jewish people to humanity are how all nations of the earth will be blessed. Less than one percent of the world's population is Jewish, but of the 663 Nobel Prizes awarded by the Nobel Foundation of Sweden between 1901 and 1995, 140 were awarded to Jews or people of Jewish descent. That's 21 percent.[1] But we are not at all certain that is how to interpret this promise. Paul seized on the singular use of the word "seed" in Galatians 3:16 when he said, "Now the promises were spoken to Abraham and to his seed. He does not say, 'And to seeds,' as referring to many, but rather to one, 'And to your seed,' that is, Christ." The promise to Abraham's descendants (literally "seed," referring not to the Jews but to Jesus, the "seed" of Abraham) of inheriting the world (v. 13) must be understood in relationship to the Messiah's future domination of this earth as "KING OF KINGS, AND LORD OF LORDS" (Rev. 19:16). This will be realized when the seed of Abraham, Jesus Christ, sits on the throne of David during the Millennium and rules the world with a rod of iron. Because of this, it is impossible that Abraham's inheritance can be obtained by Law (v. 14). No heir of Abraham, save Jesus Christ, has ever been able to entirely keep the Law. If fulfillment of this promise depended on law-keeping, our inability to keep the Law would insure that the promise would never be fulfilled and thus would be made of no effect. But God keeps His promises, and He'll keep this one through His Son, Jesus Christ.

Eventually, failure to keep the Law imposes penalties that bring to the Law-breaker the wrath of God. "But where there is no law, neither is there violation"

(v. 15). Paul appears to be drawing on a current legal maxim in the Roman Empire ("no penalty without law"), when here, as in 5:13, he claims that sin is not imputed where there is no law. The Law simply declares what is right and requires conformity to it. But the Law does not give either the power to obey it or atonement when it is not obeyed. "For this reason it is by faith, that it might be in accordance with grace" (v. 16). Since the promise of salvation is dependent on faith, the blessings of salvation are afforded by the means of God's grace. Therefore they come "not only to those who are of the Law, but also to those who are of the faith of Abraham" (v. 16). Paul is insistent that only those who possess the faith of Abraham are the seeds of Abraham, and whether we are Jew or Gentile, if we have placed our faith in the salvation provided by Abraham's God, then Abraham is the father of us all.

Abraham and Faith in the Promises of God (4:17–21)

Again by quoting from the Old Testament, this time from Genesis 17:5, Paul continues his argument that physical inheritance from Abraham is insufficient to receive God's righteousness. Abraham relentlessly believed in the God "who gives life to the dead and calls into being that which does not exist" (v. 17). Throughout this next series of verses concerning the giving and confirming of the covenant to Abraham, God interchangeably uses the words "I will" and "I have." The reason is that God is above time; He has neither future nor past, only an eternal present. When in Genesis 17:5 God said He would make Abraham "the father of a multitude of nations," Abraham was yet childless. But it didn't matter, the promises of God are better than money in the bank. They always come true. We can count God's "I wills" as God's "I haves." The same thing was true before the battle of Jericho when the Lord appeared to Joshua and said, "See, I have given Jericho into your hand, with its king and the valiant warriors" (Josh. 6:2). What was for Joshua yet to happen was for God an accomplished fact. The apostle describes the quality of Abraham's trust in God as "in hope against hope he believed" (v. 18). Grammatically this is known as an oxymoron, a figure of speech in which contradictory ideas are combined (e.g., thunderous silence, sweet sorrow). When the promise was given that Abraham would become the father of many nations, no human ground for hope existed with regard to Abraham's wife Sarah bearing a child. Although beyond hope, Abraham believed God anyway, and his faith generated hope. "Without becoming weak in faith he contemplated his own body, now as good as dead since he was about a hundred years old, and the deadness of Sarah's womb" (v. 19). Abraham believed God in spite of the circumstances. He did not consider his lack of virility at one hundred years old.

Neither did he consider the inability of his ninety-year-old wife to conceive and withstand the pain of childbirth. Adverse circumstances did not stand in the way of Abraham's faith.

Both the Old and New Testaments describe those who had faith toward God. The individuals listed below are said to have been faithful in their walk with the Lord.

Illustrations of Faith from the Bible

Description	Reference
Samuel the priest of the Lord was characterized by faith.	1 Samuel 2:35
Hananiah was a faithful commander who feared God.	Nehemiah 7:2
Abraham was the father of the faithful.	Romans 4:12
Sarah by faith believed God for the promise of a child.	Hebrews 11:11
Isaac by faith blessed Jacob and Esau.	Hebrews 11:20
Jacob by faith blessed his family when he was dying.	Hebrews 11:21
Moses' entire ministry was characterized by faith.	Hebrews 11:23–29
Rahab the harlot saved the spies because of her faith.	Hebrews 11:31
Silvanus was a Christian brother known for his faith.	1 Peter 5:12
Antipas was a martyr who died for his faith.	Revelation 2:13

"He did not waver in unbelief, but grew strong in faith" with respect to the promise of God (v. 20). The word translated "waver" (Greek, *diakrinomai*) means to separate or distinguish, and, as a deponent verb, means to dispute. With regard to his faith in God, Abraham did not have a divided mind. But how can we reconcile this with Abraham's laughter in Genesis 17:17? We need not understand Abraham's laughter as mocking. Jerome translated laughter as "marveled." Calvin and Augustine both translated it as "laughed for joy."

Abraham's questioning how a child could be born of him at one hundred years of age was more an exclamation of holy wonder that was immediately overcome by holy faith.

The fact is, not only did Abraham not waver in faith, but Paul also tells us that by hoping against all hope, Abraham actually "grew strong in faith, giving glory to God" (v. 20). And how did he give glory to God? Robert Haldane explains:

> By believing that He [God] would do what He promised, although nothing less than almighty power could effect what was promised. This is an important thought, that we glorify God by ascribing to Him His attributes, and believing that He will act according to them, notwithstanding many present appearances to the contrary. But how often is the opposite of this exemplified among many who profess to have the faith of Abraham. When unable to trace Divine wisdom, they are apt to hesitate in yielding submission to Divine authority. Nothing, however, to countenance this is found in Scripture. On the contrary, no human action is more applauded than that of Abraham offering up Isaac in obedience to the command of God, in which he certainly could not then discover either the reason or the wisdom from which it proceeded.[2]

Abraham was not just wistfully hoping that God would make him the father of many nations, but was fully persuaded that what God had promised He was able also to perform. History teaches us that God does indeed perform what He promises. Verse 22 begins, "Therefore also it was reckoned to him as righteousness." Because Abraham had faith, because he believed God in the face of adverse circumstances, his faith was imputed to him for righteousness. Bottom line? All that Abraham had—his righteousness, his inheritance, and his posterity—he gained not by works, but by faith.

This illustration of the way in which Abraham received righteousness is not recorded for his sake alone or applicable to him only. The expression "But for our sake also" (v. 24) indicates that all believers are justified by faith in the promises of God. If we "believe in Him who raised Jesus our Lord from the dead," we exhibit the same faith Abraham did in God's promises, and the result will be the same—faith counted as righteousness. God the Father delivered Jesus Christ to the cross of Calvary, not as an example, but to make atonement for our sins (2 Cor. 5:21). God the Father also raised Jesus Christ again for our justification. The meaning of the resurrection for us today is that Christ Jesus died on account of our sins and was raised from the dead to render us righteous in God's eyes. The righteousness of Abraham, David, and us is the righteousness of the risen Lord.

What can we learn from this chapter? The noun *faith* occurs ten times in these verses, and the corresponding verb, *believe,* occurs six times. Together the idea of believing faith is found no less than sixteen times in Romans 4. The word *credit,* meaning "impute" or "charge to one's account" occurs eleven times. And the word *righteousness* occurs in one of its forms eight times in this chapter while the corresponding verb *justified* occurs in one of its forms three times. Together the idea of righteousness is found no less than eleven times in Romans 4. It is significant that, apart from the common words of our language, these three words occur so frequently. The application of this chapter is simple: Faith imputes righteousness. There isn't a thing anyone can do to become clothed with God's righteousness except have faith in Jesus Christ as Savior from sin.

Study Questions

1. Define *reckoned,* or *imputed.*
2. Why does Paul dwell on the topic of circumcision in this chapter?
3. What specific promise was made to Abraham?
4. Why is it impossible to be justified by law-keeping? Explain.
5. Why does Paul show that Abraham was justified in the sight of the Lord before the giving of the Law? Explain.
6. What does the resurrection of Christ tell us about justification?

CHAPTER 10

Justification by Faith Experienced
Romans 5:1–11

Preview:

Justification comes by faith and also brings peace with God. When we were helpless as sinners, Christ died for us, justifying us by His blood and saving us from the wrath of God. Reconciliation comes by the death of Jesus; salvation comes by the fact that He is alive today.

Having established God's method of justifying sinners, and having provided an Old Testament example of that method, Paul now demonstrates that not only are benefits derived from justification at the moment of salvation, but blessings also accompany justification throughout the believer's life.

The first word of the chapter indicates that there is a close link between chapter 4 and chapter 5. In fact, it is unfortunate that there is a chapter break here, for there is no break in Paul's logical pattern of thought. "Therefore" is a bridge between the two chapters and the ideas of past justification and present blessings.

Justification Means Peace with God (5:1)

The word translated "having been justified" (Greek, *dikaioō*) is an aorist passive participle in Greek. The time of action is in the past. The voice is obviously passive, which means the subject received and did not initiate the action. So Paul says that at some point in the past, without our help, God justified us, that is, He declared us and began to treat us as if we were righteous.

[handwritten note: this action is already complete + not based on anything we did.]

Thus, we should understand this verse as saying, "Having been justified by faith, we have. . . ," and then Paul lists the benefits of our justification.

The first benefit is that justification means we have peace with God. This is not the peace *of* God, but peace *with* (Greek, *pros*) God; not a *feeling* of peace, but a *state* of peace. Between the sinner and God exists a state of enmity, hostility, and antagonism. As natural born sinners, we are the enemies of God (Is. 48:22; Col. 1:21; James 4:4). The state of war that exists between the unbeliever and God continues until a state of peace is declared. Therefore, having been justified by faith, we have a peace treaty with God through our Lord Jesus Christ. He is the mediator between the two parties at war (1 Tim. 2:5–6). As our mediator, Jesus Christ has worked out our peace treaty with God. But Jesus Christ is much more than our mediator. Since He made peace through His blood, Jesus is our peace with God (Eph. 2:13–18).

Justification Means Access to God (5:2)

The word translated "introduction" in the NASB is better translated "access." Paul chose the Greek word *prosagōgē* to name a second benefit of justification. This word is found only three times in the New Testament, used all three times by Paul, and all three referring to our access to God once we have been justified. The word means "approach" and refers to our newfound ability to approach God. Ephesians 2:18 says, "For through Him [Jesus] we both have our access in one Spirit to the Father." And again in Ephesians 3:12, speaking of Christ Jesus our Lord, the apostle says, "In whom we have boldness and confident access through faith in Him."

If you have ever attempted to call the president of the United States, you know how relatively inaccessible he is. For unbelievers, God the Father is even more inaccessible than the president. He cannot be reached, for there is no common ground, no mediator between unbelievers and God. Believers, however, have access to God because they have been justified. Each time I turn on my computer, I am asked for a password. If I don't have that password, I go no further. That's the way it is with God. If you want to approach the holy, sovereign, righteous God, you need to know the password to have access to Him. That password is Jesus Christ. God the Son gives immediate and consistent access to God the Father to all whom God has declared and treats as righteousness. Thus, having been justified by faith, we have access to God.

Justification Means a Standing before God (5:2)

A third benefit of having been justified is a place to stand. That may not seem like much of an issue, but if you search the Scriptures, you'll quickly find that this is an age-old problem. Listen to the psalmist: "If Thou, LORD, shouldst mark iniquities, O Lord, who could stand?" (Ps. 130:3). Hear the question of Asaph: "Thou, even Thou, art to be feared; and who may stand in Thy presence when once Thou art angry?" (Ps. 76:7). And what about Nahum? After describing the character of the God who reserves wrath for His enemies, the prophet asks, "Who can stand before His indignation?" (Nah. 1:6). Or the venerable Job, who records God's words, "Who then is he that can stand before Me?" (Job 41:10). And, of course, there is the prophet Malachi, who asks: "But who can endure the day of His coming? And who can stand when He appears? For He is like a refiner's fire and like fullers' soap" (Mal. 3:2).

We do not have a leg to stand on when it comes to a defense of our sinful actions. How is it possible for a sinner to stand before God? The Swiss reformer Robert Haldane said, "And it is by Him [Jesus Christ] they enter into the state of grace, so by Him they stand in it, accepted before God; secured, according to His everlasting covenant, that they shall not be cast down"[1] The only possible way we can stand before God is by His grace, and that grace is demonstrated to us when He justifies us by faith. Jesus Christ is our place to stand, and we stand before God dressed in the righteousness of Christ. He's the only place that is acceptable to God. If we want to stand in the day of judgment, we need to find our place in the Son.

Justification Means Hope of Glory (5:2)

A fourth benefit of having been justified is that we can rejoice in the "hope of the glory of God." What does it mean to rejoice or exult in the hope of the glory of God? In his massive, multivolume *Theological Dictionary of the New Testament*, German scholar Gerhard Kittel explains that the word Paul chose (Greek, *kauchaomai*) means

> "To boast," usually in a bad sense. . . . In the Old Testament there are many proverbs against self-glorying or boasting (1 Kings 20:11; Prov. 25:14; 27:1; cf. 20:9), though place is also found for justifiable pride (Prov. 16:31; 17:6). . . . In the New Testament, *kauchaomai* is used almost exclusively by Paul alone, in whom it is very common. For Paul *kauchasthai* (a form of *kauchaomai*) discloses the basic attitude of the Jew to be one of self-confidence which seeks glory before God and which relies upon itself. For this reason he sets in contrast to *kauchasthai* [boasting] the attitude of *pistis* [faith] which is appropriate to man and which is made possible, and demanded, by Christ.[2]

We have seen this again and again in the first five chapters of the epistle to the Romans.

So to exult in the hope of the glory of God means that there are big changes coming in our lives, changes that began at justification. The glory of God, of which we have fallen short, is the perfect standard of Christ's righteousness (John 1:14; 17:22–23; Heb. 1:3). We can rejoice in the fact that whatever we are like today, one of the benefits of having been justified is the hope that one day we will be like Christ (Rom. 8:29; 1 John 3:2–3).

Justification Means Exulting in Our Tribulations (5:3–4)

Some may think Paul has lost his mind at this point, but his logic is impeccable as he presents the fifth benefit of justification. If we have hope in glory—present hope, real hope, concrete hope—why should we worry about our present troubles? They are only temporary. Soon they will be gone forever. But even more than that, our tribulations are productive in the process of Christian maturing. The apostle says, "And not only this, but we also exult in our tribulations, knowing that tribulation brings about perseverance; and perseverance, proven character; and proven character, hope" (vv. 3–4). We who have been justified rejoice not in spite of our tribulations, but *in* or *because of* our tribulations.

William Barclay comments:

It was hard to be a Christian in Rome. Remembering that, Paul produces a great climax. "Trouble," he said, "produces fortitude." The word he uses for trouble (or tribulations) is *thlipsis*, and *thlipsis* literally means pressure. All kinds of things may press in upon the Christian—the pressure of want, need, straitened circumstances, the pressure of sorrow, the pressure of persecution, the pressure of unpopularity and loneliness. All that pressure, says Paul, produces fortitude. The word he uses for fortitude is *hupomonē*. *Hupomonē* means more than endurance; it means the spirit which can overcome the world; it means the spirit which does not passively endure but which actively overcomes and conquers the trials and the tribulations of life. When Beethoven was threatened with deafness, that most terrible of troubles for a musician, he said, "I will take life by the throat." That is *hupomonē*. When Scott was involved in ruin because of the bankruptcy of his publishers, he said: "No man will say 'Poor fellow!' to me; my own right hand will pay the debt." That is *hupomonē*. . . . *Hupomonē* is not the spirit which lies down and lets the floods go over it; it is the spirit which meets things breastforward and overcomes them.[3]

In charting the progression from tribulation to hope, Paul shows that there is a natural, logical connection between the four: tribulations—perseverance—proven character—hope. The tribulations of which Paul speaks

(1 Cor. 4:9–13; 2 Cor. 1:4–10; 11:23–30; Phil. 4:12; 2 Tim. 3:11–12; et al.), result in patience. This is not a passive quality but, as Barclay mentioned, is the ability to remain strong while bearing the burden of tribulation. The test of endurance in turn results in fortitude (Greek, *dokimē*) or proof of the presence of the Spirit of God in our lives (which makes perseverance possible). The result proceeds to hope, the certain knowledge that, as "heirs of God and fellow heirs with Christ" (Rom. 8:17), we will one day be glorified like the Son of God. Here is the cycle of life for the Christian. We begin with hope, that concrete knowledge that we are declared righteous through faith in Jesus Christ, the glory of God. From there we pass through tribulations: spiritual, emotional, physical, and financial difficulties. But, sustained by God's grace, those difficulties only cause us to be steadfast. We find fortitude, a proven character we never would have discovered without these tribulations. And this endurance proves that we are indeed children of God, which in turn encourages us in the hope of the glory of God. What a perfect circle. Thus, having been justified by faith, we can exult in our tribulations.

Justification Means Encouraging Hope (5:5)

Paul continues with the "benefits package" that accompanies being justified by faith. A sixth benefit is that our "hope does not disappoint." Having already been justified, we have a hope that cannot be humiliated.

The word *hope* confuses many Christians. For them, hope is nebulous, ethereal, hard to get one's hands around. It's a faint optimism in the future. But that's not the concept of hope found in the Bible. In fact, biblical hope is not something we *do* at all; it's something we *have*. Because we have been justified, we have hope. Biblical hope is concrete because it is not something we grasp at in the warmth of summer only to have it dashed in the bitter winter seasons of life; we possess it in all seasons. That's why the New Testament writers especially speak about what we have when we have hope. (See the table entitled, *The Hope We Have* on the next page.)

In each case, hope is a very tangible thing. It is something we have, not something we do. We even have a blessed hope (Titus 2:13), a better hope (Heb. 7:19), and a living hope (1 Pet. 1:3)—all nouns. Because we know hope is a present possession, we can rest in hope (Acts 2:26) and rejoice in hope (Rom. 5:2; 12:12). In fact, in my favorite expression of the concreteness of hope, the prophet Zechariah says that God's people are 'prisoners of hope' (Zech. 9:12).[4] As Christians, then, we are bound by a hope that will never make us ashamed. Thus, having been justified by faith, we exult in the hope that will never disappoint us.

The Hope Christians Have	
Hope of resurrection	Acts 23:6
Hope of the promise	Acts 26:6
Hope of Israel	Acts 28:20
Hope of glory	Romans 5:2; Colossians 1:27
Hope of righteousness	Galatians 5:5
Hope of your calling	Ephesians 1:18; 4:4
Hope laid up in heaven	Colossians 1:5
Hope of the gospel	Colossians 1:23
Hope of salvation	1 Thessalonians 5:8
Hope of eternal life	Titus 1:2
Hope set before us	Hebrews 6:18

Justification Means Experiencing the Love of God (5:5–8)

The hope we have in the glory of God will prove to be genuine even though it is tested in the caldron of fiery tribulation. Why? "Because the love of God has been poured out within our hearts" (v. 5), which is a seventh benefit of justification. God's love has been generously poured (Greek, *ekchunnō*) on us, not given grudgingly or halfheartedly. The word is the one Jesus used when He said, "This is My blood of the covenant, which is poured out (Greek, *ekchunnō*) for many for forgiveness of sins" (Matt. 26:28). God graciously and generously loved us when He justified us, and that love is an everlasting love, as strong today as it was then (Jer. 31:3). It is interesting that this passage began by speaking of faith, moved to hope, and now has come to the end of the trilogy with love. Our hearts are flooded with God's love for us because we have been justified.

Verses 6–8 relate that the distinctive quality of God's love is that it operates irrespective of merit. Human love is given to those who are lovable; but God's love embraces even the unlovely. The expression "For while we were still helpless" in verse 6 is parallel to the expression in verse 8, "while we were yet sinners." Paul uses it to show our utter helplessness in the face of our all-encompassing sin. While we were under the guilt of our sin, we were helpless to do anything about it. That's why God had to do something, and the something He did was at Calvary. "At the right time Christ died for the ungodly" (v. 6). This means that circumstances did not bring Christ to the cross; rather, the divine plan of God did (Gal. 4:1–5). At the time of our greatest need, the only remedy was the blood of Jesus.

Verses 7 and 8 expand what is implicit in verse 6. When Paul said that Christ died for the ungodly, he was indicating that the Lord did not die for those who were simply void of morality but for those who were actively opposed to God. Again, we have the contrast of Romans 1 and 2. "For one will hardly die for a righteous man [i.e., one who observes divine law or keeps the commands of God—perhaps the Jewish person of Romans 2]; though perhaps for the good man [i.e., one who is honorable, respectable—perhaps the moral person of Romans 2] someone would dare even to die." The just man is approved by God, and hardly anyone would think of dying for him. The good man is loved by men, and most would not think of dying for him, although some may be tempted. But here comes the clincher. Paul's argument is that while we would rarely find anyone who would lay down his life for a righteous or good man, "God demonstrates His own love toward us, in that while we were yet sinners [i.e., someone without redeeming qualities—perhaps the immoral man of Romans 1], Christ died for us." The sacrifice of Christ on Calvary's cross arose out of the heart of God filled with the love of God. All these blessings are ours, because at some point in the past, without our help, we have been justified by God and are now being treated as if we are righteous. Thus, having been justified by faith, we have proof of the love of God.

> Could we with ink the ocean fill and were the skies of parchment made,
> Were every stalk on earth a quill and every man a scribe by trade;
> To write the love of God above would drain the ocean dry,
> Nor could the scroll contain the whole tho stretched from sky to sky.
> — Frederick Lehman

Justification Means the Gift of the Holy Spirit (5:5)

An eighth benefit accompanies justification (v. 5), and we dare not miss it. Paul says, "The love of God has been poured out within our hearts through the Holy Spirit who was given to us." It is the Holy Spirit who pours into the hearts of believers a sense of God's love for them. Notice the apparent dual sense in which Paul uses the verb "poured out." Not only was God's love poured out to us by the Holy Spirit when we were justified, but the Holy Spirit was "poured out" to us as well. The word here is *ekcheō*. In Titus 3:5–6 the apostle remarks that God "saved us, not on the basis of deeds which we have done in righteousness, but according to His mercy, by the washing of regeneration and renewing by the Holy Spirit, whom He poured out upon us richly through Jesus Christ our Savior." Talk about team effort! God the Father justifies us "through our Lord Jesus Christ" (Rom. 5:1), and it is "through Jesus Christ our Savior" that the Holy Spirit is poured out upon us. Acts 2:17–18 also mentions the pouring out of the Holy Spirit on the Day of Pentecost.

What can we learn from this? Remember that Paul is listing the benefits package that comes as a result of having been justified by faith. Each of these benefits is unmerited, everlasting, and immediate. Immediately upon being justified we had peace with God. Immediately we had access to God and a standing in His Son. We did not have to wait; these things came with the package. Immediately we had unalloyed joy in our tribulations and encouraging hope. Immediately we had proof of God's love. And immediately we had the presence of the Holy Spirit "who was given to us" (v. 5). The verb translated "was given" (Greek, *didōmi*) means to grant, impart, or put into the heart. The clear implication is that at the moment of salvation we received the everlasting gift of the Holy Spirit Himself. Justified persons need not anxiously look to a future time when they will be baptized with the Holy Spirit, receive the second blessing, or any other empowerment of the Holy Spirit. At the moment of our salvation, Christ's righteousness is ours, God's love is ours, and the Holy Spirit's presence is ours. They are inextricably bound together in a package we call salvation. Thus, having been justified by faith, we have received the gift of the Holy Spirit.

At this point a noticeable change occurs. Paul has been enumerating what we have as a result of having been justified. Now, in verses 9–11, he speaks of what will be because God has justified us. He switches from the present to the future.

Justification Means Being Saved from God's Wrath (5:9)

Paul lists the ninth benefit in these words: "Having now been justified by His [Christ's] blood, we shall be saved from the wrath of God through Him."[5] In addition to the blessings we presently enjoy because we have been justified, there is yet the promise that we shall be saved from wrath through Christ. People don't like to see themselves this way, but all people are by nature the children of wrath (Eph. 2:3) and under God's wrath (John 3:36). The prophet Nahum warns that the Lord has reserved wrath for His enemies (Nah. 1:2). In fact, when John the Baptist saw the Pharisees and Sadducees coming out to the Jordan River for baptism, he scorched them, saying, "You brood of vipers, who warned you to flee from the wrath to come?" (Matt. 3:7; Luke 3:7). It is comforting for the believer to note, however, that "God has not destined us for wrath, but for obtaining salvation through our Lord Jesus Christ" (1 Thess. 5:9). Thus one of the future benefits of our justification is that we will be preserved from the day of God's fierce wrath.

But what is this wrath of God from which Christians have been spared? Paul is not specific, and that is likely intentional. At the point we were justified by the blood of Jesus, God removed His entire wrath from our permanent record, from our present lives, and from our future. When Jesus Christ died in our place at Calvary, He paid our debt and satisfied God's holy demands against us (Is. 53:10; Rom. 5:8; 6:23). As the Father's propitiation for our sins (see the discussion of Rom. 3:25), Jesus Christ appeased God's wrath by satisfying those demands. Once that atonement was made, we were declared righteous in God's sight and were removed from under the heavy weight of God's wrath (Rom. 1:18). We were reconciled to God (Col. 1:21–22), and that exempted us from all future expressions of God's wrath. Therefore, believers in the Lord Jesus Christ will never be condemned to hell (John 5:24; Rom. 8:1), nor will we be the objects of God's future wrath during the coming Tribulation (1 Thess. 1:10; 5:9) or on Judgment Day (Rev. 20:11–15). Thus, having been justified by faith, we shall be saved from God's wrath.

Justification Means Being Saved by Christ's Life (5:10)

Some have been confused over this tenth benefit derived from having been justified. Paul said, "For if while we were enemies, we were reconciled to God through the death of His Son, much more, having been reconciled, we shall be saved by His life" (v. 10). The answer to the question "Are we saved by Christ's death or are we saved by Christ's life?" is yes. Remember, God has always demanded a blood sacrifice to atone for sins. Always. Adam and Eve sinned, then made clothes from fig leaves to cover their nakedness (Gen. 3:7). God sought them out, told them their clothes, while maybe stylish, were unacceptable and made clothes of skins to cover their nakedness (Gen. 3:21). What's the difference? Blood. Israel's Passover in Egypt required both the shedding and the application of blood (Ex. 12:5–7). Ephesians 1:7 says, "In Him we have redemption through His blood, the forgiveness of our trespasses." "Without shedding of blood there is no forgiveness" (Heb. 9:22). Jesus Christ had both to bleed and to die to atone for our sins. Our salvation came by Christ's death.

So in what way are we saved by Christ's life if the Father required His death? Well, certainly not by His life on earth, as exemplary as it was. Jesus lived a perfect life—tempted, but perfect (Heb. 4:15). He was the epitome of kindness, gentleness, and goodness. He was the most caring person who ever walked this earth. But none of those fine qualities were required by God for our justification. So the life of Christ by which we are to be saved ("we shall be saved by His life") is not His earthly life but His heavenly life. Today Christ sits at the right hand of the Father interceding on our behalf (Heb. 7:25). He is our Advocate with the Father (1 John 2:1). He is our Great High Priest, representing our interests before God. Whenever Satan accuses us or falsely represents us to our heavenly Father, Jesus is there to save us (Rev. 12:10). So the gift of Christ's atonement just keeps on giving. Thus, having been justified by faith, we shall continue to be saved by His life.

Justification Means Continued Rejoicing (5:11)

Do you remember what your life was like before you were saved? You may have had happiness, but you had no real joy. People make up for the absence of joy with the presence of things. They buy, they travel, they collect, they network, they hook up, but they are desperate for joy. C. S. Lewis once observed, "Joy is not a substitute for sex; sex is very often a substitute for joy. I sometimes wonder whether all pleasures are not substitutes for joy."[6] Paul's final benefit of justification is that once we have been reconciled to God, wrath departs and joy makes its entrance.

When Jesus prayed for His people in the Garden of Gethsemane, He said to His Heavenly Father, "But now I come to Thee; and these things I speak in the world, that they may have My joy made full in themselves" (John 17:13). But Paul speaks of the "joy of the Holy Spirit" to the Thessalonian believers, and the Holy Spirit—who is another Helper, the gift of God to make our lives meaningful—came not only to help us pray (Rom. 8:26–28), but to allow Jesus to return to heaven, sit at His Father's right hand, and take up a full-time ministry of intercession for us. If Jesus' prayers in the garden brought joy to us, imagine how much continued rejoicing we have now that He is in heaven. Thus, having been justified by faith, we can continue to rejoice in our reconciliation.

The reason we can continue to rejoice is that our lives continue to be reconciled to God. It is the fact that God's wrath was appeased and therefore removed, and that we are now on speaking terms with Him, that brought joy in the first place. But since reconciliation continues to have effect in our lives, and always will, we continue to enjoy reconciliation rejoicing.

> Let all who seek Thee rejoice and be glad in Thee;
> And let those who love Thy salvation say continually,
> "Let God be magnified." (Ps. 70:4).

Did you notice that the benefits package that accompanies our salvation began with peace and ends with joy? This is not a bad combination. "Therefore having been justified by faith, we have peace with God through our Lord Jesus Christ. . . . And not only this, but we also exult in God through our Lord Jesus Christ, through whom we have now received the reconciliation" (vv. 1, 11).

Study Questions

1. How and why can believers now exult and have hope in their trials and tribulations?

2. What does Paul mean when he writes that hope does not disappoint?

3. Define *reconciliation*.

4. How does the blood of Christ justify us before God?

CHAPTER 11

Justification by Faith Imputed
Romans 5:12-21

Preview:

Through Adam sin entered the world of the human race. Death then followed and spread to everyone. Adam was a type of Christ in that their actions affected all humanity. Adam is not merely a type of sin, but actually brought the guilt of sin on those he represented. Likewise, Christ is not merely a type of righteousness, but actually brought the gift of righteousness, whereby those who trust in Him will have salvation and reign through Him. Christ brought the gift of grace and salvation to all who believe. With the Law of Moses the understanding of sin increased, but "grace abounded all the more" (Rom. 5:20).

Thus far in the epistle to the Romans, Paul has dealt with two great theological opposites: condemnation and justification. Before the apostle leaves the subject, he enhances our understanding by drawing contrasts between Adam and Christ (vv. 14–15), condemnation and justification (v. 16), disobedience and obedience (v. 19), law and grace (v. 20), sin and righteousness (v. 21), and death and life (v. 21).

Since these verses are so doctrinal in nature, it will be helpful to keep in mind three very important truths established in Romans 5:12–21. They are: (1) one offense, by one man, made all the world guilty of sin; (2) the resultant guilt of Adam's original sin is imputed to each of us; and (3) Adam acted as our official representative when he cast his vote against God. We'll see how each of these important truths, as well as the contrasts behind them, weaves in and out through the verses that follow.

How Sin Entered the Human Family (5:12)

This portion of Paul's epistle begins with the words, "Therefore, just as through one man sin entered into the world . . ." (v. 12). There can be no discussion as to the identity of this man. The apostle refers, of course, to Adam. Remember the words of Genesis 2:7, 15–18, 22:

> Then the LORD God formed man of dust from the ground, and breathed into his nostrils the breath of life; and man became a living being. . . .

> Then the LORD God took the man and put him into the garden of Eden to cultivate it and keep it. And the LORD God commanded the man, saying, "From any tree of the garden you may eat freely; but from the tree of the knowledge of good and evil you shall not eat, for in the day that you eat from it you shall surely die."

> Then the LORD God said, "It is not good for the man to be alone; I will make him a helper suitable for him." . . .

> And the LORD God fashioned into a woman the rib which He had taken from the man.

When the command not to eat of the tree was given to Adam, not only were there no other men around, Eve was not around yet either. So when Eve sinned, an event recorded in the next chapter (Gen. 3), it wasn't her sin that brought guilt to the world; it was Adam's sin after her.

So why is Adam's sin and not Eve's important in Paul's discussion? Because Adam was much more than the first husband; he was the first human. He stood as the head of the human race. There was much more to Adam's original sin than meets the eye. It is abundantly clear that this one man, Adam, brought sin to the human race by his disobedience. The apocryphal book of 2 Esdras asks, "O Adam, what have you done? For though it was you who sinned, the fall was not yours alone, but ours also who are your descendants" (7:118). One sin, by one man, made the entire world guilty of sin.

An Unwelcome Parasite (5:12)

[handwritten: Adam brought death / X defeated death]

But when Adam ate of the forbidden fruit, sin was not alone in entering the universe. Something sneaked in the back door with it—an unwelcome parasite—death. "Through one man sin entered into the world, and death through sin" (v. 12). Humankind's greatest enemy tagged along with the first man's greatest mistake. Sin and death cannot be separated (Gen. 2:17; 3:17–19; Rom. 1:32; 1 Cor. 15:22). Wherever you find one you will find the other.

Adam's body and mind began the process of dying the day he sinned, and eventually that process came to sin's inevitable conclusion. Perhaps the saddest words in the entire Bible are the last three in the saddest verse in the Bible—"and he died" (Gen. 5:5). Adam was created by a loving God and placed in a garden paradise filled with the finest of trees, plants, animals, gold, and precious stones. The weather was ideal; every day was perfect. Adam had no worries, no problems, and no restrictions—except one. Adam chose to break that one restriction, and when he did, he sinned. Adam's sin caught up with him just as God's Word cautions: "The person who sins will die" (Ezek. 18:20). Adam sinned; Adam died. The man God created to live forever was the first person ever to experience the pain of death.

It was not the sins of Adam's lifetime, but the one original sin that allowed death, sin's close ally, to enter the world with it. On no less than five occasions in verses 15–19, the principle of one sin by one man is asserted (vv. 15, 16, 17, 18, and 19). One act of disobedience to God was sufficient to allow sin to enter and to permeate the entire realm of humanity. And along with sin came that dreaded parasite, death. But here's the contrast: When Jesus was raised from the dead for our justification, death was defeated. Thus Paul could remark, "'O death, where is your victory? O death, where is your sting?' The sting of death is sin, and the power of sin is the law; but thanks be to God, who gives us the victory through our Lord Jesus Christ" (1 Cor. 15:55–57). Death sneaked into the human race on the back of Adam's sin. But death was defeated in the human race on the back of Christ's righteousness.

Adam as Head of the Race

Before we look at other contrasts between Adam and Christ, I must respond to the loud chorus of objectors asking, "What has Adam's sin got to do with me? If he wanted to sin, that's his business, not mine." That sounds good, but it's not true. Adam's sin has everything to do with you and me. Romans 5:12 continues, "and so death spread to all men, because all sinned."

One sin, by one man, made the entire world guilty of sin. It is true that through the process of procreation and heredity sin spread to all people. Job asked the semi-rhetorical question: "Who can make the clean out of the unclean?" and then answered his own question: "No one!" (Job 14:4). A sinful father and a sinful mother cannot bear anything but a sinful child. An old Chinese proverb speaks of "two good men; one dead, the other unborn." Clearly the process of human regeneration explains the means by which sin spread to all people, but it doesn't explain the reason. In verse 15 Paul alludes to the fact that it was due to the transgression of the one that many died.

Adam's one sin could not make the entire world guilty unless Adam stood in a unique relationship to the rest of the world, and he did. He was the head of the human race, the first man, and the first sinner. As such, his life and actions represented all who came after him.

We use this same procedure in the United States Congress. We elect representatives to go to Washington, D.C., in our behalf. When they cast a vote, theoretically at least, it is our vote they are casting. One votes for all. When Adam sinned, he cast a vote in our behalf against God and joined Satan's rebellion. That vote was our vote. He did not cast it just for himself; he cast it for the constituency he represented. It's just that simple.

Jesus as Head of a New Race

Here is the great contrast. As Adam stood at the head of one race, so Christ Jesus stands at the head of another. Adam is at the head of the family of man; Jesus is at the head of the family of God. That means that all of humanity finds itself in one family or another. If you had to choose, which family would you choose? That is not a rhetorical question. In fact, it's a question every person must answer, because choose we must.

Even if you say, "I'd like to be in Jesus' family. It looks like it has more going for it," there's a problem. When you are born, the choice has already been made for you. We are all born into Adam's family, and that's because we all find our kinship in the family of man. Adam chose to reject God's authority in the Garden of Eden, and the choice was made for everyone forever. So, like it or not, you are born into Adam's family and, unless things change, you will die in Adam's family. All of Adam's children face destruction and hell.

But if that's not what you want, how can you change your situation? If we've learned anything from the first five chapters of Romans, it ought to be that we can't change our situation by doing good things, by adopting a certain moral code, or by being of a particular ethnicity. The only way to experience change is to have faith in God's promise. Have faith in the work of Jesus Christ as your substitute on the cross, and you can be moved from Adam's family to Jesus' family. The bottom line is this: Since we all are born into the family of Adam, if we want to live in the family of God, we must be born again.

The Imputation of Adam's Sin (5:13)

We have encountered the idea of imputation before. Refer back to the story of Abraham in Romans 4. When Paul was explaining how Abraham could be treated as righteous by God, he quoted from Genesis 15:6, "Abraham believed

God, and it was reckoned to him as righteousness" (4:3). God took Abraham's rudimentary faith, faith that was genuinely expressed by the patriarch, and credited that faith to Abraham's account as righteousness. The word is *logizomai* in Greek. It means to reckon or to count or to impute to someone what he or she has not personally done. Abraham was not personally righteous, but he believed God, and God said, "Good enough. I'll take that faith and chalk it up as if Abraham were righteous." That's the principle of imputation.

It is the same principle we see in play here and the same word—*logizomai*. Just as Abraham's faith was credited to his account, Adam's sin was credited to our account. What happened in the Garden of Eden was not an isolated incident disconnected to the flow of history. It was the beginning of human history and determined the flow of history. Adam's sin was not his alone; it was ours as well. Adam was there in total innocence. He never had sinned before. He had the potential not to sin then, but he made the wrong choice, as we did. He—and in him we—chose to disregard God and do the opposite of what He commanded. We have been doing that ever since. So God took that original sin and charged it to Adam's permanent record. And since Adam was acting in our behalf, He charged it to our permanent record as well.

Before you are critical of God's methods, remember that the same thing happened when Jesus Christ died for us. God took Christ's righteousness, confirmed by His obedience at Calvary, and charged it to our account. We deserved being charged with Adam's sin; we did not deserve being charged with Christ's righteousness. That was pure grace. It is ironic, isn't it, that those who complain about the unfairness of being charged with Adam's sin are mum when it comes to the fairness of being charged with Christ's righteousness. Yet the principle is exactly the same.[1]

The Function of the Law (5:13–14, 20)

When Adam sinned, sin immediately inundated the whole world and had a mortal effect on its subsequent inhabitants. But as Paul has done so often in the past, he anticipates an argument on this point. How could there be sin before the Law? If you have no law by which to judge sin, how can you know sin is wrong? Paul answers immediately, "Sin is not imputed when there is no law" (v. 13), but even before the Law of Moses was given, physical death was clear evidence of the presence of sin in Adam and his posterity. So universal was this sin that its deadly effects were evident even in those who had not sinned "in the likeness of the offense of Adam" (v. 14). Adam is here again contrasted with Christ and said to be a "type [Greek, *tupos*] of Him who was to come." The only Old Testament character to be called explicitly a type of

Christ is Adam, probably because of Adam's position as the head of the old family and Christ's position as the head of God's new family.

Paul argued that even before the Law was given, sin was making its presence known. Is there any evidence of that? Cain killed his brother Abel (Gen. 4:8). Abraham lied twice about his relationship with Sarah to save his own life (Gen. 12:10–13; 20:1–2). Sodom and Gomorrah became so wicked that God had to destroy them both (Gen. 18:20; 19:24–25); Jacob cheated his brother (Gen. 25:29–34) and lied to his father (Gen. 27:18–19); Joseph's brothers plotted to kill him and sold him into slavery (Gen. 37:18, 28). Moses committed manslaughter and had to flee Egypt (Ex. 2:11–15). It is evident that even before the Law, sin had permeated human society.

So how did people know they were doing wrong before God gave Moses the Law? Think back to his arguments in Romans 1. Even those who did not have the Law, or do not have it today, have the law of nature and the law of conscience to condemn them. The witness of nature and conscience to sin is sufficient to convict anyone who does not suppress the truth.

What, then, does the Law do that nature and conscience cannot do? God's intention was that the Law would highlight our sin, show it in bold relief. At Sinai, the Mosaic Law "came in that the transgression might increase" (v. 20). That means, by the Law, human consciousness of sin would become sharpened. A vague knowledge of right and wrong was transformed into a precise and crystal-clear knowledge by the Law. But the Law also gave evidence that people could not adequately keep it and drove humankind to look for the Savior and the grace of God, a grace greater than all our sin (v. 20; Gal. 3:24). This is the contrast between Law and grace. "Where sin increased [by the knowledge of the Law], grace abounded all the more" (v. 20).

The Gift of God's Grace (5:15–17)

[handwritten margin note: sin of Adam vs much greater grace of God]

Paul's continued contrast between Adam and Christ shows a correspondence both in similarity and dissimilarity. Through the offense of Adam, the many (i.e., all of Adam's descendants) incurred the penalty of death. Similarly, the many (i.e., all the redeemed) have incurred the free gift of eternal life through the Last Adam, Jesus Christ. The dissimilarity is seen in the phrase "much more did the grace of God." The grace of God, which is the ground of our justification, is contrasted with the sin of Adam, because it is greater in quality and greater in degree than Adam's sin. In Adam we got what we deserved— condemnation and guilt. In Christ we have received much more of what we do not deserve—mercy and grace.

The comparative of choice for the apostle Paul was the Greek *pollō mallon*, meaning "much more" or "all the more." It was a favorite of Paul's when he wanted to show that one thing was much greater than another. Paul uses this comparative expression no less than five times in Romans 5 (vv. 9, 10, 15, 17, 20). He also uses it twice in Romans 11, comparing God's benefits to the Jews and the Gentile nations (vv. 12, 24). Paul uses it elsewhere frequently in his epistles: see 1 Cor. 6:3; 12:22; 2 Cor. 3:9, 11; 8:22; Phil. 1:14; 2:12; Philem. 1:16. Some examples: "Where [man's] sin increased, [God's] grace abounded *pollō mallon*" (Rom. 5:20); "If the ministry of condemnation has glory, *pollō mallon* does the ministry of righteousness" (2 Cor. 3:9); "Just as you have always obeyed, not as in my presence only, but now *pollō mallon* in my absence" (Phil. 2:12).

What keeping the Law could not do, believing in grace did. The Law was powerful in that it demonstrated our inability to keep it, but it was weak in providing that ability. What the Law could not do, God did in the gracious act of sacrificing His only begotten Son for us. It is through the "abundance of grace and of the gift of righteousness" (v. 17) that Christ created a new family, a new breed, a new creation—born again men and women who are trusting in Christ rather than in the works of the Law to save.

Condemnation in Adam; Justification in Christ (5:16)

In verse 16 the contrast turns to condemnation in Adam and justification in Christ. "For on the one hand the judgment arose from one transgression resulting in condemnation, but on the other hand the free gift arose from many transgressions resulting in justification." Notice again that Paul never refers to the "offenses" or "transgressions" of one man, but to the "offense," "transgression" (singular) or "disobedience" of one man (vv. 14, 15, 17–20). The *sins* of Adam's lifetime have not been imputed to us, but only his original *sin*. That one sin brought condemnation. However, the righteousness that is imputed to us by Christ, through the free gift of God's grace, covers not just that one offense but many offenses.

As the representative head of the human race, Adam's offense dethroned him as the ruler of God's creation. Consequently, death became the ruler of nature. Adam became the representative of a death-destined society. All who are born into that society have death as their destiny as well. The Last Adam, Jesus Christ, is also the representative of a society. Through the gift of righteousness, He will reign in life. Since all are born into the society of death, the only way to enter Christ's society, in which people are born unto justification of life, is to be born again. By the new birth experience, we pass from our old relationship to Adam into a new and living relationship with Christ.

Comparing Adam and Jesus	
Romans 5:12, 15	The man Adam brought death.
Romans 5:15	The man Jesus brought the gift of grace.
Genesis 1:27	Adam was created.
Romans 5:14	Jesus was He "who was to come."
Romans 5:19	Adam's disobedience made many sinners.
Philippians 2:8	Jesus' obedience unto death made many righteous.
Romans 5:16	Adam's transgression resulted in condemnation.
Romans 5:16	Jesus' free gift resulted in justification.
Romans 5:17	Death reigned through one—Adam.
Romans 5:17	The gift of righteousness will reign through one—Christ.
Genesis 3:21	Adam needed a sacrifice for sin.
Isaiah 53: 7	Jesus was a sacrifice for sin.
1 Corinthians 15:21	By one man, Adam, came death.
1 Corinthians 15:22	By one Man, Christ, came the resurrection from the dead.
1 Corinthians 15:45	The first Adam became a living soul.
1 Corinthians 15:45	The last Adam (Christ) became a life-giving spirit.
1 Corinthians 15:47	The first Adam is from the earth, earthy.
1 Corinthians 15:47	The second Adam (Christ) is from heaven, the heavenly.

The Contrast Between Disobedience and Obedience (5:19)

Here the contrast drawn is between blatant disobedience and willful obedience. How is it possible that "through the one man's disobedience the many were made sinners" (v. 19)? Theologian Charles Hodge reviews the various interpretations of this clause.

1. That the sin of Adam was the mere occasion of other men becoming sinners; whether this was by the force of example, or by an unfavourable change in their external circumstances, or in some other unexplained manner, being left undecided. 2. That in virtue of community, or numerical oneness of nature between Adam and his posterity, his act was strictly their act, and made them sinners as it made him a sinner. 3. That as the apostasy of Adam involved a corruption of nature, that corruption was transmitted to his descendants, by the general physical law of propagation. 4. That the sin of Adam was the judicial ground of the condemnation of his race. They were by his sin constituted sinners in a legal and forensic sense; as by the righteousness of Christ we are constituted legally righteous.[2]

The difference, of course, was not just between Adam and Christ, but also between Adam's disobedience and Christ's obedience. God's command to our representative Adam concerning the tree of the knowledge of good and evil was, "You shall not eat" (Gen. 2:17). Almost immediately the head of the human race disobeyed that divine command. That's how, as Hodge says, "his sin constituted sinners in a legal and forensic sense." However, Christ Jesus, the Last Adam and Head of the heavenly race, totally obeyed the will of God and testified to that when He said, "I glorified Thee on the earth, having accomplished the work which Thou hast given Me to do" (John 17:4). Again, using Hodge's words, that's how "by the righteousness of Christ we are constituted legally righteous." The difference between obedience and disobedience is the difference between life and death, between unrighteousness and righteousness.

If Jesus Christ had not obeyed the Father's will and voluntarily sacrificed His life at Calvary, we would have had another case of the head of a race disobeying God. The whole of our salvation rested on Christ's obedience. Thank God that His Son was of a mind to obey.

The Contrast Between Death and Life (5:20–21)

These verses contain the double contrast between sin and righteousness and between death and life. When Adam fell, with his sin came the parasite of death. It seemed as if sin was about to triumph over God's creation completely. From the very moment sin entered the universe, it has reigned, bringing about physical and spiritual death. Its principle of rulership has been to separate people from our Creator and to cause our end to be a mortal one. That's why, even though they lived extended lives, all but Enoch are listed as dead men among the generations between Adam and Noah (Gen. 5). But through the blood of Jesus Christ, sin has been dethroned, and righteousness now rules in its stead. Whereas death was the order of the day in Adam's society, now life eternal is the order of the day for those who have believed in Jesus Christ. The contrast is great. It is a contrast between man's sin and Christ's obedience, between the wages of sin and the gift of God (Rom. 6:23), between death and life.

As one act of sin brought guilt and condemnation to all people, so too one act of righteousness brought freedom from guilt and condemnation. Just as the sins of Adam's life did not condemn us, the acts of goodness or kindness in Christ's life do not justify us. The principle of one still applies. Jesus' one act of obedience in going to the cross and dying atoned for our sin. It was not repeated crucifixions that saved us, but one crucifixion. That's why, in a much contested passage, the writer of Hebrews says, "For in the case of those who have once been enlightened and have tasted of the heavenly gift and have been made partakers of the Holy Spirit, and have tasted the good word of God and the powers of the age to come, and then have fallen away, it is impossible to renew them again to repentance, since they again crucify to themselves the Son of God, and put Him to open shame" (Heb. 6:4–6). The issue here is not whether those once enlightened could fall away, but rather, if they could, how could there be any atonement for them? They cannot possibly fall away, because Christ cannot possibly return to the cross. The principle of one means that Christ was crucified once for all, never to return to the cross.

We have life rather than death because Jesus endured death rather than life. We are all born into the family of Adam, a family that brings death to all members. But if we have been born again into the family of Christ, we are part of a family that brings life to all members. That only happens with Jesus Christ. "In Him [Jesus] was life, and the life was the light of men" (John 1:4). "I [Jesus] am the way, and the truth, and the life; no one comes to the Father, but through Me" (John 14:6). "My sheep hear My voice, and I know them, and they follow Me; and I give eternal life to them, and they shall never perish; and no one shall snatch them out of My hand" (John 10:27–28). Born in Adam; reborn in Christ—that's the secret to eternal life.

Study Questions

1. How can it be said that "all men sinned in Adam"? Explain.

2. What does Paul mean when he writes, "But sin is not imputed when there is no law"?

3. How could Adam's sin bring condemnation to everyone?

4. In what way can it be said that death has reigned through Adam?

5. What does Paul have in mind when he says that those "who receive the abundance of grace and the gift of righteousness will reign in life through the One, Jesus Christ"?

6. What kind of *life* does the believer ultimately receive in Jesus the Lord?

SECTION IV: SANCTIFICATION

The Christian's Need for Holiness

Romans 6:1 — 8:39

Once we have been justified, our journey into life has just begun. The Christian life is the walk from new birth to heaven, and that requires spiritual growth along the way. Spiritual growth is the process by which the Holy Spirit feeds us from God's Word, takes away sinful and childish attitudes, and conforms us more and more to the image of Jesus Christ. We call the process sanctification.

CHAPTER 12

Sanctification Explained in Principle
Romans 6:1–14

Preview:

Paul writes of a spiritual baptism that places believers into the death, burial, and resurrection of the Lord. Those who experience this spiritual baptism will be raised from the dead, in the likeness of Christ's resurrection. Since we died with Him in this spiritual way, we will also live with Him. Believers then are to consider themselves dead to sin but alive to God!

Having established in 3:21—5:21 that justification is provided by faith alone, Paul now turns his attention to the provision for sanctification. In the preceding chapter, he drew some conclusions concerning the contrasts between Adam and Christ. In chapters 6 and 7, however, the contrast is between justification and sanctification. Paul transitions smoothly between the discussion of justification in chapter 5 and sanctification in chapter 6. Although there is a sharp contrast between the two; nevertheless, the intimacy of the relationship between justification and sanctification is clearly seen in the way they are connected in these chapters.

Basically, the contrast between the two is this: justification deals with the penalty for sin; sanctification deals with the power of sin. As was seen in 5:1, justification is a declarative act of God. As will be seen in chapter 6, sanctification is a progressive act of God. Both deal with the sinner: justification with the unsaved sinner; sanctification with the saved sinner. The end result

The end Result

of justification is salvation; the end result of sanctification is holiness. Although distinctly different, justification and sanctification are flip sides of the one work of God in saving people.

The Unspeakable Question (6:1–2)

In every age, some have denounced the doctrine of justification by faith on the incorrect supposition that it logically leads to sin. In some quirky way, they reason that if our sin gives rise to greater expressions of God's grace, it is good for us to continue to sin. If believers are treated as righteous by God, and if good works will not save them, then evil works will not condemn them either. Why, then, should people be concerned about their sin or attempt to live a godly life? Theologically, this belief is known as antinomianism—living as if there were no law, no binding moral code.

Thus, Paul asks the rhetorical question: "Are we to continue in sin that grace might increase?" We expect Paul's usual expression of horror—*mē genoito*—and we are not disappointed. Just because where sin increases grace abounds even more, believers are not automatically given license to live a sinful lifestyle. On the contrary, a mature understanding of justification by faith leads us to appreciate God's grace so that the end result is obedience to God out of a heart filled with gratitude. Paul's characteristic expression "May it never be!" shows how appalled he is at the mere suggestion that we continue in sin once we have experienced the grace of God. The reason we cannot mindlessly continue in sin is because, through our identification with Jesus Christ, we are dead to sin (v. 2). To die to sin means that we are dead to the guilt of sin. Sin can no longer make any legal claim on believers, because we are viewed by God as if we ourselves died that dark day at Calvary.

At this point, Paul begins to relate the secret to living a holy and sanctified life, a life characterized by being dead to sin. The secret of sanctification is not found in some sanctimonious formula or some deeper, mystical experience with the Lord. The secret is found in three words or principles: know (v. 3); consider (v. 11); and present (v. 13). Let's be especially aware of these principles as we seek to understand the relationship between justification and sanctification.

To live a sanctified and holy life after we are saved and squelch the desire to continue in sin, we must adhere to these principles:

Principle #1: The Need to Know (6:3–5)

So what is the apostle teaching? What's the meaning of this word that is central to his thinking? In his question "Do you not know . . . ?" (v. 3) he uses the Greek word *agnoeō*. It is formed by joining the root word *gnoeō* (meaning to understand, perceive, or consider) with the negative particle *"a"* as a prefix. When the alpha (*a*) prefix is attached to a word, it has the effect of negating it. So to know is *gnoeō*; not to know is *agnoeō*. That's why a person who knows is called a gnostic; a person who does not know is called an agnostic. To the apostle, knowledge of why we deserved condemnation is the foundation for sanctification. And knowledge of what happened to us when we were justified is essential to understand sanctification. So sanctification is built on knowledge, not on feeling. Paul will explain in later verses.

To show the immaturity of those who would continue in sin after justification so that grace may abound, Paul introduces the subject of baptism as evidence that a life of unrestrained, unrepentant sinful behavior cannot coexist with death to sin. The apostle says we should know that "all of us who have been baptized into Christ Jesus have been baptized into His death" (v. 3). Baptism into Christ means to be incorporated into Him, to become a member of His body (1 Cor. 12:13), and to share with Him those experiences that were historically His but are vicariously ours (i.e., His crucifixion, death, burial, and resurrection). Therefore we are buried with him by baptism into death. Burial with Christ Jesus signifies that sin no longer judicially has a hold on us. The ordinance of Christian baptism beautifully portrays this burial into Christ in which the old order of a death-controlled life comes to an end and the new order of a Christ-controlled life begins. Therefore, having already been justified, a believer demonstrates that fact to the world by submitting to the ordinance of water baptism. When a Christian has been symbolically raised up from the dead from the waters of baptism, even as Christ was raised from His Jerusalem grave, the purpose of that Christian's resurrection is that he or she should walk in newness of life. This should entirely preclude the foolish idea of continuing in sin so that a display may be made of the grace of God. Just as we were united with Christ in the likeness of His death, we will be also in the likeness of His resurrection. Hence we enter into His life and become a part of Him spiritually, yielding to Him our desires, our wishes, ourselves.

Crucified and Dead (6:6–8)

Paul is still expounding the first principle of true sanctification—knowledge. Hence, as in verse 3, he repeats the word that is characteristic of this first principle. "Knowing this, that our old self was crucified with Him" (v. 6). The old man referred to here is our old self, the person we once were before we were crucified with Christ. This crucifixion is not a present, daily experience, but is rather a past event, expressed by the aorist tense in Greek. Some make the hermeneutical mistake of appealing to 1 Corinthians 15:31 as proof that we must "die daily." But that's a serious hermeneutical mistake. First Corinthians 15 was written by Paul in the context of physical, not spiritual death. Our old man is not constantly being crucified, day by day, but has been crucified at the cross of Calvary. The reason is that "our body of sin might be done away with" (v. 6). A better rendering of "might be done away with" (Greek, *katargeō*) is "might be rendered inoperative." At the cross of Calvary, a victory was won that provided the believer with the power not to live as he or she once did, serving the old master (i.e., sin), but to live eternally serving a new master (i.e., Christ).

F. F. Bruce refers to this truth as stated in Galatians 2:20 and then continues,

> Similarly in Galatians 6:15 Paul speaks of "the cross of our Lord Jesus Christ, by which the world has been crucified (perfect tense) to me, and I to the world" (RSV). In these two passages from Galatians the perfect tense denotes a present state produced by the past event of Romans 6:6. Moreover, in Galatians 6:14 there is probably a side glance at an alternative meaning of the verb "crucify" *(stauroō)*, namely "fence off"; so that Paul's words may also imply: "that cross forms a permanent barrier between the world and me, and between me and the world." For "the old man" cf. Colossians 3:9 and Ephesians 4:22. He belongs to the "present evil age" from which the death of Christ delivers His people (Gal. 1:4, RSV).[1]

Now here's a truth we must take hold of: "He who has died is freed from sin" (v. 7). Death wipes the slate clean. The death of our Lord completely removed the guilt and penalty of our sin. We must be convinced of that truth, know it cold, and cement it in the pathway of our mind, if we are to live a holy and sanctified life before God. Those who have not firmly latched on to the truth that we are freed from the penalty of sin are constantly wrestling with that sin and its guilt. To be freed from sin doesn't mean we will never sin again, it means we will never enter a courtroom and be judicially sentenced by God for that sin. Jesus' death took it away. It is past, gone, dead. We are free to live in Christ as we once lived in Adam. That's why the apostle hurries on to express, "Now if we have died with Christ, we believe that we shall also live with Him" (v. 8). Living with Christ precludes the possibility of carnally continuing in sin so that grace may abound. New life in Christ is to be celebrated, not soiled by ongoing forays into sinful habits.

Death No Longer Our Master (6:9–10)

In chapter 5, Paul hammered home the principle that in Adam all die. In Adam death passed to all people. In Adam death reigned. We know that to be true. But for the Christian, that was then and this is now. Now, in Christ, we know something far different. "Knowing that Christ, having been raised from the dead, is never to die again; death no longer is master over Him" (v. 9). Even a casual reader has to be struck with the fact that this is the third time the word "know" in one of its forms has appeared in the first nine verses of this chapter on sanctification. It should be increasingly evident that the sanctified life begins with the informed mind, not with inspired emotions.

Paul had no doubt that Jesus was alive. He had beaten death, and because He would never die again, He was master over death, not the other way around. "He died to sin, once for all; but the life that He lives, He lives to God" (v. 10). Paul's reason for pointing that out is that when Christ died, we died; and when Jesus was raised from the dead, we were raised from the dead. We were buried with Him, and thus we are completely identified with Christ. Justification is a completed transaction by which we have once and for all passed into the resurrection life of our Lord. Jesus Christ can never die again. After we die with Him to sin, we never die to sin again. Death has no more dominion over him, and it has no more dominion over us. After Jesus went to the cross and paid the debt in full for our sin, death could no longer claim Him or those who died with Him. Therefore, the foundation of sanctification is knowing what Christ has already accomplished for us through His death. The starting point is realizing that we are holy in Him.

To live a sanctified and holy life after we are saved and squelch the desire to continue in sin, we must adhere also to the following principle.

Dead to sin, HS allows us to grow spiritually — making us more like X

Principle #2: Consider Yourself Dead (6:11–12)

Knowing what has been accomplished on our behalf at Calvary is not in itself sanctification. It is but the first principle in the process of sanctification. Paul couples to that principle a second one: "Even so consider yourselves to be dead to sin, but alive to God in Christ Jesus" (v. 11). We have encountered this verb before. It's the Greek *logizomai*, which we saw so frequently in the story of Abraham in Romans 4 (vv. 3–6, 8–11, 22–24). Abraham believed God, and it was reckoned *(logizomai)* or credited to him as righteousness. We also saw this word in Romans 5:13: "For until the Law sin was in the world; but sin is not imputed *(logizomai)* when there is no law." As a reminder, the word means to credit something to the account of another. In his epistle to Philemon, Paul says to the slave owner, "But if he [Onesimus, the runaway slave] has wronged you in any way, or owes you anything, charge *(logizomai)* that to my account" (Philem. 1:18).

"This 'reckoning' is no vain experience but one which is morally fruitful," says F. F. Bruce, "because the Holy Spirit has come to make effective in believers what Christ has done for them, and to enable them to become in daily experience, as far as may be in the present conditions of mortality, what they already are 'in Christ' and what they will fully be in the resurrection life."[2] When we daily count ourselves to be dead to the penalty of sin and alive unto God, there will be no temptation to continue in sin. We will refuse that temptation out of thankfulness to God for counting us and treating us as if we were righteous.

To live a sanctified and holy life after we are saved and squelch the desire to continue in sin, we must adhere to yet a third principle.

Principle #3: Present Yourself to God (6:13)

The third and final principle in living a sanctified life is stated negatively: "Do not go on presenting the members of your body to sin as instruments of unrighteousness; but present yourselves to God as those alive from the dead, and your members as instruments of righteousness to God" (v. 13). As those who have been justified, we are not to allow our members (e.g., our hands, feet, tongues, and minds) to become the weapons or resources of unrighteousness. Don't let that word "instruments" throw you. It sounds like the implements on a doctor's surgical tray or the pieces of brass in a band. The English translation hides more than it reveals. The word Paul chose is *hoplon*, which clearly means weapons or arms used in warfare. When Judas and the Roman cohort came with the chief priests and Pharisees to arrest Jesus in the Garden of Gethsemane, they "came there with lanterns and torches and weapons *(hoplon)*" (John 18:3). Paul uses the same word in 2 Corinthians 10:3–4: "For though we walk in the flesh, we do not war according to the flesh, for the weapons *(hoplon)* of our warfare are not of the flesh." Knowing that what Christ accomplished for us in the past resulted in our justification, and considering or reckoning ourselves dead to the penalty of sin because we have been justified, we are now to keep our weapons from being given to sinful purposes.

There is a subtle distinction here that is not evident in English. The Greek word Paul chose for "presenting," or yielding our members is *paristēmi*. It means to set at one's disposal, so "presenting" or "yielding" are both good translations. But here's the subtle distinction: When Paul uses the word the first time with regard to not presenting our members as weapons of unrighteousness, he chooses the present active imperative tense of the verb. Literally he says, "Do not keep on continually presenting your members as instruments of unrighteousness." In other words, once you have been justified, there is no place for you to continue to do the things you did before you were justified. You cannot continue living in an adulterous relationship after you are saved.

You cannot continue to click on your favorite porn sites after you have been justified. The word is a continuous present verb, and it is an imperative. On the other hand, when Paul uses the word with regard to God—"but present yourselves to God"—he switches to the aorist active imperative tense. The aorist tense is equivalent to the past tense in English. What happens in the aorist tense happens at a point in the past and is not constantly repeated (see comments on 5:1). Once we have been justified, we present ourselves to God; and while the fruit of that presentation continues day by day, we do not repeat the process day by day. There comes a point in a believer's life (at salvation) when he or she must decide to live for God and abandon the habits of the past. If one who claims to be a Christian doesn't exhibit that kind of commitment to God, there is every reason to question whether that person has really experienced salvation.

No More Master (6:14)

With this in mind, what Paul wants to communicate here in Romans 6 is that once we have been justified, we cannot even consider continuing to live the sinful lifestyle we exhibited in Adam. Now that we are born again, as those alive from the dead, we must continually offer the parts of our bodies as weapons of the righteousness of God. You'll remember that righteousness (Greek, *dikaiosunē*) is the key word in the epistle to the Romans (Rom. 1:17; 3:5, 21, 22, 25, 26; 4:3, 5, 6, 9, 11, 13, 22; 5:17, 21; 6:13, 16, 18–20; 8:10; 9:30; 31; 10:3–6, 10; 14:17).

Paul's concept of sanctification, then, is not a daily dying to one's self. It is rather being mature enough to rest wholly on the finished work of Calvary, knowing that we have been justified there, daily reckoning that work to be finished, and constantly presenting ourselves to be used of God. As William Barclay says, "Christianity can never be only an experience of the secret place; it must be a life in the market place."[3] When we, as believers, are obedient to these commands, we find ourselves on a road climbing progressively toward the resurrection life of the Lord. The Lord has a promise for those who seek sanctification in this manner: "Sin shall not be master over you." That's good news!

Study Questions

1. What shows that this baptism Paul writes about is spiritual and does not mean baptism by water?

2. What does Paul mean when he writes, "Our old self was crucified with Him"?

3. From verses 10–14, list the ways the apostle says we are now to live for the Lord and walk in a more obedient manner.

4. Since Christians do sin and wrestle with sin problems, what does the apostle Paul mean when he writes, "Sin shall not be master over you"?

5. What is the difference between being under law and being under grace?

CHAPTER 13

Sanctification Explained in Practice
Romans 6:15-23

Preview:

Believers in Christ are to <u>live obedient to the Lord, not to sin.</u> In a positional sense, the children of God are now "slaves" to righteousness. They must present their bodily members to Him as instruments of righteousness, not unrighteousness. Being a slave to sin brings wages of death, but belonging to Christ brings eternal life.

In the second half of Romans 6, Paul repeats the Antinomian argument of verse 1 but with a significant difference. In verse 1 the question was, "Are we to continue in sin that grace might increase?" Here Paul dealt with the principle of the continuation of a sinful lifestyle after the believer recognized he or she was dead to sin. Is it possible for someone born into Adam's family and now born again into Christ's family to go on living as he or she did before being saved? Paul's characteristic expression of appalled horror is his response: "May it never be!" (v. 2).

Now the question is, "Shall we sin . . . ?" Here the apostle is not speaking of a lifestyle of sin, but rather of an occasional excursion into iniquity. Is it acceptable for a Christian to repudiate being addicted to sex but still visit a pornographic website once in a while? Now, you may think that's a strange question, but it is the kind of question Paul is addressing here. Why? "Shall we sin because we are not under law but under grace?" Since we are no longer under the restrictions of the Mosaic Law but are now living in the age of grace, is it not permissible to fall into sin once in a while? After all, God's grace is always there to understand and forgive. Paul's abhorrence is seen in his usual answer, *mē genoito!* "May it never be!" (v. 15).

The Slave Trade (6:16–17)

But the apostle does more than show his horror. He furnishes an answer. "Do you not know that when you present yourselves to someone as slaves for obedience, you are slaves of the one whom you obey, either of sin resulting in death, or of obedience resulting in righteousness?" (v. 16). Paul uses the analogy of the slave market to illustrate that sanctified believers dare not even occasionally fall into sin. His point is that if we start to obey sin even a little, we are opening the door for the mastery of sin in our lives.

Every drug addict in the world understands this principle all too well. A young executive begins to take some drugs to handle the unexpected pressures of his job—not much, maybe just a few pills. But soon pills aren't enough; he needs more. One drug leads to another. At after-hours office parties, he gets into heavier drugs. The first thing you know he is on the street looking for methamphetamines and ends up using crack. Still unsatisfied, he seeks the ultimate buzz with heroine. The story is repeated daily throughout the world. That's why Paul develops our Lord's words, "No one can serve two masters" (Matt. 6:24). Yielding to sin even a little almost always means yielding to eventual control by that sin. People become slaves to their sin of choice, and eventually, when that sin no longer satisfies (and it won't forever), they search for even greater ways to enslave themselves to sin. Ultimately the mastery of sin results in their death (v. 16).

But there is good news. The same pattern that drags people down when they yield to sin builds them up when they present their bodies for righteous living. They begin by attending the Sunday service and hiding out in the crowd at church. They are safely tucked away as spectators. But it's not enough. The Spirit prompts them to get involved in a Bible study. They like it and want more. Soon they are assisting a small group. The first thing they know, they're hooked. They want to learn more. Now they are teaching the group and studying the Bible even when they don't have to prepare a study session. They're yielding themselves to obedience to Christ, and that brings righteousness.

What made the difference in these two scenarios? The truthful proposition of verse 16: "You are slaves of the one whom you obey." Whatever we yield to in a small way in the beginning is what we ultimately become servants of. If we present ourselves to be slaves to sin, slaves to sin we'll become. If we present ourselves to be slaves to righteousness, slaves to righteousness we'll become. The key word *present* (Greek, *paristēmi*) is one we have seen before (v. 13); it means "to place yourself at the disposal of another." This is why Paul answers so strongly that believers can't even allow themselves to take side excursions into sin. Occasional visits will escalate into frequent stays that eventually lead to death.

Reason for Giving Thanks (6:17–18)

Here Paul turns from admonition to thanksgiving. "But thanks be to God that though you were slaves of sin, . . . having been freed from sin, you became slaves of righteousness" (vv. 17–18). The apostle was ever mindful that God was to be thanked for the Roman believers following the patterns of teaching that were embodied in Christ Jesus. This "form of teaching" (v. 17) as Paul calls it, is sound doctrine, the kind of doctrine that was handed from Paul to Timothy and then to other faithful people after him (2 Tim. 2:2). While others are trying to find some new doctrine, gain some new insight, this is the stuff of which Christianity is made. It's the body of truth taught from one generation to another and always based on the inerrant Word of God.

For the twenty-first-century Christian, there is a very important distinction in Paul's words. He does not say, nor does he imply, that the Romans were obedient to the form of teaching they chose or enjoyed. Rather, they were obedient to the form of teaching that was committed to them. Today we are accustomed to the smorgasbord form of religion in which Christians pick and choose which doctrines, which portions of the Bible, which commands of God's Word they like, and then they obey only those they feel are most meaningful or beneficial to them. But mature Christians do not pick and choose from God's Word; mature Christians are shaped by every page of the Bible, which is why they are mature. Because they are ever being conformed to the image of Christ through obedience, they have been made free from service to sin and, in turn, have become the servants of righteousness. They are growing "in the grace and knowledge of our Lord and Savior Jesus Christ" (2 Pet. 3:18).

The Freedom of Slavery (6:19–20)

The apostle used the human analogy of a slave because he knew that, as residents in the capital city of the empire, where as many as one third of the inhabitants were slaves, his readers could identify with it. Slaves were constantly paraded through the streets of Rome. The Arch of Titus at the entrance to the Roman Forum, which depicts slaves at work, is a perfect example of how slavery was constantly before the Romans. Since spiritual truth is sometimes difficult to understand, Paul used a familiar analogy to make what he was about to say next more understandable.

"For just as you presented your members as slaves to impurity and to lawlessness, resulting in further lawlessness, so now present your members as slaves to righteousness, resulting in sanctification" (v. 19). For twenty-first-century Christians, the concept of being a slave to righteousness is unattractive at least, repulsive at most. Nobody wants to be a slave to anything, even to Christ and His righteousness. We are free people; just leave us alone. But it doesn't work that way when we have already been slaves all our lives. When we moved from the family of Adam, which was mastered by sin, into the family of Christ, which is mastered by righteousness, we moved from one master to another, but with a huge difference: Sin brought nothing but disharmony, disarray, and destitution. Righteousness brings love, joy, peace—all the fruit of the Spirit (Gal. 5:22–23).

Slavery to Christ is liberating. Martin Lloyd-Jones explains it this way:

At one and the same time it combines the elements of slavery and freedom. In this new slavery there is a kind of compulsion, but it is not comparable to the compulsion that preceded it. A Christian is, in a sense, a slave; but he is not a slave in the same sense as he was before. There is a difference. It is that he is now a slave to love. The element of loves comes in, and that changes the entire situation. A man who is in love is, of course, a slave. He lives for the other, for the object of his love; and the one whom he loves really controls him in a totalitarian sense. But what a difference there is between that and the slavery imposed by some terrible potentate or tyrant! There is a sense in which it is right to say that both are conditions of slavery, and yet you cannot leave it at that; you have to explain the difference in the slavery. In the second case it is a willing slavery.[1]

Because slavery to Christ is really freedom, Paul now counsels the Roman believers to yield themselves to holiness with the same gusto they once yielded themselves to uncleanness. When they were servants of sin, it was their master. Now that they are servants of Christ, righteousness must be their master. They cannot serve the master of righteousness and dabble in sin at the same time.

Once we were bound to the ruthlessness of sin. That's what life was like for our old man. But the old man is now gone, and we are unbound from the penalty of Adam's sin and are enjoying the freedom of Christ's righteousness. As freed slaves, we now enslave ourselves in love to the One who loved us enough to die for us. And in the process of being constrained by the love of Jesus Christ to serve Him, we discover the secret of sanctification and holiness. It's obedience in love.

Slavery to Sin Versus Slavery to Christ

Verse	Slavery to Sin	Slavery to Christ
Romans 6:16	Is an obedience issue	Is an obedience issue
Romans 6:16	Results in death	Results in righteousness
Romans 6:17	Slavery to sin	Obedience, commitment
Romans 6:18		Freed from sin Slaves of righteousness
Romans 6:19	Presented their members to slavery Results in impurity, lawlessness Weakness of the flesh	Presented their members to righteousness Results in sanctification
Romans 6:20	Free from righteousness	
Romans 6:21	Results in death	
Romans 6:22		Freed from sin, enslaved to God Results in sanctification, eternal life
Romans 6:23	Wages is death	Free gift of eternal life

A Final Observation (6:21–22)

Paul's case is made, but he can't help one final observation. When we are set apart to God, those things we once enjoyed in Adam are an embarrassment to us now. We look back on our old life, not with regret, but with shame. Too often those who have had a life of exciting wickedness before becoming a Christian pander to that excitement in their testimony. Paul could have as well, but he was too embarrassed by who he was to trade on his past life. He was very happy, however, with who he was becoming. Hence Paul's biting question to those who would dare to practice sin: "What benefit were you then deriving from the things of which you are now ashamed?" (v. 21). He asks what fruit has been derived from that sin. What good has come from those years of immorality and guilt? Paul knows well that sin always promises more than it can deliver. None of sin's fruit is worth having, and the final result of being a slave to sin is the ghastly horror of death.

But what benefit do those have who are freed from the bondage of habit-ual sin and are "enslaved to God" (v. 22)? They have sanctification now and eternal life forever. What a deal! The fruit of righteousness is holiness, and the end result of holy living is everlasting life. There is a drastic contrast between the outcomes of the two bondages. Bondage to sin has shame as its by-prod-uct. Bondage to Christ has as its by-product the status of being positionally holy and the process of becoming conformed to the image of Christ. This is biblical sanctification. Negatively, it is separation from personal sin (Col. 3:8), from unrepentant sinning believers (Matt. 18:15–17; 2 Thess. 3:14–15), and from worldliness (1 John 2:15). Positively, it is dedication to God and willing service to Christ. And the end result of being sanctified to God is eternal life. Bondage to sin has death as its end. Bondage to Christ has everlasting life as its end. The choice is yours.

Getting Paid the Right Wages (6:23)

The final verse of chapter 6 is one known to every Christian. It succinctly states what we must all believe if we are to see the need of trusting Jesus Christ as our Savior: "The wages of sin is death." And while this verse clearly has appli-cation to the person still in the first Adam, it was just as clearly written to those who are in the Second Adam.

Paul's summary statement relates to all that he has said about the contrast between our old life and our new life in Christ. Everything about our old life—our bondage, our sin, our thoughts, our shame—was heading in one direction—death. The reason is that when you are a slave and are paid a wage, that wage is indicative of your master. The wages of sin is death, because the paymaster is Satan, the disciple of death. But when you are paid a wage by the Savior, that wage is life, because, as Jesus said, "I am the way, and the truth, and the life; no one comes to the Father, but through Me" (John 14:6).

William Barclay points out:

Paul uses two military words. For pay he uses the word *opsonia. Opsonia* was the soldier's pay, something that he earned with the risk of his body and the sweat of his brow, something that was due to him and could not be taken from him. For gift he uses the word *charisma.* The *charisma,* or, in Latin, the *donativum,* was a totally free and unearned gift which the army sometimes received. On special occasions, for instance on his birthday, or on his accession to the throne, or the anniversary of it, an emperor hand-ed out a free gift of money to the army. It had not been earned; it was a present; a gift of the emperor's kindness and grace. So Paul says: "Sin has earned death. If we got the pay we had earned it would be death. It is death that is due to us as a right." And then he goes on: "But what we have received is a free gift; we did not earn it; we did not deserve it; we have earned death; but out of His grace God has given us life."[2]

I said previously that this verse was written in the context of the believer, not the unbeliever. Therefore, there must be an application to all who are in Christ, and there is. Warren W. Wiersbe says:

> If you serve a master, you can expect to receive wages. Sin pays wages—death! God also pays wages—holiness and everlasting life. In the old life, we produced fruit that made us ashamed. In the new life in Christ, we produce fruit that glorifies God and brings joy to our lives. We usually apply Romans 6:23 to the lost, and certainly it does apply; but it also has a warning for the saved. (After all, it was written to Christians.) "There is a sin unto death" (1 John 5:17). "For this reason many among you are weak and sick, and a number sleep" (1 Cor. 11:30, NASB). Samson, for example, would not yield himself to God, but preferred to yield to the lusts of the flesh, and the result was death (Jud. 16). If the believer refuses to surrender his body to the Lord, but uses its members for sinful purposes, then he is in danger of being disciplined by the Father, and this could mean death. See Heb. 12:5–11, and note the end of v. 9 in particular.[3]

What lesson is to be learned? If we choose Christ but do not present ourselves to Him as servants, we are on shaky ground. Jesus Christ expects to be Lord of those for whom He is Savior. You cannot take the one and skip the other. If you see Jesus as a convenient way to escape the penalty of sin but are not serious about yielding all the parts of your body to Him in sanctification, you are not really serious about salvation. Jesus is a loving Savior, but He is also our Judge. There are wages to be paid. Make sure you receive the right wages.

Study Questions

1. Can Christians go about willfully sinning because they are under grace and not under law?

2. What is the new "position" that children of God now enjoy?

3. What role does the heart play in obedience?

4. What were believers in Christ once free of?

5. In this section, what does Paul mean by "sanctification"?

CHAPTER 14

Sanctification and the Demands of the Law
Romans 7:1–6

Preview:

The principle of law rules over its subjects. For example, a married woman is bound by law to her husband while he is living. But if he dies, she may be joined to another. In similar manner, believers in Christ who once had a passion for sin have been released from the Law, having died to it. They may now be joined to the Lord in a newness of the Spirit.

Paul continues his teaching on sanctification in a particularly difficult chapter. Perhaps more controversy has surrounded Romans 7 than any other chapter in the epistle. But just as this is a controversial passage, it is likewise an extremely tender portion in Paul's letter. He refers to the Romans as "brethren" in the double sense of the word. Specifically, he is "speaking to those who know the law" (v. 1), his racial kin, fellow Jews now worshiping in the church at Rome. But he also is speaking to them as his brothers and sisters in Christ. Paul has used the affectionate appellation "brethren" only once so far in this letter (1:13), but there are plenty more times coming (see 7:4; 8:12; 10:1; 11:25; 12:1; 15:14, 30; 16:17). In each case, Paul addresses a topic of enhanced emotion. Here it probably relates to certain Jews in the church of Rome who were still having difficulty accepting that salvation is by grace alone without the presumed benefit of keeping the Law.

Authority and Adultery (7:1–3)

To help his Jewish friends in Rome understand their relationship to the Law now that they had become messianic Jews, Christians, believers in the Lord Jesus Christ, Paul latched onto the analogy of marriage. Theologian Charles Hodge explains that many interpreters do not regard this verse as presenting an example, but as an allegory. Those who take this view give different explanations. Following Augustine's lead, Melanchthon, Beza, and others say: "The husband is our corrupt nature, the wife is the soul, or our members. When, therefore, the corrupt nature (or old man) dies, the soul is free from that husband, and is at liberty to marry another." "Others, with much more regard to the context, say that this wife is the Church, the husband the Law; so Origen, Chrysostom, Olshausen, Philippi, etc. This is indeed the application that the apostle makes in the following verses, but it is not what is said in verses 2, 3. Here we have only an example, illustrating the truth of the assertion in verse 1."[1] Hodge is right; this is just an example. He uses the analogy of marriage only to teach a truth.

"For the married woman is bound by law to her husband while he is living; but if her husband dies, she is released from the law concerning the husband" (v. 2). The teaching of the Bible regarding marriage is clear. It is a sacred vow, a very solemn bond, one that is to be honored and treated as permanent. God's feeling towards divorce, the voluntary dissolution of marriage, is equally clear. "'For I hate divorce,' says the LORD, the God of Israel. . . . 'So take heed to your spirit, that you do not deal treacherously'" (Mal. 2:16). And while there may be exceptions to His rule (Matt. 5:32; 19:9), God's intent is for marriage to be a binding commitment between a man and a woman all the mutual days of their lives. Marriage is not only for better or worse, marriage is for life. Not only does a woman who divorces her husband become an adulteress should she remarry, Paul uses the intransitive *chrēmatizō*, a word that implies this woman should be publicly branded as an adulteress. That may sound harsh and unnecessary in the twenty-first century, but it is the same word used in Acts 11:26 to say, "The disciples were first called Christians in Antioch." Initially the term *Christian* was used in a derogatory way, branding one as a follower of a spurious sect. The woman who is still bound to a husband but sleeps around with other men is to be publicly known as an adulteress. But the stigma is gone if the woman's husband has died. She is not permitted unlawful or illicit sex, but she is permitted to remarry. To the Corinthians Paul says, "A wife is bound as long as her husband lives; but if her husband is dead, she is free to be married to whom she wishes, only in the Lord" (1 Cor. 7:39).

Thus the husband is bound to his wife as long as she lives, and the wife is bound to her husband as long as he lives. Karl Barth notes, "The distinctive and critical meaning of the words 'as long as he liveth' (7:1) can be brought out by an analogy. As long as he lives, yes! But no longer! The conception of death, which is both the characteristic feature and the boundary of this life, enables us to reach a decision concerning the existence or nonexistence of that which constitutes a man's 'life.'"[2]

Remarriage while the husband is alive is called adultery; remarriage after the husband is dead is called freedom. The law of marriage, both in Jewish and Roman law, has authority over a married couple as long as either partner is alive. But should one die, death brings the loss of that authority. "She is released from the law concerning the husband" (v. 2). Death severs the bond of marriage (Luke 20:33–35).

Joined to Another (7:4)

Now let's get to the point of the marriage analogy. "Therefore, my brethren, you also were made to die to the Law through the body of Christ, that you might be joined to another, to Him who was raised from the dead, that we might bear fruit for God" (v. 4). Three truths are evident from Paul's thinking about the relation of the believer and the Law.

First, as brothers and sisters in Christ, we did not set out to divorce ourselves from the Law. It was not our goal to see that marriage end. It may not have been a happy marriage, but we knew of no better prospects. Thus, for the marriage with the Mosaic Law to end, the Law had to die to us and we to it. "You also were made to die to the Law" (v. 4) uses the aorist passive of *thanatoō*, meaning to put to death (Greek, *ethanatōthēte*). It was not we, nor was it the Law, that put us to death. It was God. God alone both planned and carried out our salvation. It was God who engineered and accomplished the plan for us to be severed from the bonds of the Law. He did this "through the body of Christ," who was crucified for our sins and raised from the dead for our justification.

Second, the reason God engineered the death of the Law to us and our death to it is so we "might be joined to another" (v. 4). The Law of Moses was good, but it wasn't God's ideal; it was His prerequisite for holy living. God never intended the Law to be a tool of salvation; it lacked the power to be such a tool (Gal. 2:16). But we were married to the Law because of necessity until God demonstrated His grace at Calvary. That's when our marriage of convenience and necessity to the Law was annulled and our marriage to the One who truly loved us became possible. Having been freed by death from bondage to the Law, we are now free to enjoy our destined love relationship with Jesus Christ. Galatians 2:19 says, "For through the Law I died to the Law, that I might live to God."

Third, the results of being joined to Christ should bring forth "fruit for God" (v. 4). Fruitbearing in the Christian life is a common theme in Paul's writings (Rom. 1:13; Gal. 5:22–23; Eph. 2:10; 5:9; Phil. 4:17; Col. 1:6), having to do with the good works and spiritual works that come forth from believers for the sake of the Lord (John 15:1–4; Gal. 5:22–23). Just as Christian parents bring forth offspring dedicated to the Lord, new believers are spiritual offspring who become children of God through accepting Christ as Savior. Procreation is the grand design in the physical realm as are reproduction and fruitbearing in the spiritual realm. What could not be produced when we were married to the Law is not only possible but also expected in our new marriage to Christ.

The Body Outlet (7:5–6)

In our old life, our thoughts and motives and actions were governed by our sinful human nature. That's all our old man could produce. Paul repeats here what he has already so eloquently asserted—that "while we were in the flesh, the sinful passions . . . were at work in the members of our body" (v. 5). These sinful passions—jealousy, bitterness, illicit sexuality, anger, hatred, envy, and more—always found expression through the body. Therefore every part of our bodies—our minds, feet, hands, sex organs, eyes, ears—was completely engaged by our sinful nature. The angry heart found expression in the clenched fist. The jealous soul found expression in the slandering tongue. Sexual lust found expression in addiction to pornography or hooking up for brief and meaningless sexual encounters. But it was always the body where our sin found a means of expression. This does not mean that the flesh is itself sinful.

Sin, because of its nature, cannot reside in physical matter. Sin, by definition, is an attitude or an act; it is the violation of God's law by a rational creature; it is not a physical substance nor does it have physical existence. No material object, therefore, is sinful within itself. Any object may be used wrongly, but the object itself is not sinful. For example, a knife may be used to murder someone, but this does not make the knife sinful. The sin is in the heart of the one who violates God's law by willfully and maliciously taking the life of his fellow man. The same is true of a deck of cards, a glass of whiskey, a bottle of poison, or any other material object. Regardless of how such things are used (or misused!), they can never be sinful within themselves.[3]

The truth remains, nonetheless, that the body is the outlet for the sinful heart. Our sinful instincts manifest themselves in the flesh, but we are not without help in controlling them. We have the Holy Spirit of God who lives within us. Whereas before our flesh worked "to bear fruit for death," now when we give our bodies over to the control of the Holy Spirit, our flesh can work to bear fruit for life. As newborn babes in Christ, our bodies no longer need to be governed by our sinful nature. We have a new nature through which the Spirit of God can work and govern our lives to make them eternally productive. "We have been released from the Law, having died to that by which we were bound, so that we serve in newness of the Spirit and not in oldness of the letter" (v. 6).

We were released from the Law when our old man died and our new man was born. When we who were born in Adam were born again in Christ, our relationship with the Law changed forever. No longer are we bound by our old nature to serve as a slave to our sinful instincts. Now, having been given a new nature, we are free to reject those sinful instincts and allow the Spirit of God to guide us in a new and fulfilling lifestyle. The old way of keeping the letter of the Law in order to attempt to be righteous has given way to the new way of the Holy Spirit, who can empower us to live in the righteousness of Christ (Rom. 8:3–4). Now that we are married to Christ, we need to give our bodies to Him and Him alone. That's the principle of being severed from one by death in order to be married and faithful to another.

Study Questions

1. Why does the apostle Paul address those who are under the Law?

2. What is the main reason a wife may be released from her husband?

3. By what means have believers "died" to the Law?

4. How can the Law arouse those in the flesh to sinful passions?

5. List the ways the apostle compares living unto the Law and living unto Christ.

CHAPTER 15

Sanctification and the Battle Within
Romans 7:7–25

Preview:

The Law is not evil, but good. For without the Law we would not know what is good and acceptable or what is wicked and forbidden. As a holy and righteous commandment, the Law brought sin to life and death followed. By the Law's demands, our flesh brings about slavery to sin. The Law cannot free us from this slavery and make us holy, but it can convict us of our sin. Though delivered from the penalty of sin by the imputation of Christ's righteousness, believers now struggle on a daily basis with the power of sin. So with the mind, the children of God serve the law of God, but with the flesh, they serve the law of sin.

We have come to the most controversial section of the most controversial chapter in Paul's epistle to the Romans. How are we to interpret what Paul says? Is he writing hypothetically? Is he writing about an unbeliever? Is what he writes biographical? As is often the case, good people differ on how this passage should be understood.

Who Is the Wretched Man?

Many have seen Paul's reference here to that of an unsaved person and argue that it would be impossible for Paul to make these statements about himself—for example, "I died" (v. 9); "death for me" (v. 10); "it killed me" (v. 11); "a cause of death for me" (v. 13). In verse 14 Paul says, "For we know that the

Law is spiritual; but I am of flesh, sold into bondage to sin." How could one who has experienced the freedom that comes through justification by faith ever speak of being "sold into bondage to sin"?

Others believe Paul is speaking hypothetically here and argue that this chapter does not represent his personal experience but rather his attempt to show what the Christian life would be like if his readers did not learn the biblical principles of sanctification in chapter 6. Accordingly, chapter 6 would represent the right way to be sanctified, chapter 7 the wrong way. Some see the person depicted in Romans 7 as making frequent derogatory statements about himself: "I am of flesh, sold into bondage to sin" (v. 14); "For I am not practicing what I would like to do" (v. 15); "For I know that nothing good dwells in me" (v. 18); "I practice the very evil that I do not wish" (v. 19); "Wretched man that I am" (v. 24). If these are the words of a believer, they must be of a very young and inexperienced believer. Surely they would not have been uttered by a mature Christian who has grown in the grace and knowledge of the Lord and Savior, Jesus Christ.

The final view is that Paul was actually speaking of himself and his struggles against sin in his Christian life. Could Paul say such things of himself as a Christian? He did elsewhere. Often the apostle spoke of himself and his weakness in the flesh. "I am the least of the apostles" (1 Cor. 15:9); "To me, the very least of all saints" (Eph. 3:8); "Christ Jesus came into the world to save sinners, among whom I am foremost of all" (1 Tim. 1:15). Therefore, most believe that this is the actual experience of the apostle during the course of his Christian life.

I don't believe this passage refers to an unsaved person. The flow of Paul's argument from chapter 6 to chapter 8 does not permit introducing an unbeliever into the context. At one time, Augustine believed that Paul was referring to an unsaved person, but he eventually abandoned that opinion. John Calvin said, "Augustine was for a time involved in the common error, but having more thoroughly examined the passage, not only retracted what he had falsely thought, but in his first book to Boniface proves, by many forceful arguments, that what is said cannot be applied to any but the regenerate"[1] Martin Lloyd-Jones says that Romans 7 is not a hypothetical case. It is an actual picture of the internal strife caused by the law of sin against the law of the Spirit in the apostle Paul. He notes that this need not be the normal Christian experience, for Paul has already instructed us how to avert this internal strife. Chapter 6 presents the proper way to sanctification; this chapter presents the improper way.[2] "The person described in Romans 7:14–25 hates sin (7:15), wishes to do what is good (vv. 19, 21), in his inner being delights in God's law (v. 22), deeply regrets his sins (vv. 15, 18–24), and thanks God for his deliverance (v. 25). Is it at all possible that such a person has not been regenerated by the Spirit of God?" asks William Hendriksen.[3]

"A characteristic of Romans 7," observes Theodore Epp, "is the use of the first person singular pronoun. It occurs six times in verse 15, 38 times in verses 15–25, and 47 times in all of Chapter 7."[4] This would strongly indicate this is an autobiographical passage. F. F. Bruce says the autobiographical interpretation "is the most natural way to understand this section, and the arguments against it are not conclusive. Paul, of course, did not think of his own experience as unique; he describes it here because it is true in a greater or lesser degree of the human race."[5]

Romans 7 is not a description of Paul before his salvation, but describes the continuing struggle of the believer with the power of sin. It may reflect any period of his life, even those mature years as a Christian, but most appropriately refers to the early years in his Christian experience when he was wrestling with how to reconcile his newfound faith with his rabbinical training. Or it may reflect those times of weakness when he struggled to give the Holy Spirit complete control over his life. Whichever, it certainly relates to his experience after salvation.

The Law and Sin (7:7–8)

Here is yet another series of Pauline questions about the relation of the Law to sin. "What shall we say then? Is the Law sin?" (v. 7). Paul responds with his characteristic abhorrence, "May it never be!" and quickly provides an explanation for his answer. "I would not have come to know sin except through the Law." So what is the true function of the Law? Paul claims it does not make us sin but rather reveals what sin truly is. He illustrates this truth by quoting from the Decalogue: "I would not have known about coveting if the Law had not said, 'You shall not covet'" (v. 7). Had there been no Law, covetousness would still exist. But it was the Law that said, "Cross this line, and you have sinned." That is the function of the Law. "But sin, taking opportunity through the commandment, produced in me coveting of every kind" (v. 8). The word translated "opportunity" is the descriptive Greek word *aphormē*, which describes a place from which a military commander would launch an attack. The Law was not evil, but it became the base of operations from which Satan could assault Paul with the desire to covet. Thus he says, "Apart from the Law sin is dead." He means that if you remove the tenth commandment, with its varied possibilities for transgression, sin lies dormant, since by definition, sin is the violation of God's Law.

Life and Death and the Law (7:9–11)

These verses record the dawn of conscience in the life of the apostle Paul. He had lived a self-complacent, self-righteous life in which he was free from conviction of sin. It is difficult to say exactly when this period existed in Paul's life. Hendriksen explains:

The feeling of not I'm not really a bad person

> There was a time when I felt secure, under no conviction of sin. At that time the full implication of the law had not yet registered in my consciousness, had not yet become an unbearable burden upon my heart. I thought that morally and spiritually I was doing quite well. But when the commandment came, that is, when it was brought home to me what the law really demanded (nothing less than that which is summarized in Mark 12:29–31), I realized what a great sinner I was. It was then that I died; that is, that was the end of me as a self-satisfied, self-secure person.[6]

When the commandment came to him—an apparent reference to "You shall not covet" in verse 7—for the first time, Paul became conscious of his lack of ability to keep the Law. At that point sin sprang back to life and, says Paul, "I died" (v. 9). This must be put in contrast with "I was once alive apart from the Law" and therefore should be understood as death to his complacent attitude toward sin.[7]

"For sin, taking opportunity through the commandment, deceived me, and through it killed me" (v. 11) means that, since the commandment was intended to produce life, Paul expected the commandment to yield life as a result. But instead it became the occasion for sin and consequent death. Since the commandment yielded the opposite of what Paul expected, he felt deceived. The perpetrator of this deception, however, was not the commandment itself, but sin. The commandment was merely the instrument by which sin deceived him. The Law was designed to bring life. Sin always brings death. Therefore Paul was deceived by the promise of the Law but only because he himself did not keep the Law. Had he obeyed the Law, he would not have been deceived, nor would he have had to live with the consequences of his sin. But we all make choices, and when we choose to disobey God and His Law, that sin brings death.

Who's to Blame? (7:12–14)

Paul now comes to the only conclusion an honest person can make. "So then, the Law is holy, and the commandment is holy and righteous and good" (v. 12). Paul is driven to conclude that it is a holy Law, just and good, and immediately asks a rhetorical question to expand on the principle that it is sin that is the deceiver and not the Law: "Therefore did that which is good become a cause of death for me?" Did the Law lose its intended purpose? Was what God intended for our good the cause of death for Paul? By now you can guess what the apostle's response will be. *Mē genoito.* "May it never be!" (v. 13). The Law isn't the cause of death; sin is. The Law is but the instrument by which we may be shown that sin is causing our physical and spiritual death.

Paul's conclusion concerning the Law is this: "For we know that the Law is spiritual" (v. 14). The apostle is convinced that the Mosaic Law is holy and just and good because it is derived from God. The word "spiritual" (Greek, *pneumatikos*) is not used in contradistinction to corporeal, but is used to indicate that the Law finds its roots in the Holy Spirit. The word is used the same way in 1 Corinthians 2:13 of "spiritual" words, in 1 Corinthians 2:15 of the "spiritual" person, and in Colossians 3:16 of "spiritual" songs. The tone of these verses certainly squares with the understanding that Paul is speaking of his own experience.

The Problem with the Flesh (7:15–17)

The apostle continues to speak in the first-person singular, using the present tense. Suddenly there is an inward tension present that was not evident in his discussion of the Law (7:1–14). Autobiographically, Paul points out that even the believer is constantly beset by the tugs and pulls of a self-seeking and self-centered ego. Paul designates this ego "the flesh." This is no straw man Paul sets up, but it in fact pictures the anguish of his own soul. He knows to do right and to obey the law, but in himself he cannot do either.

This passage presents the tension between Paul's knowledge and his ability in three phases: (1) We know that the law is spiritual (v. 14); (2) I know that nothing good dwells in me (that is, in my flesh) (v. 18); (3) I find then a law, that, when I would do good, evil is present (v. 21). Each of these phases presents significant knowledge by Paul. Each of them is immediately followed by proof that, even though he knows what is right, he cannot do what is right. The conclusion of the whole matter, which he draws in verse 25, should be an encouragement to all believers.

"For that which I am doing, I do not understand" (v. 15). While recognizing that the Law is spiritual because it is God's Law, Paul also must admit that he is carnal (Greek, *sarkinos*), of the flesh (v. 14). When Paul speaks of his flesh, he means his sinful propensity inherited from Adam. There is nothing good in it (7:18); with it, he says he serves "the law of sin" (7:25). It is still present with him, even if progressively disabled—and this in spite of the fact that it has been "crucified." Compare Galatians 5:24, "They that are Christ's have crucified the flesh with the affections and lusts," with Romans 6:6 (KJV), "Our old man was crucified with him [Christ], that the body of sin might be done away." This apparent paradox is one that we meet repeatedly in the Pauline writings, where believers are enjoined time and again to be what they are—to be in actual practice what they are as members of Christ. Thus they are said to "have put off the old man with his deeds" and to "have put on the new man" (Col. 3:9–11), while elsewhere they are exhorted to "put off . . . the old man" and "put on the new man" (Eph. 4:22, 24). The old man is what they were "in Adam"; the new man is what they are "in Christ." Therefore to put on the new man is to put on Christ, and while Paul tells the Galatians that "For all of you who were baptized into Christ have clothed yourself with Christ" (Gal. 3:27), he tells the Romans to "put . . . on the Lord Jesus Christ" (Rom. 13:14).[8]

Paul has been delivered from the penalty of sin through justification, but daily he still faces the struggle with the power of sin. Often he finds himself a virtual prisoner to that power, and it confuses him. Paul knows what he wants to do, yet he cannot do what he wants. Conversely, those things he knows he must not do, he gravitates toward. A historical parallel to this is Horace's statement, "I pursue the things that have done me harm; I shun the things I believe will do me good" (Epistle 1.8.11). Paul differs from Horace, however, in his conclusion (see below).

The Battle of Wills (7:18–20)

Paul continues to describe his struggle for spirituality. "For I know that nothing good dwells in me, that is, in my flesh" (v. 18). In this second phase of tension between what Paul knows and what he practices, the apostle recognizes that in himself there is not the ability to do good. He wills to do good, but how to accomplish his will is not found within himself. He cannot do the will of God as he wants as long as sin holds dominion over him. When sin is Paul's master, lord, and king, Jesus Christ cannot fill the same position. He wants to break the power of sin in his life, but by himself he cannot do it. Paul knows this is a battle of wills—his will and Satan's will—and he is outmatched. When Satan's will prevails, Paul is a defeated Christian. This is not to say there is anything wrong with his justification. God has declared Paul to be righteous as a result of his faith in Jesus Christ as Savior. God even treats Paul as if he were righteous. But like Abraham before him, Paul is only treated as righteous, he often does not live in righteousness. Gleason Archer explains, "It is not the new man in Christ who carries on this life of defeat, but it is the sin-principle in him, engendered by the unyielded flesh and occupying the Lord's temple as a trespassing squatter like the Tobiah, whom Nehemiah expelled" (cf. Neh. 13:7–9).[9]

Isn't it refreshing to find someone as honest as Paul? He has been justified by faith in Jesus Christ. He is being sanctified by the power of the Holy Spirit. One day he will be glorified by the grace of the Father. But as was pointed out at the beginning of our discussion on chapter 6, while justification is a declarative act of God, sanctification is a progressive act. It doesn't happen all at once but continues throughout the Christian's life. Hence, the kind of honest struggle with sin that Paul reports is the very kind of struggle you and I experience almost daily. Don't make the mistake of sweeping your struggle with sin under the proverbial carpet. There is a battle of wills going on inside of you. The only way to win that battle is to know that it exists, admit it every day, and submit all the parts of your body to God's will.

A Principle Within (7:21–23)

Moving toward a conclusion to chapters 6 and 7, Paul declares, "I find then the principle that evil is present in me" (v. 21). If you have tried to live for God, you have discovered that law too. The law to which Paul refers has been variously interpreted as the law of God (v. 22) and the law of sin (v. 23). Either interpretation is plausible. It seems likely, however, that the law prohibits him from doing good and therefore must be the law of sin. This unrelenting, inflexible, unbearable, persistent law is that, despite his best intentions, he tends to sin when he wants to live righteously. It's not that Paul has wrong motivations or desires. He admits, "For I joyfully concur with the law of God in the inner man" (v. 22). It is the desire of Paul, as it should be with every believer, to love and obey the law of God. However, opposed to the law of God is the law of sin, which brings his members (i.e., all the parts of his body) into captivity.

I mentioned earlier that this passage presents the tension between Paul's knowledge and ability in three phases: (1) We know that the Law is spiritual (v. 14), which is the foundation for his subsequent comments; (2) I know that nothing good dwells in me (that is, in my flesh) (v. 18); and (3) I find then a law, that, when I would do good, evil is present (v. 21). The law, which he finds and references in verse 23, is the third phase of his knowledge. Paul has come to the conclusion that as long as the believer is alive, war will constantly be waged between the old sinful nature, which most often expresses itself through the parts of Paul's body, and his delight in the law of God, which is expressed only when he is controlled by the Holy Spirit. Unfortunately, when Paul or any other believer attempts to win this battle in himself, he is always defeated. Self-attempts to rid our members of the tyranny of indwelling sin cause the frustration that underlies this passage. No one knew that better than the apostle Paul. As long as that principle of sin remained within him, Paul would struggle with the flesh. What's true for the apostle is true for you and me too.

What Believers Should Do When They Sin	
Seek restoration: the Spirit intercedes for our weakness.	Romans 8:26
Return to walking by the Spirit.	Galatians 5:16, 25
Run from partaking in the sins of sinners.	Ephesians 5:7
Return to pleasing the Lord.	Ephesians 5:10
Seek to understand God's will for their life.	Ephesians 5:17
Put on the full armor of God.	Ephesians 6:13–18
Put no confidence in the flesh.	Philippians 3:3
Turn back to the truth.	James 5:19–20
Return to walking in the light.	1 John 1:7
Confess their sins for forgiveness and cleansing.	1 John 1:9
Watch carefully what they do in the future.	2 John 1:8

There is one phrase in these verses we dare not allow to slip by: "I see a different law in the members of my body, waging war" (v. 23). The war depicted here uses as its battleground our flesh, the various parts of our bodies. That this is important in Paul's discussion of sanctification is evident from his use of this expression in 6:13 (twice), in 6:19 (twice), in 7:5, and in 7:23 (twice). While we may have our heart right with God, often by the time the message goes from our heart to our hands, something goes awry. So often Paul and other writers of the Bible emphasize the need for "clean hands and a pure heart" (Ps. 24:4). This implies that we must not only know our own heart, but we must also control our own bodies. That is an integral part of the process of sanctification. Let those who claim to have a pure heart always demonstrate that they have clean hands as well.

Wretched Man (7:24)

Helplessly, Paul throws up his hands and exclaims how wretched a believer is when he has not gained mastery over sin. "O wretched man" (Greek, *talaipōros*) is an expression used in pagan Greek drama to express tragic misfortune and woe. Paul recognizes that he is in a helpless state of despair because he cannot rid himself of his bent toward sinning. "The body of this death" (literally, "this body of death") probably does not refer to a physical body. Sin is much more deeply rooted than the body. Paul is speaking of human nature, which has inherited guilt and sin from Adam. Paul knows there hangs over his life a cloud of guilt and death imputed with sin. The main purpose of this statement, however, is in the question, "Who will set me free?" Paul indicates that if he is to be delivered from the mastery of sin, that deliverance must come from without. He is unable to live the Christian life in himself. He is incapable of gaining mastery over sin. You and I do not possess the power either to control sin or to live righteously. We are unable to live the Christian life in ourselves. Even the great apostle couldn't do so. That's why the final verse of Romans 7 is so important to every Christian who struggles with doing what we don't want while not doing what we do want.

The Secret of Success (7:25)

Perhaps you have been waiting for a definitive statement throughout all the confusion and seemingly contradictory statements of Romans 7. Your wait is now rewarded. To the problem of obeying the Spirit while we are living in the flesh, Paul's final answer is, "Thanks be to God through Jesus Christ our Lord!" You can feel a climax approaching. Suddenly, in the midst of a chapter that could easily lead to despair, hope is building. Everything is going to be all right. Paul inescapably comes to the conclusion that only Jesus Christ can enable us to live a sanctified life. It is not our life for Him that we live in the body, but it is His life we live. "I have been crucified with Christ; and it is no longer I who live, but Christ lives in me; and the life which I now live in the flesh I live by faith in the Son of God, who loved me, and delivered Himself up for me" (Gal. 2:20). The secret of successfully living in the body of this flesh is not trying to outwit Satan, nor is it trying to overpower the flesh. The secret is to submit to the lordship of Jesus Christ and ask Him to live His life through you.

Paul would like to serve the law of God. He honestly admits that. But he is equally honest in his admission that his flesh causes him to serve the law of sin. He can't change that, but Jesus can. In justification, Jesus saved Paul's inner man (v. 22), including his mind (v. 25). In sanctification, Jesus empowers Paul's inner man, including his mind, to defeat the influences of sin as displayed in his body.

Study Questions

1. List the ways the Law amplifies sin and brings about condemnation.

2. Is the Law the direct cause of the lost living out a sinful life?

3. What sells people into sin?

4. List the things Paul says about himself when he uses the pronoun *I*.

5. Does the apostle Paul say the struggle with sin in the Christian life is hopeless?

CHAPTER 16

Sanctification and Freedom from Sin's Power
Romans 8:1–13

Preview:

Because they are justified by faith, there is no condemnation for those who are in Christ Jesus. Since the Law could not save, Christ came in the flesh and offered Himself for sin. The Law then was fulfilled for those who walk according to the Spirit. Now the Spirit who comes from God, and from Christ, dwells within believers. This same Spirit will someday give new resurrected life to the mortal bodies of the children of God. Therefore, Christians have no obligation to live in the flesh.

Once we have been justified by faith, the process of sanctification begins. The old man we were in Adam is gone; the new man we are in Christ is here to stay. But now the old nature, that penchant to sin within us, hangs around and badgers us through our flesh. If we allow this old nature to dominate our new life in Christ, it will be impossible for us to enjoy a life of victory over sin. That's why we must yield our lives to the control of the Holy Spirit and make every part of our body available to him to set apart for service to God. When we do, we are certain of God's blessing now and His reward in the future. Romans 8 is all about assurance, being certain because we have been justified.

The Assurance of the Righteousness of God (8:1–4)

Paul begins this chapter with a bold statement. "There is therefore now no condemnation for those who are in Christ Jesus" (v. 1). The word *condemnation*

(Greek, *katakrima*) is much more than an antonym for justification. F. F. Bruce writes:

> If "condemnation" were simply the opposite of "justification," Paul would be saying that those who are in Christ Jesus are justified; but that stage in the argument was reached in 3:21ff. The word *katakrima* means "probably not 'condemnation,' but the punishment following sentence" (Arndt-Gingrich)—in other words, "penal servitude." There is no reason why those who are "in Christ Jesus" should go on doing penal servitude as though they had never been pardoned and never been liberated from the prison-house of sin.[1]

Freedom from condemnation means we are not servants to the penalty for our sin, but that guilt and penalty have been removed at the cross. Therefore, those who are "in Christ Jesus" do not live under the constant threat of judicial punishment by God. Justification brings the possibility of that freedom; sanctification is how we live once we have left sin's prison house. The expression "who walk not after the flesh, but after the Spirit" found in the King James Version is not in the original. There should be an exclamation point after the expression "There is therefore now no condemnation for those who are in Christ Jesus!" This is one of the greatest truths in the Bible, a book filled with great truths.

The apostle continues, "For the law of the Spirit of life in Christ Jesus has set you free from the law of sin and of death" (v. 2). We should understand the law of the Spirit of life here to be the principle on which the Holy Spirit works. The reference to the Spirit of life is the first time (with the exception of Romans 1:4 and 5:5) the Spirit of God is mentioned in this epistle. In this chapter alone, however, the Spirit and His activity are mentioned nineteen times. Even a casual reading of Romans 8 will leave us with the impression that without the Spirit of God in our lives we are headed for defeat. Life in the Spirit enables us to live free from the law or principle of sin and death. This does not mean that believers are free from sin or free from the prospect of death, but that the principle of sin and death does not have dominion over him. It is possible for those for whom there is no condemnation to live a life that is not inundated with sin, a life that will not end in spiritual death. James A. Stifler comments on the liberating effect of the law of the Spirit of life in Christ Jesus:

> By faith in Christ a man finds not only acquittal from sins, but also the power by which he no longer commits them; for this law of the Spirit sets him at liberty ("free") from the "law of sin and death". . . . The spiritual law is set against the carnal and overcomes it. The law of gravity ever keeps the serpent crawling on the earth, and he cannot rise above it; but give

him wings and now he has a power superior to gravity by which he can fly. . . . In Christ Jesus there is a power that sets one at liberty from the sinful force in his members. Gravity never ceases, but it may be overcome. The law of sin in the members exists as long as they do, but "in Christ" it cannot operate.[2]

"For what the Law could not do, weak as it was through the flesh, God did" (v. 3) is a statement of contrast. The Law of Moses could not justify us; it could not sanctify us because it was weak through the flesh. The Mosaic Law is good and holy, but our flesh is weak, and we are unable to keep the Law; therefore, the Law does not have the power to justify. However—and here's the contrast— God sent His own Son in the likeness of sinful flesh and for sin condemned sin in the flesh. What the Law could not do, the Lord could. Paul chose his words carefully. Had he said that Jesus came "in sinful flesh," he would have been guilty of the Docetic heresy. Instead, he said that Jesus Christ came in the flesh, in the likeness of a man, but was not Himself in sinful flesh for He "knew no sin" (2 Cor. 5:21). The word "sin" (Greek, *hamartia*) is the equivalent of the Old Testament "sin offering" (Hebrew, *chattath*). Since the Law could not be that offering, God provided our atonement by offering the person of Jesus Christ in order that the requirement of the Law might be fulfilled in us, who do not walk according to the flesh, but according to the Spirit" (v. 4). Thus we are assured of the righteousness of God the Law could not provide but the atonement of Christ does provide.

The Assurance of the Indwelling Spirit of God (8:5–11)

Paul turns a page here to another certainty of the Christian life. "For those who are according to the flesh set their minds on the things of the flesh, but those who are according to the Spirit, the things of the Spirit" (v. 5). The verb translated "set one's mind on" (Greek, *phroneō*) means to have something as the habit of your thoughts; something in which you place a total interest. Those who place their total interest in the things of the flesh cannot have their interest in the things of God. "For the mind set on the flesh is death" (v. 6). If the mind is not Christ-centered and our interest is constantly on carnal things, the results are the symptoms of spiritual death. However, if the interests of the mind are placed on the things of the Spirit of God, we have a peace in life that passes all understanding. Why? "Because the mind set on the flesh is hostile toward God" (v. 7). If our minds have an interest in carnal things, they cause us to be the enemy of God. This is why James counsels, "You adulteresses, do you not know that friendship with the world is hostility toward God? Therefore whoever wishes to be a friend of the world makes himself an enemy of God" (James 4:4). The carnal mind "does not subject itself to the law of God, for it is not even able to do so" (v. 7). Paul is not speaking here of two types of Christians, one spiritual and one unspiritual. He is speaking of believers and unbelievers, as verse 9 plainly indicates. Those still living in the flesh, those not yet born from above, cannot please God. Until faith is placed in Jesus Christ, no person can be pleasing to God the Father in any spiritual way (Heb. 11:6).

But here comes the great contrast. The Roman Christians have been born from above. Old things have passed away. They are new creatures in Christ, indwelt by the Holy Spirit. Paul affirms, "However, you are not in the flesh but in the Spirit, if indeed the Spirit of God dwells in you" (v. 9). The Holy Spirit of God is the decisive factor in salvation. If a person does not have the Spirit, that person does not have Christ and "does not belong to Him." Paul clearly teaches that no one can receive Christ's atonement for salvation unless the Spirit of God dwells within that person. It is therefore irrational to say that there are Christians who have not fully received the blessing of the Spirit of God. There is no scriptural basis for a "second work of grace" or a "baptism of the Holy Spirit" subsequent to salvation. At salvation either we have all of the Spirit of God or we have none of Him. There may be a time subsequent to salvation in which the Spirit of God gets more of us, but there is never a time when we get more of Him. "If Christ is in you, though the body is dead because of sin, yet the spirit is alive because of righteousness" (v. 10). This does not mean that we have already died physically; it means that the energizing Spirit of God within us has given us new life, a life of righteousness.

The Assurance of Resurrection (8:11–12)

Paul's letter has a footnote of hope: "But if the Spirit of Him who raised Jesus from the dead dwells in you, He who raised Christ Jesus from the dead will also give life to your mortal bodies through His Spirit who indwells you" (v. 11). As in 1 Corinthians 6:14, 2 Corinthians 4:14; and 1 Thessalonians 4:14, our resurrection from the dead is both foreshadowed and dependent upon Christ's resurrection. Jesus promised His disciples, "Because I live, you shall live also" (John 14:19). Not only are we not alone in this life, for the Holy Spirit dwells in us, but we also will not be left alone after this life. Death is not the end. The grave couldn't hold Jesus; it won't hold us either. Because of Jesus Christ, we have freedom to be a victor instead of a victim.

The Resurrection of Christ

Old Testament Prophecies of His Resurrection

Psalm 16:9	*The Messiah's flesh will "dwell securely."*
Psalm 16:10	*God will not abandon His soul in Sheol. God will not allow His Holy One to undergo decay.*
Psalm 16:11	*The Messiah will know from God the path of life.*

Christ's Prophecies of His Resurrection

Mark 14:28	*"After I have been raised."*
John 2:19–20	*He would raise His body [temple] in three days.*
John 11:25	*"I am the resurrection and the life."*

Evidence of His Resurrection

John 20:1	*Mary Magdalene saw the empty tomb.*
John 20:2–8	*Peter and probably John saw the empty tomb.*
John 20:11–13	*The two angels showed Mary Magdalene the burial place.*
John 20:14	*Mary Magdalene first saw Jesus at the tomb.*
Matt. 28:9	*The "other" Mary also saw Him.*
Mark 16:7; 1 Corinthians 15:5	*He was seen by Peter.*
Luke 24:13–35	*He appeared to Cleopas and another disciple.*
Luke 24:43	*He ate with Cleopas and the other disciples.*
John 20:19–31	*He showed His hands and feet to Thomas and the other disciples.*
John 21:1–14	*He showed Himself to the disciples by the Sea of Tiberias.*
Acts 1:3	*He showed Himself to the disciples for a period of forty days.*
Matthew 28:16–20; Mark 16:14	*He appeared to the disciples while they were eating and gave them the Great Commission.*
1 Corinthians 15:6	*He appeared to an additional five hundred disciples.*

Consequently, "we are under obligation, not to the flesh, to live according to the flesh" (v. 12). Because we have new life in Christ and the Holy Spirit within us, we are not obligated to live the way those who do not have the Spirit within them live. There should be a sharp contrast between the lifestyle of the believer and the unbeliever if only for the presence of the Holy Spirit in the life of the believer. We have the assurance of being resurrected, but until that becomes a reality, Paul cannot help but remind his readers that when the Spirit of God comes to us at salvation we are under new management, and therefore we are debtors to that management. Thus we live the "resurrected life," a life that is indicative of someone who has the assurance of being resurrected.

How different the Christian hope of resurrection is from the Hindu doctrine of reincarnation. Hindus live under obligation to the flesh, to do those things that they believe will earn them a better lot in their next life. Consequently, reincarnation brings dejection and despair, "for if you are living according to the flesh, you must die" (v. 13). Resurrection, on the other hand, brings hope and optimism. We do not live under obligation to work for our salvation. Instead, we enjoy the benefits of what Jesus Christ already did for us at the cross of Calvary. "But if by the Spirit you are putting to death the deeds of the body, you will live" (v. 13). That's a difference too distinct to miss—the difference between death and life.

Study Questions

1. Specifically, what has set believers free from the law of sin and death?

2. How was the Law fulfilled in us?

3. Are children of God in the flesh or in the Spirit?

4. How will believers in Christ be raised from the dead? Explain.

5. How do believers put to death the deeds of the body?

CHAPTER 17

Sanctification and the Benefits of Sonship
Romans 8:14–17

Preview:
Those being led by the Holy Spirit are called the sons of God and have received a spirit of adoption whereby they can call God "Abba." The Holy Spirit bears witness that they are the children of God and fellow heirs with Christ.

For the Christian, the news of Romans 8 just keeps getting better. Living a sanctified life is proof that we are in God's family. We live like our Father in heaven desires us to live. If we were of our father the devil, we'd live like the devil. But since we are part of the family of God, we are to live like a family member and not be an embarrassment to our Father. This portion of Paul's letter to the Romans addresses the benefits of being a member of the heavenly family.

The Benefit of Being Led by the Spirit (8:14)

"For all who are being led by the Spirit of God, these are sons of God" (v. 14). What does it mean to be "led" by the Spirit of God? The verb *ago* means to guide, direct, impel, or lead away. Luke 4:1 records, "And Jesus, full of the Holy Spirit, returned from the Jordan and was led *(ago)* about by the Spirit in the wilderness." When the devil tempted Jesus the third time, "he led *(ago)* Him to Jerusalem and had Him stand on the pinnacle of the temple" (Luke 4:9). And when Jesus was arrested in the garden, "they led *(ago)* Him away, and brought

Him to the house of the high priest" (Luke 22:54). Later that night "the whole body of them arose and brought *(ago)* Him before Pilate" (Luke 23:1).

Some conclusions can be drawn both from how the word is used elsewhere and how it is used in Romans 8:14. First, it is obvious that to be led does not merely mean to be influenced. Jesus was not "influenced" as a sheep to the slaughter, nor was Paul "influenced" before King Agrippa. *Led* means to be moved by a force external to oneself. When we are led by the Spirit of God, it is not by suggestion but by exertion. Second, the leading of the Holy Spirit is not harsh but gentle. He is not repressive but kind, saying, "This is the way, walk in it" (Is. 30:21). He does not lead as a tyrant but as a teacher (John 14:26). Third, the leading of the Spirit is not sporadic or haphazard but steady and sustained. The verb *ago* is in the third person present indicative form, which implies continuous action. Finally, the leading of the Holy Spirit is authenticating. By His constant, gentle leading, the Spirit assures us that we are indeed the children of God, born again into the line of the Second Adam and on our way to heaven.

The Benefit of Being Adopted (8:15)

"For you have not received a spirit of slavery . . . but you have received a spirit of adoption" (v. 15). When Paul says that we have not received the spirit of slavery, he means that when the Spirit of God dwells in us, God does not treat us as servants, but as sons (cf. 1 Cor. 2:12; 2 Tim. 1:7). We do not fear God as the slave fears his master. Rather, we love Him as a son loves his father. The slave does his master's bidding because he knows he will be punished if he does not. But for all in whom the Spirit of God dwells, there is no element of fear that can intrude in our service for the Lord. We serve the Lord as a son lovingly serves his loving father.

William Barclay's lifelong study of Roman history and culture is useful here. He says:

> In this passage Paul is introducing us to another of the great metaphors in which he describes the new relationship of the Christian to God. Here Paul speaks of the Christian being adopted into the family of God. It is only when we understand how serious and complicated a step Roman adoption was that we really understand the depth of meaning in this passage. Roman adoption was always rendered more serious and more difficult by the Roman *patria potestas*. The *patria potestas* was the father's power over his family; that power was absolute; it was actually the power of absolute disposal and control, and in the early days it was actually the power of life and death. In regard to his father a Roman son never came

of age. No matter how old he was, he was still under the *patria potestas*, in the absolute possession, and under the absolute control, of his father. Obviously this made adoption into another family a very difficult and a very serious step.

In adoption a person had to pass from one *patria potestas* to another. He had to pass out of the possession and control of one father into the equally absolute possession and control of another. There were two steps. The first was known as *mancipatio*, and it was carried out by a symbolic sale, in which copper and scales were symbolically used. Three times the symbolism of sale was carried out. Twice the father symbolically sold his son, and twice he bought him back; and the third time he did not buy him back, and thus the *patria potestas* was held to be broken. After the sale there followed a ceremony called *vindicatio*. The adopting father went to the praetor, one of the Roman magistrates, and presented a legal case for the transference of the person to be adopted into his *patria potestas*. When all this was completed then the adoption was complete. Clearly this was a serious and an impressive step.

But it is the consequences of adoption that are most significant for the picture that is in Paul's mind. There were four main consequences. (1) The adopted person lost all rights in his old family, and gained all the rights of a fully legitimate son in his new family. In the most literal sense, and in the most binding legal way, he got a new father. (2) It followed that he became heir to his new father's estate. Even if other sons were afterwards born, who were real blood relations, it did not affect his rights. He was inalienably co-heir with them. (3) In law, the old life of the adopted person was completely wiped out. For instance, legally all debts were canceled; they were wiped out as if they had never been. The adopted person was regarded as a new person entering into a new life with which the past had nothing to do. (4) In the eyes of the law the adopted person was literally and absolutely the son of his new father.

Roman history provides an outstanding case of how literally and completely this was held to be the case. The Emperor Claudius adopted Nero, in order that Nero might succeed him on the throne. They were not in any sense blood relations. Claudius already had a daughter, Octavia. To cement the alliance Nero wished to marry Octavia. Now, Nero and Octavia were in no sense connected; they were in no sense blood relations; yet, in the eyes of the law, they were brother and sister; and before they could marry, the Roman senate had to pass special legislation to enable Nero to marry a girl who was legally his own sister. Nothing shows better how complete adoption in Rome was.[1]

Being adopted as adult sons brings an added benefit to us as Christians—intimacy with the Father. We can call the Sovereign God of the universe "Abba, Father." This tandem of terms occurs only in two other places in the New Testament—Mark 14:36 and Galatians 4:6. *Abba* is an Aramaic word that was used by Jews as a term of endearment, a familiar term like *Papa*, which children might use in addressing their father. The idea of God being a father was extremely foreign to Jewish thinking in the Old Testament. But being adopted as sons and daughters of the Most High God has given us a special, intimate, and unique relationship with Him. "The same word is used here that Christ Himself used in addressing His heavenly Father—'Abba'—in the Garden of Gethsemane according to Mark 14:36. Because we are in Him, we may use the very word He used."[2] We may not defame Him nor disrespect Him, but we can call God "Daddy," and that's something special. Only children can do that.

The Benefit of Family Confirmation (8:16)

"The Spirit Himself bears witness with our spirit that we are children of God" (v. 16). What does it mean to "bear witness"? The verb is *summartureō*, a word composed of the prefix *sun* ("with") and the verb *martureō* ("to give honorable testimony"). Thus, *summartureō* means to bear joint witness or to give supporting testimony with another. The Spirit bears joint witness with our spirit that we are born again into the family of God.

This is the sense in which Paul uses the word elsewhere in Romans. Besides here, Paul utilized this word both in Romans 2:15 and 9:1, and nowhere else. In Romans 2:15 what is written on the heart of the immoral person is also the voice of his conscience. The heart and conscience bear joint witness. In Romans 9:1 Paul testifies that he is burdened for Israel's salvation, and his conscience confirms that testimony. In all three cases, two sources of testimony confirm each other. But what does this mean to the Christian? It means we have become convinced that we were estranged from God as sinners and have believed that Jesus Christ paid the penalty for our sin at Calvary, and as a result, we have invited Him into our lives and been born again into God's family. That knowledge brings a sense deep in our hearts that we are God's children and on our way to heaven. But our feelings are not always trustworthy indicators of reality. So we have the Spirit of God within us confirming those feelings, providing independent and reliable testimony that what we feel is fact.

The Benefit of Being God's Heir (8:17-18)

We now come to the final benefit of sonship—being God's heir. Four facets of being God's heir are worthy of our consideration: (1) the One who bequeaths an inheritance; (2) the ones who receive the inheritance; (3) the inheritance itself; and (4) the consequences of being an heir.

There can be no inheritance if there is no testator, the person who provides the inheritance. In this case, there can be no question who that person is. Paul speaks of "heirs of God." The Holy One of Israel provides an inheritance for us. Immediately when you think of a testator you want to know, "What kind of inheritance does this person have the ability to leave to His heirs? Will it be a little or a lot?" With God, the inheritance is more than sufficient. After all, He is "God Most High, possessor of heaven and earth" (Gen. 14:19, 22). He is the One who says,

> Every beast of the forest is Mine,
> The cattle on a thousand hills.
> I know every bird of the mountains,
> And everything that moves in the field is Mine.
> If I were hungry, I would not tell you;
> For the world is Mine, and all it contains. (Ps. 50:10–12).

Since everything belongs to God, everything belongs to His heirs.

That God gives an inheritance to His Son, Jesus Christ, should surprise no one. If a good man gives an inheritance to his children's children (Prov. 13:22), you would expect the same of a good God. And the Father did say of His Son, "This is My beloved Son, in whom I am well-pleased" (Matt. 3:17; 17:5). He also said,

> "'Thou art My Son,
> Today I have begotten Thee.
> 'Ask of Me, and I will surely give the nations as Thine inheritance,
> And the very ends of the earth as Thy possession.'" (Ps. 2:7–8).

Jesus Himself said, "All things that the Father has are Mine" (John 16:15). So for Jesus to be the heir of His Father is expected. The miraculous and marvelous truth of Romans 8:17 is that we are "fellow heirs with Christ." All that belongs to the Father belongs to the Son, and those who are children of God share equally with the Son all that belongs to the Father. It's amazing!

We know two things for sure about our inheritance from God. First, it is a future inheritance, and second, it will be shared with Jesus Christ. That it is a future inheritance is implied from the next verse (v. 18), which speaks of "the glory that is to be revealed to us." That it will be shared with Jesus Christ is both indicated in the words *fellow heirs* (Greek, *sugklēronomos*) and in the reference to the believer being qualified by the Father "to share in the inheritance of the saints in light" (Col. 1:12). So what is the inheritance that we share as an heir of God? The Bible speaks of golden crowns (Rev. 4:4; cf. 14:14), a new name (Rev. 3:12), a "well done" from our Master (Matt. 25:21, 23), and a position of responsibility in God's kingdom (2 Tim. 2:12; Rev. 20:6) as just a few features of our future inheritance.[3]

Blessings Believers Inherit	
Upon the one to whom God imputes righteousness.	Romans 4:6
Upon those who are blessed with Abraham by faith.	Galatians 3:9
For those in Christ in the heavenly places.	Ephesians 1:3
Blessed hope of Christ's return.	Titus 2:13
For persevering under trial.	James 1:12
For enduring suffering.	James 5:11
For giving a blessing instead of giving evil and insults.	1 Peter 3:9
For suffering for righteousness' sake.	1 Peter 3:14
For being reviled for Christ's sake.	1 Peter 4:14
For especially reading the book of Revelation.	Revelation 1:3
"Called . . . that you might inherit a blessing" (1 Peter 3:9)	

Being God's heir is better than being a billionaire's heir. The benefits are greater, and we have a holy and righteous Father as well. Sanctification is a serious matter and should be taken seriously by believers. Living a life that pleases our Father now means that we have all the benefits of God's family now. And in the future, we will have all the benefits of being God's legitimate heirs. Furthermore, having a clear view of the future will cause us to live differently in the present.

Study Questions

1. What constitutes being called the sons of God?

2. Explain some characteristic differences between the privileges of a slave and the privileges of an adopted son.

3. From this passage, what is one of the most important works of the Holy Spirit?

4. What are the results of being a child of God?

CHAPTER 18

Sanctification and the Prospects for the Future
Romans 8:18–30

Preview:

Sufferings cannot be compared to the glory that is yet to be revealed. Even the creation waits for the revelation of the sons of God, and it also groans to be released from its corruption. Believers in Christ also groan to be adopted. Because of human weakness, children of God do not know what to pray for, but the Spirit makes intercession with God for us. All things work together for good for those called of the Lord according to His purpose.

While we may be thrilled at being heirs of God and fellow heirs of Jesus Christ, there are consequences to our position that may not thrill us. Suffering is the necessary prelude to glory. The glory awaits us; the suffering is now.

The Prospect That Suffering Is the Ground of Glory (8:18)

How do we presently suffer as heirs of God? We are not likely to suffer as martyrs who are called to give their lives for their faith. Suffering can mean bearing with grace the final painful days of life. It can mean keeping your cool when a university professor ridicules your Christian beliefs. People suffer by not receiving a deserved promotion because they have witnessed to their faith. Some women suffer the persecution of abusive husbands who don't share their faith. But however suffering comes, it is important to remember that "the sufferings of this present time are not worthy to be compared with the glory that is to be revealed to us" (v. 18).

Paul mentioned the sufferings of the present without going into much detail about his personal life. But we know the apostle suffered greatly for his faith. To the Corinthians he wrote, "We have this treasure in earthen vessels, that the surpassing greatness of the power may be of God and not from ourselves; we are afflicted in every way, but not crushed; perplexed, but not despairing; persecuted, but not forsaken; struck down, but not destroyed" (2 Cor. 4:7–9). A fuller description of the extent of Paul's afflictions can be read in 2 Corinthians 11:22–28. But read it with caution, because many of the events recorded there are not known to us from the pages of Scripture. Nevertheless, the apostle is confident. If we presently endure great hardship, cruel and unusual punishment, severe persecution, or even death itself, none of these evils can compare with the heavenly bliss that is awaiting those who are in Christ Jesus.

The Prospect of a Transformed Creation (8:19–23)

In verse 19 the apostle speaks of the "anxious longing of the creation," and in verse 22 he says, "The whole creation groans and suffers." What does he mean? "The whole creation" means all of nature, with some notable exceptions. These exceptions, however, are not the rule. Almost everything that was created by God in this world yielded control of itself to futility through the consequences of sin. The ground, as a part of God's creation, was cursed because of sin (Gen. 3:17), and the birds and animals groan (Gen. 3:14), waiting for the day when they will no longer be under the curse of sin. God's created nature was not cursed "of its own will" (v. 20), because it was man who sinned, not the earth, the trees, or the animals. Nature was cursed as a result of God's curse on humans, and this shows how inextricably linked humans are with the world in which they live.

But just as humans are linked with the pain of the curse on the earth, so humans are linked with lifting that curse and its attendant pain. The whole creation is anxiously awaiting "the revealing of the sons of God" (v. 19), for it is only then that the pain that creation endures as a result of God's curse will cease. Today the curse covers the world and brings the groaning of pain even to that which is inanimate. Yet one day God will remove the curse and save the earth from its pain when He establishes His Millennial Kingdom here on the earth (Rev. 20—21). The Millennium is when the wolf will dwell with the lamb and the little child will put his hand into the snake's nest and not be hurt (Is. 11:6–9). And as glorious as that messianic age will be, it will be only a prelude to eternity when "creation itself also will be set free from its slavery to corruption into the freedom of the glory of the children of God" (v. 21). That's when "there shall no longer be any curse; and the throne of God and of the Lamb shall be in it [the whole earth]" (Rev. 22:3). Little wonder when Isaac Watts wrote the hymn *Joy to the World* he included, "No more let sins and sorrows grow, nor thorns infest the ground; He comes to make His blessings flow far as the curse is found."

As the preacher of Ecclesiastes observed, there is nothing in this life (apart from Jesus Christ) that provides lasting significance to life. If the hand of God were today removed from His creation, all that existed would be found pursuing a course of ultimate frustration. "For the creation was subjected to futility, not of its own will, but because of Him who subjected it, in hope" (v. 20). This can only mean God, for only God can subject His creation in hope. Apart from God, creation is meaningless; it is plunging headlong into decay and death. God, however, promises that even creation will one day be delivered from bondage to liberty. That's why "the whole creation groans and suffers the pains of childbirth together until now" (v. 22). The pains with which the whole creation groans are not death pains but birth pains. Paul has in mind the Jewish expectation of a coming Messiah, but he knows that a time of great tribulation will precede that millennial rule of the Messiah. Both humankind and the rest of God's creation will share in these birth pains as they together anticipate the joy that follows the pain of birth. "And not only this, but also we ourselves, having the first fruits of the Spirit, even we ourselves groan within ourselves" (v. 23). As the creation groans for the coming of the Messiah, so also do believers groan. We are said to have the first fruits of the Spirit. That is, the indwelling Spirit is the first installment or down payment on the eternal glory that awaits both the believer and God's creation. As believers we await the adoption, that is, the redemption, of our bodies. Though today we may be attacked by physical pain, surrounded by financial distress, or discouraged by failing health, we know that because we possess the Holy Spirit as our down payment, God will certainly redeem our bodies as He has already redeemed our souls. As the sons of God, we will one day be clothed with immortal and incorruptible bodies (1 Cor. 15:51–55; 2 Cor. 5:2–3; Phil. 3:21).

Paul's statement in verse 24, "For in hope we have been saved," does not imply that salvation comes through the instrumentality of hope. The uniform teaching of Paul, as well as Scripture in general, is that we are saved by faith (cf. 1:16–17; Eph. 2:8). The words "in hope" refer to that ingredient that is inseparable from salvation and a natural accompaniment to it. Hope can never be divorced from salvation, because salvation is the ground of our hope. But hope that is seen is not hope. Once we have realized the heirship and the redemption of our bodies that has been promised to us, we will no longer hope in them. Therefore, if we hope for what we do not see, we wait with patience for it. This expression of patience is a fitting conclusion to the chapter that deals with the provision of assurance. Looking to a future adoption of the body provides opportunity for our faith to grow and mature. Consequently, the virtue of patience is developed in addition to hope and faith. Therefore, although we are assured of eternal heirship, nevertheless, we develop patience in waiting for the coming of the Lord.

The Prospect of Present Intercession (8:26–27)

Here's good news. The great consolation we have during this period of waiting for the Lord's return is the presence of the Holy Spirit. He is the One who helps our "weakness" (Greek, *astheneia*). We have one great weakness or need while waiting the Lord to return for us, and that is "we do not know how to pray as we should" (v. 26). The only thing our Lord's disciples asked Him to teach them was how to pray. Each believer encounters the same difficulty in knowing how to pray and for what to pray. Have you ever had to choose between your current job and accepting another? Did you pray? Was the answer forthcoming? Maybe not. Have you struggled in knowing how to ask God to guide you? We all have. Even Paul three times struggled with asking God to remove his thorn in the flesh (2 Cor. 12:7–8), but apparently he was asking for the wrong thing. God gave him what he needed—sufficient grace to endure the thorn so Paul would see that God's power is often demonstrated in our pain.

Because praying is hard work and we are not always successful at knowing how or for what to pray, God has given His Holy Spirit to make intercession for us "with groanings too deep for words" (v. 26). The Holy Spirit's groanings never fail to be noticed by God, because "He who searches the hearts knows what the mind of the Spirit is" (v. 27). The Scriptures are unambiguous that God knows the hearts and secrets of all. "The Lord searches all hearts, and understands every intent of the thoughts" (1 Chr. 28:9). The Lord "knowest the hearts of all men" (Acts 1:24). "All things are open and laid bare to the eyes of Him with whom we have to do" (Heb. 4:13). When your whole world collapses around you and you can't even pray, the Spirit grieves with you and prays for you. But His grief exceeds yours, and He groans with feelings too deep for words. The Father searches the mind of the Spirit, interprets these groanings, and knows what His Holy Spirit is thinking as He prays in your behalf. The Spirit groans with thoughts that always concur with the will of God (v. 27). Sometimes you and I pray for things that clearly are not God's will—for example, the desire for sexual relations outside of marriage. Other times we pray for things that may not be God's will—for example, the victory of your favorite football team. If we only knew God's will, we could pray more intelligently, effectively, and spiritually. The Spirit of God is a superb intercessor for us in that He always knows and prays for God's will. Every time the Spirit groans in prayer in your behalf, you can be certain that God's will is being addressed.

The Prospect of God's Eternal Purpose (8:28–30)

Often when we are in a situation so desperate that we cannot pray, we are joined by those who pray for us. We appreciate that. They come to empathize with us and to comfort and cheer us. But occasionally with their good intentions they offer us hollow advice and, like Job's three friends, become sorry comforters (Job 16:2). "Cheer up," they say, "don't you know that all things work together for good?" Yes, we know, but sometimes that doesn't appear evident.

Romans 8:28 is not a crutch, a "feel good" adage to be used to prop us up. This is a promise of the living God and should always be claimed in that light. "And we know that God causes all things to work together for good to those who love God, to those who are called according to His purpose" is an iron-clad promise from a sovereign God who can perform what He promises. This we can "know" about God and His ability to keep this promise. Here the word "know" (Greek, *oida*) implies knowledge deriving from what we perceive with our eyes or discover by our senses; we know by experience. Paul's point in using this verb is that knowing all things work together for our good and God's glory is not something we know innately or intuitively; it is something we understand from observation. We know God works out His plans in our lives because we have watched Him do so.

"All things" is not a promise that every detail or event in your life will immediately turn around from bad and be observably for your good. Rather, the "all things" promise is that nothing is excluded from God's sovereign control. Not only the prosperity of our lives but also the adversity, not only the good times but also the bad, not only the days of joy but the days of sorrow, not only the periods of good health but the periods of ill health—God will use "all things" in the wonder of His will to benefit us. Nothing is excluded. God doesn't promise we will "see" all things work together for good, He simply promises that He will make all things work together for good. That requires faith, fortified by the knowledge of experience.

The promise of Romans 8:28 has sometimes been taken as a universal, unqualified, blanket statement of everything working out to be good for us. And when that doesn't happen, people often blame God. But Romans 8:28 is not a universal, unqualified, blanket statement. It has two qualifiers, the first of which is that it is made "to those who love God." Someone who does not love God does not know God. Thus the promise in Romans 8:28 is made to those who know God, those who have come to trust Jesus Christ as their Savior. The second qualifier for Romans 8:28 is that this promise is only to a special group. Romans 8:28 does not say "to those who are called according to His purpose" as the NASB and other versions read, but "to those who are *the* called according to His purpose." The definite article strengthens the intent of the apostle. This promise is not for the world; it is made only to those who are "in Christ Jesus." Only those who have been effectively called by God and have embraced the Lord Jesus as Savior can expect all things to work together for their good (Rom. 1:7; 8:30; 9:24; 1 Cor. 1:2, 24; 7:17–24). We are *the* called, according to God's purpose, which Paul is about to explain.

The Significant Events of Our Salvation	
Foreknown	Beforehand and previously known in an intimate, personal way. Rom. 8:29; 11:2; 1 Pet. 1:2.
Predestined	Beforehand encircled and destined for salvation. Rom. 8:29, 30; Eph. 1:5, 11.
Called	Specifically called and chosen for salvation. Rom. 8:30; Eph. 1:4; 1 Pet. 1:1–2; 2:4; 9.
Justified	Legally acquitted, to receive imputed righteousness from Christ. Rom. 3:5, 21; 4:3, 5; 8:30, 33; 2 Cor. 5:21; Gal. 5:5; Eph. 4:24.
Sanctified	"Set aside," made holy by being joined to Christ. Rom. 1:7; 1 Cor. 1:2; 6:11; Eph. 1:4, 5:26; 1 Pet. 1:2.
Glorified	Positionally, already glorified in the mind of God. Is. 43:7; Rom. 8:30.

Past

Present

Future

The Prospect of the Unbroken Chain (8:29–30)

You can't think of the Christian's prospects for the future without reflecting on the past. Paul does this as he strings together the works of God on our behalf to show us our glorious future. He uses five theological words—foreknew, predestined, called, justified, and glorified—to describe five works of grace that God performs in our behalf to insure that our future is what He intended it to be before the world began. Notice these are all past tense verbs, but their impact is not locked into the past. Actually, two of these works of God occurred in eternity past—foreknowledge and predestination; two occur in the present—calling and justification; and one will occur in eternity future—glorification.

Paul begins, "For whom He foreknew, He also predestined to become conformed to the image of His son" (v. 29). The last word of the preceding verse is "purpose." Paul now expands on God's purpose in verses 29 and 30 by means of a sorites, a construction in which the predicate of one clause becomes the subject of the next clause. In the salvation provided by God, there is a link from eternity past, through the present, to eternity future. That link includes foreknowledge, predestination, calling, justification, and glorification. We must understand, however, that the key word in this passage is "purpose." All the others arise out of the purpose of God, and our understanding of them must be in connection with God's eternal purpose.

Probably no doctrine has evoked a greater variety of interpretations than that of God's foreknowledge. Although it is true that foreknowledge means "to know beforehand," in the context of God's purpose, to interpret the expression this way would be an oversimplification. For God to preview history to discern our response to the gospel and then act accordingly, would make the creature sovereign over the Creator. The word *foreknow* occurs infrequently in the New Testament, and therefore a clear understanding of its import must be seen from the way it is used in the Old Testament as well. When God takes knowledge of His people, it is more than just a basic understanding of them (cf. Amos 3:2; 1 Cor. 8:3; Gal. 4:9; et al.). It is the knowledge that a father has of his child. God knows and loves the world, but His foreknowledge of His own is an intimate knowledge that results in an abiding love (Rom. 5:8) for us that draws us to Him in salvation.

"Whom He foreknew, He also predestined to become conformed to the image of His Son" (v. 29). God's foreordination or predestination must not be equated with fatalism. Fatalism says that the world is plunging headlong toward an indeterminate end. Paul teaches that there is a very determinate end for those who are "the called." Their end or goal is to be conformed to the image of God's Son, Jesus Christ. We are not plunging downward toward increasing evil as the world is, but we are progressing upward toward increasing likeness with the Son of Righteousness. As believers, we should become more and more like the Master every day. But God has planned for us a final and complete conformity to the resurrection glory of the Lord, for He is the "first-born among many brethren" (cf. 1 Cor. 15:49; 2 Cor. 3:18; Phil. 3:21; 1 John 3:2). Since the term *firstborn* always implies a position of supremacy, it is the eternal purpose of God that we become increasingly more conformed to the image of Him who is the Supreme Being in the universe.

As Paul progresses toward the third link in the chain of God's purpose, he says, "Whom He predestined, these He also called" (v. 30). As believers, we were foreknown and foreordained prior to our birth. Yet God does not manipulate us like puppets. Rather, He calls us, He beseeches us to receive His offer of salvation. When we are quickened by the Spirit of God and respond to His call in faith, we are then justified and made useful for His service.

> Paul had been thoroughly drilled in the contents of what we today call the Old Testament. He knew that during the old dispensation there were certain places, objects, and people that had been "set apart" and "consecrated" for the service of God; for example, the holy place (1 Kings 8:10) and the Holy of Holies (Ex. 26:33), the tithe of the land (Lev. 27:30), the priests (Lev. 21:6, 7), and even the Israelites as a whole, viewed in distinction from the other nations (Ex. 19:6; Lev. 20:26: Deut. 7:6). It is this idea which in the New Testament is applied to Christians generally. They are the "elect race, royal priesthood, holy nation, people for God's own possession" of the new dispensation, chosen to declare God's praises (1 Peter 2:9).[1]

Link number four is justification, that which much of the earlier chapters of this letter are about. "And whom He called, these He also justified" (v. 30). Justification is a vital doctrine in Pauline thinking. As was seen in Romans 3:24, justification occurs when God charges the penalty for our sin to the account of Jesus Christ. When what Jesus did at Calvary's cross is charged to our account, the transaction of justification is complete. God lays on Jesus' shoulders the sins of the world. "He [God the Father] made Him [God the Son] who knew no sin to be sin on our behalf, that we might become the righteousness of God in Him" (2 Cor. 5:21). Thus, when we are justified by God, we don't actually become righteous, but we are cloaked in the righteousness of Jesus Christ, who became sin for us. There will be a future day when we are righteous, confirmed in Christ's righteousness, but for now, God considers us as if we are righteous because of the atoning death of Jesus Christ. And just as important as reckoning us as righteous, God treats us as if we are righteous. All this happens when we trust Christ as Savior, shed the filthy rags of our sin, and take on the righteousness of Christ as a robe covering our sin and inadequacy.

When a monk named Martin Luther finally understood this concept by reading his Bible rather than listening to others, he clearly saw that if he ever were to be righteous, he would not become so by saying the rosary, repeating the Lord's Prayer, taking the sacraments, or celebrating mass. Luther said, "For

God does not want to save us by our own but by an extraneous righteousness, one that does not originate in ourselves but comes to us from beyond ourselves, which does not arise on earth but comes from heaven."[2] Justification comes only as we respond in faith to the work God is already doing in us, convicting us, drawing us to Himself, and saving us. Along with calling, it is the present work of God in the five golden links in His chain of salvation.

Because God has cloaked us with Christ's righteousness and counts us as righteous, He cannot complete the five links of salvation until He actually makes us righteous in heaven. So Paul continues, "And whom He justified, these He also glorified" (v. 30). The final step in the purpose of God is the glorification of His people. Ultimately, we will be completely conformed to the image of God's Son. "When Christ, who is our life, is revealed, then you also will be revealed with Him in glory" (Col. 3:4; cf. 1 John 3:2). This is God's view of salvation. Foreknowledge and foreordination belong to the eternal past, in the eternal counsel of the Godhead; calling and justification take place in the believer's present experience; the glory that begins now will not ultimately and completely be known until the future. Although salvation from our viewpoint is an instantaneous act, it has in fact stretched from eternity past to eternity future and finds its basis, not in our merit or in the works of the law, but in the purpose of God. In the depression and turmoil of these days, nothing can be of greater encouragement to believers than to know that God is working all things together for our good and His glory.

Study Questions

1. What does Paul mean when he says, "the creation was subject to futility"?

2. How and why was the creation enslaved to corruption?

3. What does "our groaning" cause us to do?

4. List the things the Holy Spirit is doing presently on behalf of the children of God.

5. Explain the meaning of *foreknew* as used by Paul in this context.

6. Explain in your own words how verse 30 shows that our salvation is a completed happening in the mind of God.

CHAPTER 19

Sanctification and the Power of God
Romans 8:31–39

Preview:

Since we belong to the Lord, can any charge be laid against us? Nothing can separate us from the love of God. We are conquerors because God has loved us in Christ, and nothing on the earth, or even in this universe, can separate us from the love of God!

Paul wants his readers, including you and me, to stop and ponder the ground he has just covered. He has demonstrated that for those who are "in Christ" there is no more threat of judicial condemnation (vv. 1–8). He has helped his readers to understand that living a sanctified life is possible because they are indwelt by the Holy Spirit (vv. 9–10) and that one day God will raise up their bodies just as Jesus' body was resurrected (vv. 11–13). And there are other benefits to the Holy Spirit indwelling them—namely, they are guided by Him (v. 14), and they know they are heirs of God and fellow heirs with Jesus Christ (vv. 15–17) and will one day celebrate their new birth in God's heaven (v. 18). Paul has encouraged them that a day is coming when creation will no longer groan in pain (vv. 19–22) because the curse will be completely removed by God, and that those who also groan (vv. 23–25) will one day experience the wonder of a fully redeemed body. The apostle has given his readers hope by reminding them that God promises that both the good and the bad of life will be used to mold them into the redeemed masterpiece that has always been God's purpose for them (v. 28). For all of this, every believer in the Lord Jesus can be extremely and eternally grateful. As is usually the case, Paul's method to get his readers to ponder something is to ask questions.

The Power of God's Eternal Advocacy (8:31–32)

Paul's first question is, "What then shall we say to these things?" (v. 31). In essence, this verse is the conclusion Paul draws to the first eight chapters of Romans. What will our response be to what has been said? "If God is for us, who is against us?" This is not one of the rhetorical questions but rather the answer to the first question. Paul's only response to "What can we say?" is his complete assurance that the eternal purpose of God will come to fruition because God is God. "Who can be against us?" does not mean that we have no adversaries. Verses 35 and 36 list a great number of adversaries. But by this Paul means that there is no adversary so great as to be able to thwart the eternal purpose of God.

As evidence of the fact that God will bring His eternal purpose to its proper conclusion, Paul argues that God "did not spare His own Son, but delivered Him up for us all" (v. 32). These words are reminiscent of the classic example of the redemptive efficacy of martyrdom which is given in Genesis 22:12. There God says to Abraham, "You have not withheld [Greek, *pheidomai* in the Septuagint, as here] your son, your only son, from Me." So significant was God's love for us that He did not stop short of sacrificing His only begotten Son to provide atonement for us. We let that thought slip too quickly from our minds. What incredible sacrifice; what amazing love. If we take a moment to think about it, we are inspired to sing with Charles Wesley, "And can it be that I should gain an interest in the Saviour's blood? Died He for me, who caused His pain? For me, who Him to death pursued? Amazing love! How can it be that Thou my God shouldst die for me?"

In light of the superiority and scale of God's sacrifice, Paul then argues from the greater to the lesser in the rhetorical question, "How will He not also with Him freely give us all things?" (v. 32). If God did not spare His own Son, but delivered Him up to the cross of Calvary, it isn't logical, it isn't even thinkable, that He would fail to bring to its completed end the purpose for which Christ was sacrificed. Hence, all the gifts and blessings that accompany salvation are promised to us, and they will be ours just as salvation is ours.

The Power of God's Eternal Plan (8:33–34)

Paul's next rhetorical question is, "Who will bring a charge against God's elect?" This question is along the same line as that in verse 31. This question asks who is capable of bringing a charge against God's elect that is serious enough to cause them to be judicially condemned. Who is in a position to charge as guilty those whom God has declared righteous? Paul is issuing a challenge to the universe that if there is any man or woman, any angel or demon, anyone or anything at all who can make a charge against God's elect that can stick, let him do so now. That's the issue. What is Paul's response? It is classic and it is double-sided.

"God is the one who justifies" (v. 33). Since "the called" are justified by God, no one will be able to appeal God's verdict of justification. He is the highest court there is. Every tongue that attempts to do so will be silenced (cf. Is. 50:8–9; 54:17). Again there is an echo here from the Old Testament. In the clearly messianic passage found in Isaiah 50, the Servant of the Lord says,

> I was not disobedient. . . .
> I gave My back to those who strike Me,
> And My cheeks to those who pluck out the beard;
> I did not cover My face from humiliation and spitting. (Is. 50:5–6).

And then the Messiah issues this challenge:

> He who vindicates Me is near;
> Who will contend with Me?
> Let us stand up to each other;
> Who has a case against Me?
> Let him draw near to Me. (Is. 50:8)

With God at His side, who dares stand toe to toe and complain with the way God has vindicated His Son? Paul makes this same argument for the believer. It is God who justifies us. Who is capable of disputing our justification? No one.

But there's a second reason why no one can bring a charge against God's elect. "Christ Jesus is He who died" (v. 34). If someone were to object to God justifying us when we were yet sinful, it could not be a sinful person himself. Why? Because a sinful person has no room to talk, no ground upon which to object to God. We all are in the same boat. If anyone were to object, it would have to be a sinless person who would say, "Hey, God, that's not fair. I am sinless; they aren't. You have justified and treated as righteous people who really aren't. That's not fair to me who is righteous." Only one who is righteous could legitimately object to God's method of justifying us. It's remarkable, isn't it, that the only one who is righteous is Jesus Christ. That means the only one who could legitimately condemn us is the very person who died for us. Only God could come up with a plan like that!

The Power of God's Eternal Presence (8:35-39)

Now the apostle deepens his questions and expands his search area. "Who shall separate us from the love of Christ?" Our assurance in the eternal presence of God is based on the unfailing love of God as demonstrated in the atoning sacrifice of His Son, Jesus Christ (5:8). Paul then amplifies the question by asking if it is possible that tribulation, distress, persecution, famine, nakedness, peril, or the sword can enter our lives and undo what Christ has accomplished on our behalf at the cross. But why these threats? What individual challenge does each represent?

Tribulation (Greek, *thlipsis*) means "pressure" or denotes something that is pressed together as in a vice. This word is used some forty-five times in the New Testament, more than half the times by Paul. It is the word he chose in Romans 12:12, "persevering in tribulation." A good translation of the word is "affliction," probably of the variety that comes from without.

Distress (Greek, *stenochōria*) denotes a narrow place, a tight squeeze, and hence difficulty. We have already seen it in Romans 2:9, "There will be tribulation and distress for every soul of man who does evil." Paul uses this word three times in connection with the word above (Rom. 2:9; 8:35; 2 Cor. 6:4), perhaps to distinguish between outward tribulation and inward distress.

Persecution (Greek, *diōgmos*) is any form of harassment. Not a common word (used once by Matthew, twice by Mark, and twice by Luke in Acts), Paul used it only five times including here.

Famine (Greek, *limos*) is the dearth of anything, but especially food, and therefore means "hunger." Jesus predicted, "Nation will rise against nation, and kingdom against kingdom, and in various places there will be famines and earthquakes" (Matt. 24:7). While the word is used a dozen times in Scripture, Paul uses it only here and in 2 Corinthians 11:27.

Nakedness (Greek, *gumnotēs*) means nakedness of the body. Paul used this word of himself both here and when, in 2 Corinthians 11:27, he said, "I have been in labor and hardship, through many sleepless nights, in hunger and thirst, often without food, in cold and *exposure* (emphasis added)." Nakedness and hunger often accompany each other.

Peril (Greek, *kindunos*) denotes any kind of danger or jeopardy. At Ephesus, Demetrius the silversmith wanted to get rid of Paul because he caused "danger *(kindunos)* that this trade of ours fall into disrepute" and that "the temple of the great goddess Artemis be regarded as worthless" (Acts 19:27).

Sword (Greek, *machaira*) identifies either a large knife like that used for killing animals or a small sword. Jesus advised His disciples, "Do not think that I came to bring peace on the earth; I did not come to bring peace, but a sword" (Matt. 10:34). It was this kind of large knife that Peter used to cut off the ear of the high priest's servant (John 18:10).

William Hendriksen makes a good point when he says,

> We should not forget that when Paul spoke about these adverse circumstances which Satan and the other enemies of the cross used in order to bring about separation between believers and their Lord, he was not speaking as an armchair theologian or philosopher. On the contrary, as 2 Corinthians 11:23–29 indicates, he had already suffered the first six of these seven hardships before writing this epistle to the Romans. Moreover, by means of the seventh, i.e., the sword, he was going to be put to death. The apostle was speaking not only by inspiration but also from experience, therefore, when he stated that none of these things can bring about separation between believers and their Lord, He knew what he was saying![1]

Before Paul answers his question about any of these things having the ability to separate us from the love of Christ, he quotes Psalm 44:22. This quote (v. 36) is introduced to indicate that God's people shall endure affliction even as the faithful did in the Old Testament. However, the persecution and tribulation that enters our lives, which has been featured so prominently in this chapter, is not sufficient to separate us from God's love demonstrated at the cross of Christ. Now for Paul's answer: "But in all these things we overwhelmingly conquer through Him who loved us" (v. 37). In the midst of illness, suffering, and life's afflictions, we have God's assurance of His eternal presence, and therefore we not only succeed, we overwhelmingly conquer. The word Paul chose to portray the idea that we are superconquerors is *hupernikaō*, which means just that. We do not merely hold our own in the face of testing, but through suffering we are drawn closer to Christ and become more conformed to His image. Notice, however, the means by which we are superconquerors. It is "through Him who loved us" (v. 37). Personal heroism and inner strength are not contributors to success in the Christian life. As we owe our justification and sanctification to Him, we also owe the staying power of our salvation to Him. All we have we owe to Him.

And finally, we have in verses 38 and 39, Paul's great doxology, his summary hymn of praise to God, the certainty of his salvation. Paul searches the entire universe to see if there is anything that can possibly separate us from the eternal presence of God. He goes first to the realm of death and finds nothing there. Then he turns to the realm of life and again finds nothing. He looks to the angels, and they have no power to separate us. He turns to prin-cipalities, which, in this case, may refer to the angelic hosts representing Satan. There is nothing there. He proceeds to examine "things present" and finds nothing. He explores the future, and in the "things to come" he finds nothing that can separate us. Nothing can happen now or in the future to remove the love of God from us or us from His eternal security.

Paul does not stop here. Next he searches the entire universe, and noth-ing in the expanses of space, "height nor depth," can be found to prohibit the presence of God from us. But just in case he has missed something, Paul then says that there is no other creature or creation of God that is able to separate us from the love of God in Christ Jesus. Nowhere can the apostle find any-thing in the whole universe of God that can sever the relationship the children of God have with their Father's love. This great assurance comes to those who are "the called" in Christ Jesus our Lord.

"Blessed assurance, Jesus is mine! Oh what a foretaste of glory divine! Heir of salvation, purchase of God, born of His Spirit, washed in His blood." The power of God is such that once we have been justified, there is nothing, no one, no sin, no fault, no creature in the entire universe that can separate us from "the love of God, which is in Christ Jesus our Lord." That's security. That's assurance. That's divine power. All these wonderful promises belong to us because we belong to Christ.

Study Questions

1. What has God's Son imparted to us?

2. From verse 33, describe the two main reasons no one can lay a charge against the child of God.

3. From verse 36, why does the apostle Paul quote Psalm 44:22?

4. How can weak and helpless believers be made conquerors in Christ?

5. Explain in your own words how Christ presently intercedes for the believer.

SECTION V: REDEMPTION

The Divine Purpose for Israel

Romans 9:1 — 11:36

So much of what we know about God's future plans for His chosen people we know from these three chapters in Romans. Before Paul can address those "nuts and bolts" issues that impact the daily life of the Christian, he chooses first to explain God's future program for Israel.

CHAPTER 20

The Sovereignty of God and Israel's Past
Romans 9:1–33

Preview:

The apostle Paul has great compassion for his fellow Jews. He explains that just because they are Jews in the flesh does not mean they all are children of the "promise" made by the Lord. <u>God is the one who chooses; He is the sovereign potter who determines the fate of people.</u> In a paradoxical way, He waits for those who are vessels of wrath, but He has before prepared the vessels of mercy for glory. The Gentiles are now being saved by faith, but the Jews stumble over Christ, who is their Rock of offense!

Although in many ways Romans 9—11 is parenthetical, nevertheless, it is an integral part of Paul's argument for justification by faith alone. Paul may have been accused of being so dedicated as the apostle to the Gentiles that he had completely forgotten about his Jewish kith and kin. He therefore addresses the question of Israel and its future before proceeding to the practical section of this epistle. Also, the original believers in Rome appear to have been Jews; but in Paul's day the church was predominantly Gentile. Those Jewish believers at Rome needed the apostle's reassurance of their place in the kingdom of God. But above all, the many messianic promises to the Jews of old necessitated an understanding that God would yet honor those promises. If Paul's message of salvation by faith was true, why didn't Paul's own people receive that message? Thus, Paul had to deal with the problem of Jewish unbelief before he could proceed to a conclusion concerning life in Christ Jesus. The only way to reconcile God's promises with Jewish unbelief is to see the sovereignty of God underlying all of history. Hence, this chapter is all about divine sovereignty and corresponding divine choices.

Paul's treatment of the problem is daring. He readily admits that the Jewish nation has rejected the gospel, yet he takes a firm stand in declaring that God is not finished with the Jew. Paul views everything that happens as part of the eternal purpose of God and therefore moving toward God's desired end. Furthermore he teaches that God maintains His righteousness regardless of how people respond to Him. Righteousness is the key concept of this letter. Having established that humans lack righteousness but that God can provide what they need, Paul is not about to back away from that promise when it comes to God's wayward people, the Jews. Here's the proof.

Sovereignty Exhibited in Paul's Passion for Israel (9:1–5)

Paul immediately arrests the attention of his readers by certifying the truthfulness of what he is about to say. He says, "I am telling the truth in Christ," and then he adds the negative "I am not lying" to emphasize the double veracity of his statement (cf. 2 Cor. 11:31; Gal. 1:20; 1 Tim. 2:7). And, as if he needed to seal the truthfulness of what he is about to say, he adds, "my conscience bearing me witness." Now we have a positive declaration, followed by the corresponding negative declaration, further strengthened by an appeal to his conscience, and finally sealed with the witness of the Holy Spirit (v. 1). Paul's conscience will attest to that which his tongue will speak concerning the absolute veracity of the Holy Spirit.

So after all that posturing to insure that the Jewish apostle to the Gentiles is speaking the truth, what does he have to say? In the midst of Paul's expression of joy and great assurance (chapter 8), he also has to admit that he has "great sorrow and unceasing grief" in his heart. He bears this unceasing grief and sorrow for his fellow Jews. So deep is Paul's sorrow that he sighs, "For I could wish that I myself were accursed, separated from Christ for the sake of my brethren" (v. 3). This statement about being anathema from Christ is reminiscent of Moses' statement made upon returning from Mount Sinai. As the great leader viewed the children of Israel involved in the idolatrous worship of the golden calf, he lamented to God that he would prefer to have his name blotted out of God's book in return for the salvation of Israel (Ex. 32:30–33). Paul's understanding, however, in relation to justification by faith, does not allow him to actually wish himself accursed from Christ (i.e., separated from Christ for everlasting destruction). Paul knows that his life is not his own.

Therefore he is not the master of his fate and does not have the power to cast away the eternal life that was purchased for him by the blood of Christ. The verb is in the imperfect tense ("I could wish"), meaning that Paul would accept everlasting destruction in return for the salvation of Israel, but God would not allow him to do so.

Now Paul describes the Jewish people in terms that no one could misunderstand. Paul says he speaks of the Jews, "who are Israelites: to whom belongs the adoption as sons, and the glory and the covenants and the giving of the Law and the temple service and the promises"; and there's more—that's just his description of the Jews in verse 4. Paul does not address his kinsmen according to the flesh by their racial name, but as "Israelites," their theocratic name. The adoption (i.e., sonship; cf. Ex. 4:22–23; Deut. 14:1–2; Hos. 11:1; Mal. 1:6); the glory (which appeared on Mount Sinai, Ex. 24:16–17 and filled the tabernacle, Ex. 40:34–38); the covenants (made to Abraham, Moses, and David); the giving of the Law (the Mosaic constitution); the service of God (the ordinance of worship and sacrifice in the sanctuary, Heb. 9:1–6); and the promises (of forgiveness of sins, of the inheritance of the Promised Land, but most especially of the Messiah, Gal. 3:16) are all further descriptions that indicate the apostle is not talking about the Romans, the Gentiles, the descendants of Ishmael, or anyone other than the children of Jacob—the Jews. The further description of Paul's ethnic kin as "whose are the fathers, and from whom is Christ according to the flesh" (v. 5) is solid proof that the promises of God were not made to the Chinese, the Arabs, the Swedes, or anyone but the Jews.

Divine Sovereignty and Significant Distinctions (9:6–8)

Paul has not forgotten who He is, nor is he confused as to who God is. The apostle is committed to the belief that the promises of God are better than money in the bank; they always come true. The Word of God has not failed with regard to Jehovah's promises to Israel. Why, then, does it appear as if God has turned away from the Jews? The reason is a twofold distinction that must always be made when speaking of God's descendants, the recipients of God's promises. First, "they are not all Israel who are descended from Israel" (v. 6). Is that some sort of apostolic double-talk? No, this distinction is one that Paul has been making throughout his letter to the Romans. The true Jews are those who believe in the God of Abraham and have had their faith imputed to them for righteousness, as was his. This distinction is seen between the lines throughout the New Testament (cf. John 8:31–32). The Lord Jesus spoke of Nathanael as "an Israelite indeed, in whom is no guile!" (John 1:47). Paul speaks of the Israelites as being true Israel when they are "born according to the Spirit" (Gal. 4:29). Thus, since not all who are racially Jewish are descended in faith from Israel, but only those who trust in Israel's God, Paul makes a distinction between those who are descendants of Abraham and those who are descendants of Abraham who exhibit the faith of father Abraham.

But there is a second distinction made in the sovereignty of God with regard to His promises. "Neither are they all children because they are Abraham's descendants" (v. 7). Has Paul lost his mind? Weren't the promises of Jehovah made to all the descendants of Abraham? No. God has always worked on the principle of divine sovereignty. Sovereignly God made a distinction between Abraham's descendants. "Through Isaac your descendants will be named." Being of the seed of Abraham does not make one an Israelite, for Abraham had two sons, Ishmael and Isaac. Only "the children of the promise are regarded as descendants" (v. 8). We must always keep these two distinctions in mind when reading Paul. One wasn't a Jew and heir to God's promises just because he could trace his ancestry to Abraham; only through Abraham's son Isaac were the promises made. And even then one wasn't a faithful Jew and heir to God's promises just because he could trace his ancestry to Abraham through Isaac. He had to have faith in Jehovah, as Abraham did, and have that faith reckoned as righteousness. If it appears that the Word of God has failed the Jews, it is because the Jews have failed the God of their fathers. God still sovereignly declares righteous all who put their faith in Him for salvation.

Sovereignty Exhibited in God's Personal Choices (9:9–13)

Continuing to show that God will keep His promises to provide righteousness to all who believe in Him, Paul notes that God's choices reflect His righteous sovereignty. "For this is a word of promise: 'At this time I will come, and Sarah your wife shall have a son.'" This quotation from Genesis 18:10 aligns with the promise that, although Abraham had fathered a son by Hagar, the handmaiden of Sarah, nevertheless Isaac, the son of Sarah, would be born in fulfillment of a promise that seemed so unlikely that it provoked Sarah to laughter (Gen. 18:12). Still Isaac was born, and although not the firstborn of Abraham, he was God's choice as the son through whom the promises of God would be evidenced. For a good illustration of how God deals on the principle of His divine sovereignty through personal choices, just look at Abraham's two sons, Isaac and Ishmael. God chose Isaac, not Ishmael.

But Paul concedes that someone might say that the example of Isaac is inappropriate because Ishmael was the son of the bondwoman and therefore not truly legitimate. Consequently, he introduces a second example of God's election of grace through personal choices. This time it is Jacob. Had the principle of sovereign election been seen only in the life of Isaac, it would not have produced a biblical pattern. But this principle is seen as well in God's choice of Isaac's sons.

Paul gives the background to the story. "And not only this, but there was Rebekah also, when she had conceived twins by one man, our father Isaac" (v. 10). There is no question that the sons, Jacob and Esau, are both legitimately in the line of Isaac, the promised child. Yet Paul advances that God, by His sovereign personal choice, superseded the process of natural primogeniture-ship[1] and chose Jacob, the younger, to be served by Esau, the elder. The reason for this choice is "in order that God's purpose according to His choice might stand" (v. 11). Every action of God arises out of His eternal purpose (Rom. 8:28). The selection of Jacob to be the heir of the promise instead of his older brother, Esau, is even a better example of the sovereignty of God exhibited in God's personal choices. Jacob was chosen even before he was born, before he could do anything good to win God's election or anything bad to lose it. Salvation is never on the basis of human merit, "not because of works, but because of Him who calls" us to Himself in divine grace.

In case Paul's readers aren't convinced, he appeals to the prophet Malachi and a prophecy with which the Jews were very familiar. "Just as it is written, 'Jacob I loved, but Esau I hated.'" While there are good people who differ on how these words are to be understood,[2] in the context of Malachi 1:1–5, we don't appear to do justice to the context if we believe the expression "Esau I hated" means an innocuous "love less." In that Old Testament passage, God actually directed His wrath toward Esau and his descendants. John Murray comments:

> It can readily be suspected that in the original context, as it pertains to the Edomites (Mal. 1:1–5), the mere absence of love or favour hardly explains the visitations of judgment mentioned: "Esau I hated, and made his mountains a desolation, and gave his heritage to the jackals of the wilderness" (v. 3); "they shall build, but I will throw down; and men shall call them the border of wickedness, and the people against whom the Lord hath indignation for ever" (v. 4). These judgments surely imply disfavour. The indignation is a positive judgment, not merely the absence of blessing. In Scripture God's wrath involves the positive outflow of his displeasure. What we find in Malachi 1:1–5 is illustrated by instances in the Old Testament where God's hatred is mentioned and where either persons or things are the objects (cf. Psalms 5:5; 11:5; Prov. 6:16; 8:13; Is. 1:14; 61:8; Jer. 44:4; Hos. 9:15; Amos 5:21; Zech. 8:17; Mal. 2:16).[3]

Still, God displayed His wrath on the sins of Edom not in unholy rancor but in righteous judgment. He does the same with individuals who sin and do not repent.

Sovereignty Exhibited in God's Powerful Will (9:14–17)

Do you have questions? Paul's readers had plenty, as we do today. To forestall those questions, Paul engages in his usual tactic of asking and answering a question before others have opportunity to do so. When Paul asserted his teaching on the election of God's grace, he was well aware that the objection of many would be embodied in the question, "There is no injustice with God, is there?" (v. 14). Wouldn't God be unrighteous if He chose one man over another? To the human observer, the choice of Jacob in preference to the elder Esau prior to their birth must appear to be arbitrary and unjust. But this is because we as human observers are acting on the basis of limited knowledge. Paul's response to the thought that God could ever be unjust in choosing one over another is the strongest negative he can express, his characteristic, "May it never be!"

Paul answers this potential objection the same way we should learn to answer objections, with the Word of God. Jehovah said, "I will have mercy on whom I have mercy." This divine statement is a quote from Exodus 33:19 and is God's response to Moses' request, "I pray Thee, show me Thy glory!" (Ex. 33:18). Paul quotes this verse without commentary. It needs none. He intends to show that even Moses had no particular claim to any favor with God. God operates on the just principle of His eternal purpose and on that alone. It's the only way He can insure fairness, righteousness, and justice. Paul continues, "So then it does not depend on the man who wills or the man who runs, but on God who has mercy" (v. 16). In a nutshell, that is the principle of salvation. God's mercy finds its cause in Himself and not in any human activity. As in Galatians 2:2 and Philippians 2:16, "running" is symbolic of human activity and has no effect whatsoever on the mercy or purpose of God. Salvation is not won like a race; it is awarded on the basis of God's sovereign grace.

> I declared the former things long ago
> And they went forth from My mouth, and I proclaimed them.
> Suddenly I acted, and they came to pass. (Is. 48:3)

More doctrine requires more illustration, and Paul goes back to the Bible to prove that God always has operated on the basis of His sovereign personal choices. He says, "For the Scripture says to Pharaoh" (v. 17). The case of the pharaoh of the Exodus strikingly illustrates this principle of divine mercy. Pharaoh is said to have been raised up by God that Jehovah could demonstrate His power in the Egyptian ruler and "that My name might be proclaimed throughout the whole earth" (v. 17). Both goals of God were accomplished well. Not even the power of the great Egyptian pharaoh was sufficient to thwart the eternal purpose of God or to prohibit Him from blessing and delivering His people. The Scripture Paul quotes is Exodus 9:16, where the

Hebrew verb *amadth,* meaning "stand," is used for the expression "I raised you up." God put Pharaoh in a position of being the Egyptian king. He also preserved him there in spite of his disobedience so that God's purpose might be fulfilled. The purpose was that His name might be declared throughout the earth (cf. Ex. 15:14; Josh. 2:10; 9:9; 1 Sam. 4:7–9). Who doesn't know the story of the Exodus and the parting of the Red Sea? The whole world knows what God did that day.

Common Objections to God's Sovereignty

If God is sovereign, how can He find fault with people?
Answer: "Does not the potter have a right over the clay?" (Rom. 9:21).

People are the masters of their own lives.
Answer: "You ought to say, 'If the Lord wills, we shall live and also do this or that'" (James 4:15).

People die simply by accident.
Answer: Man's days are determined and numbered; God sets limits so that man cannot pass beyond those days (Job 14:5).

God does not force Himself upon people; they can do what they want to do.
Answer: No one can be delivered from God's hand; He acts and no one can reverse His decisions (Is. 43:13).

Mother Nature is in charge of natural events, not God.
Answer: God sets a limit for the rain, a course for the thunderbolt (Job 28:26).

God is not involved in the affairs of history.
Answer: God makes the nations great, then destroys them (Job 12:23).

God does not determine all future events.
Answer: God declares the end from the beginning, from ancient times things that have not been done (Is. 46:10).

God does not see everything people do. Their actions are hidden from the Lord.
Answer: "The eyes of the LORD are in every place, watching the evil and the good" (Prov. 15:3).

Divine Sovereignty Exhibited in Divine Actions (9:18–24)

Again Paul quotes from the Old Testament to teach truth to New Testament believers. "So then He has mercy on whom He desires, and He hardens whom He desires" (v. 18). The initial phrase of this verse echoes Exodus 33:19, but the latter phrase refers to the occasions on which Pharaoh's heart was hardened. It must be recognized that Pharaoh hardened his own heart (cf. Ex. 5:2; 7:13) by his deliberate opposition to the will of the God of Israel. A time came, however, when he was judicially bound over in hardness by God, and the initial indifference of Pharaoh's heart was cemented by God into a permanent hardness (cf. Ex. 7:23; 9:12; 10:1, 20, 27; 11:10; 14:4, 8). That begs the question, "Why does He still find fault? For who resists His will?" (v. 19). Paul knows there will be objections to the idea that God purposefully hardened Pharaoh's heart. Even those who love God dearly will believe that you cannot find fault with a sinner for acting the way God made him. Some will say, "If God is sovereign, and He is, and it is impossible to resist His will, and it is, humans are not accountable for their lost condition." Although there is a fallacy in this type of reasoning (God did not make humans the way they are; He created them in His own image, and humans are what they are today because of their own sin), Paul does not argue that point. Rather, in reply he quotes Scripture: "On the contrary, who are you, O man, who answers back to God?" (v. 20). The apostle knows that the creatures God created are not competent to sit in judgment on their Creator. To judge the validity of God's actions is to imply that humans are more righteous than God; to judge the wisdom of God's movements is to imply that humans are wiser than God. Neither is true, and thus Paul sternly rebukes any type of reasoning that inverts the divine order of creature to Creator. "The thing molded will not say to the molder, 'Why did you make me like this,' will it?" (v. 20). God is not answerable to humans for what He does, but He is answerable to something much higher than the moral aptitude of humankind. God must act consistent with His own character, and that's the safeguard of sovereignty. Divine sovereignty does not permit God to do what divine character will not allow. If we can trust the character of God, we can trust the wisdom of His sovereignty as well, even if we do not always understand.

The apostle now engages in a bit of philosophical argumentation. "Or does not the potter have a right over the clay, to make from the same lump one vessel for honorable use, and another for common use?" (v. 21). The implied answer is yes, so Paul continues. "What if God, although willing to demonstrate His wrath and to make His power known, endured with much patience vessels of wrath prepared for destruction?" (v. 22). Such a question demands a reasonable answer. Here Paul argues that the justice and grace of God are displayed in humans, both through the persistent unbeliever (whom he calls a vessel prepared for wrath) and through the believer (a vessel of mercy). Notice that Paul does not say God created one vessel for wrath and another for mercy. It says He endured the vessels of wrath that were prepared for destruction. The expression "fitted for destruction" is in the Greek middle voice and should be interpreted "man fits himself for destruction." On the other hand are those who were prepared by the grace of God through faith in His Son for eternal life. With a thankful heart, Paul notes that God has sovereignly called to glory those of the Jews and also those of the Gentiles. As believers, whether Jews or Gentiles, we have been the recipients of God's mercy and have been prepared for the glory of His presence. For this we should be eternally thankful.

Sovereignty Exhibited in Israel's Partial Blindness (9:25–29)

Paul now appeals to a number of Old Testament prophecies concerning God's people and the principle of divine election. He paraphrases Hosea 2:23, "I will call those who were not My people, 'My people.' And her who was not beloved, 'beloved'" (v. 25). In the tragedy of his domestic life, this Old Testament man of God saw a parable of the relationship between God and Israel. Hosea took Gomer to be his wife, and a child was born which he named Jezreel. But when Gomer's second and third children were born, of whom Hosea was not convinced he was the father, names were given that expressed his dismay. They were named in Hebrew, Lo-ammi ("no kin of mine") and Lo-ruhamah ("one for whom no natural affection is felt"). These names strikingly indicate God's attitude toward His people Israel when they broke their covenant with Him and forsook His commands. "And it shall be that in the place where it was said to them, 'You are not My people,' there they shall be called sons of the living God" (v. 26). Paul does not make an application here to the prophecy of Hosea, but it is evident that he is extracting from this prophecy the principle of divine election. He shows that great numbers of Gentiles, who had never been "the people of God," could now lay claim to the same relationship with God that Israel had by faith in the promises of God.

Next Paul appeals to the prophecy of Isaiah 10:22–23. The meaning of Isaiah's prophecy is that although Israel was numerous as a people, nevertheless only a small minority would survive the judgment of God by the Assyrian empire. Tragic as that is, if only a remnant of Israel would survive, there would still at least be a remnant. God has always had a people. Paul applies Isaiah's teaching of the remnant principle to his own day. Although Israel rejected God due to spiritual blindness and hardness of heart, nevertheless, there are some who, through the grace of God, have received salvation. The spiritual blindness of God's chosen people is only partial, not total. Thus verse 28 indicates that the punitive judgment of God on His people who have rejected Him will exhibit both thoroughness and great dispatch. God will cut short His working on the earth to prevent Israel from spiritually destroying itself. Yes, Israel is blind, but not entirely. Yes, Israel will destroy herself spiritually, but not entirely. In His eternal purpose, God will preserve a remnant. It has always been that way. "Except the Lord of Sabaoth had left to us a posterity, we would have become as Sodom, and would have resembled Gomorrah" (v. 29). This quote from Isaiah 1:9 reveals that Isaiah attributed solely to the grace of God the fact that a posterity (i.e., a remnant, the very germ of the nation) had been saved and they had not been obliterated like Sodom and Gomorrah. To the Lord of Hosts alone belongs the praise for the salvation of any of the wicked Israelites. It is God's sovereignty that keeps Him from destroying Israel for its unbelief just as it is God's sovereignty that draws us to Him in salvation and belief.

Final Questions and Conclusions (9:30–33)

Paul's summary question in this chapter follows the same form as we have seen elsewhere in this epistle (cf. 3:5; 4:1; 6:1; 7:7; 8:31; 9:14). "That Gentiles, who did not pursue righteousness, attained righteousness, even the righteousness which is by faith; but Israel, pursuing a law of righteousness, did not arrive at that law" (vv. 30–31). This is a summary of Paul's teaching in this chapter that is all about God's sovereignty and divine choices. God has always saved on the basis of faith and never on the basis of good works. Therefore Gentiles can come to the Savior and follow the path to righteousness, which is the path of faith, even without the privileges of the Jews. The Jews, on the other hand, who had great privileges and knew well the Old Testament Scriptures, tragically attempted to establish their own righteousness by adherence to the works of the Mosaic Law. Consequently, Paul concludes that the partial blindness of Israel exhibits God's sovereignty in allowing those who were most distant from Himself (the Gentiles) to come unto Him by faith.

How could what Paul has just described possibly happen to Paul's kinsmen? The Jews sought God's righteousness, but they sought it in the wrong place. Instead of having the faith of their father Abraham, they attempted to secure righteousness by meticulously adhering to the works of the Law. The result was that the chosen people of God became a spiritual Humpty Dumpty—they had a great fall just as it was written: "Behold, I lay in Zion a stone of stumbling and a rock of offense, and he who believes in Him will not be disappointed" (v. 33). The great tragedy of the Jewish nation was that the Messiah they so long awaited became to them a stumbling stone rather than a shelter in which to hide. The quotation here is from Isaiah 28:16, which is set in the context of Israel trusting Egypt for deliverance from the Assyrians instead of trusting in the power of God. Those who trust in God need never fear that their trust has been ill-placed or is ill-founded. Whoever believes on Him will not be disappointed (Is. 28:16; Rom 10:11). Had Israel trusted in their God rather than their Law and their neighbors, they would not have been defeated and dispersed throughout the world.

As bad as that dispersion was for the chosen people of God, it was good for the rest of the world. The partial blindness of Israel, in the eternal purpose of God, has opened the door of God's grace to those who are not the chosen people of God. God is now calling out a people for His name from both Jews and Gentiles, and this too is His sovereign choice. If we learn anything from the ninth chapter of Romans, it must be that God has always, and will always, operate out of His eternal purpose, which is unchanging. And it is His purpose that gives rise to His sovereign choices, and His sovereign choices are demonstrated in His sovereign actions. God is sovereign and is willing to demonstrate that sovereignty, not when we demand it, but when He sovereignly wills it.

Study Questions

1. From Romans 9:4–5, what spiritual advantage did the Jews have over the Gentiles?

2. Why does Paul use Pharaoh as an illustration in this chapter?

3. Is God unjust and unfair in His sovereign "molding" and election?

4. What does the apostle have in mind when he speaks of a Jewish remnant?

5. From verses 30–33, list the ways the Jewish people fell short of obtaining salvation.

CHAPTER 21

Human Responsibility and Israel's Present
Romans 10:1–21

Preview:

Though people may not know of God's righteousness apart from His Word, they are still responsible their sin and for attempting to establish their own right-eousness! Human beings have to turn from their ways, confess Christ, and turn to Him. Those who call on the Lord will be saved. The Lord uses people to carry the good tidings of salvation. Despite the blindness that sin brings, God stands waiting for both Jews and Gentiles to turn to Him.

The groundwork for chapter 10 has already been laid in 9:30–33. The emphasis here is on righteousness and why Israel lacks it. Paul will lay the responsibility for the lack of righteousness squarely on the shoulders of individuals. He knows that when sinners are brought into the presence of divine sovereignty, their frequent response is to justify themselves by placing the responsibility for their sin on God. Paul does not apologize in any way for what he has said about God's sovereignty in chapter 9. He does not retreat at all from his strong belief that God has always worked by the principle of divine election. He does demonstrate, however, that God is not responsible for unbelievers' lost condition. Humans alone are responsible, and it is futile to try to hide behind divine sovereignty and the doctrine of election as an excuse for personal sin.

The Opportunity for Personal Responsibility (10:1–10)

It's déjà vu all over again. As we've seen on other occasions, most recently in the last chapter, Paul sympathetically expresses his deep compassion and concern for the Jewish people. "Brethren, my heart's desire and my prayer to God for them is for their salvation" (v. 1). Even though Paul is the apostle to the Gentiles, he takes no satisfaction in Israel's rejection of God. He bears personal testimony from his own life to the fact that the Jews have a definite zeal for God. Paul himself had had such zeal (Acts 9:1–3; Phil. 3:6), but like his former zeal, the Jewish zeal for God was an ill-informed zeal. The problem with the Jews was that their improper motives caused them to have a zeal for keeping the Law but not for being the nation God would have them to be. They read and memorized the Law, they dissected its truth and catalogued its teachings, but they never internalized the truth of God's Law. Thus, instead of accepting the gift of God's righteousness by faith as Abraham had done, they set out to establish their own righteousness by assiduously keeping the Law. In so doing, "they did not subject themselves to the righteousness of God" (v. 3). Any attempt to establish one's own righteousness is open rebellion against God and His method of imputing righteousness to us. This brought Paul great grief, for he truly desired to see His people submit to the righteousness of God in faith, but most did not.

Here's what the Jews missed: "For Christ is the end of the law for righteousness to everyone who believes" (v. 4). Take note of the "everyones" and "whoevers" in this chapter. It clearly is speaking about the worldwide opportunity for people to have faith in Christ as Savior and Lord. But in what respect is Christ the end (Greek, *telos*) of the law, any law, whether the Mosaic Law, the Levitical law, or the law of the jungle? The word may indicate, on the one hand, that Christ is the goal or purpose for which law was established. In this respect it would mean that the Mosaic Law was aimed at bringing us to Christ but lacked the power to do so. Hence Jesus came to fulfill that Law and thereby give it validity (cf. Is. 42:21; Matt. 5:17). On the other hand, this word may properly mean that Christ is the terminal point of all law. With the advent of the Lord Jesus, the old order, of which the law was a significant part, was done away with, and the new order of the Holy Spirit of God was instituted. Either understanding is appropriate, because both are true. There is, however, one qualification to Christ being the goal or terminal point of law, one qualification for receiving God's righteousness. Jesus Christ is only the end "to everyone who believes." Those who attempt to establish their own righteousness do not find Christ as the end of the Mosaic Law or any other law and consequently do not discover true righteousness. They are left with self-righteousness and thus are left with nothing.

The antithesis seen in verses 3 and 4 between self-established righteousness and God-established righteousness is now alluded to as recorded by Moses. Moses speaks both of the righteousness that is of law and of the righteousness that is of faith. For the righteousness based on law, Paul quotes Leviticus 18:5, "that the man who practices the righteousness which is based on law shall live by that righteousness" (v. 5). Any person who lives by any law is subject to the outcome of that law, and since keeping any law will not generate righteousness, the man or woman who lives by the law in order to produce righteousness will be left disappointed. In reference to Moses' teaching concerning the righteousness that is of faith, the apostle quotes Deuteronomy 30:12, 14, "Do not say in your heart, 'Who will ascend into heaven?'" (v. 6). The righteousness that is the desired end of the Law taught people to *do* and live. But the righteousness that is by faith teaches people to *believe* and live (v. 6). The Pentateuch clearly shows that the Law was to be written on the hearts of people. It was not to be an external means of external justification. Unfortunately, the Jews mistakenly perverted the Law and were attempting to keep the Law outwardly without the right inward heart attitude.

Throughout this passage, Paul is interested in establishing the accessibility of the message of God's righteousness. The gospel is available to everyone, even the Jews who have decided to reject Jesus and therefore reject the gospel. Thus, "Do not say in your heart, 'Who will ascend into heaven?' (that is, to bring Christ down), appears to be something of a taunt. The Jew feels the righteousness of God is inaccessible because no one can ascend into heaven to inquire about it. Paul teaches, however, that we do not have to ascend into heaven, because God came down from heaven and lived among us in the person of Jesus Christ, to demonstrate for us the righteousness of God. Similarly he asks, "'Who will descend into the abyss?' (that is, to bring Christ up from the dead)" (v. 7). Again, there is a taunt of unbelief. This smacks of a denial of the resurrection of Christ. We do not need to descend into the abyss to learn of God's righteousness, for Christ is living proof of that righteousness. So having proof is not the requirement for righteousness; having faith is.

In putting an end to these foolish questions, the apostle quotes Deuteronomy 30:14, "But the word is very near you, in your mouth and in your heart, that you may observe it." Paul maintains that the true word concerning the righteousness of God was always very near the Jews. He even goes so far as to say that it was in their mouths and in their hearts. But how can this be? One answer is that when entering a town to preach, Paul immediately proceeded to the synagogue. Whether the Jews believed his message or not, when he left they remained behind to discuss what Paul had taught. The very message of the gospel of Christ was in their mouths and in their hearts, but they did not believe. The truth of righteousness was as close to them as it could possibly be, but they failed in their responsibility to receive that truth by faith. So the apostle tells them what they must do with their mouths: "If you confess with your mouth Jesus as Lord" (v. 9). Paul builds on what the Jews had when he explains that the confession "Jesus is Lord" refers to the authority Jesus exercises as the resurrected and exalted Christ. The Jews, and everyone else, had failed to understand the truth that reading, memorizing, or scrutinizing the Word was no substitute for believing the Word. If they were to believe the Word of God, they would come to confess that Jesus was the long-awaited Messiah and Lord. Salvation must entail, not just faith, but faith in One who is Lord. Confession of the lordship of Christ presupposes His incarnation, death, and resurrection. Jesus is not just another way to God; He is the only way to God. The apostle goes on to say that in order to be saved one must believe in his or her heart that God has raised Jesus from the dead. The only faith that saves is faith in the resurrected Lord. New life for the believer is contingent upon having a living Lord.

How Responsible Are People for Their Unbelief?

The Jews have a zeal for God. Is that not enough?
Answer: Their zeal is not according to truth, or biblical "knowledge" (Rom. 10:2).

The Jews do not know about God's righteousness. Are they not then faultless?
Answer: They refuse to submit themselves to God's righteousness (v. 3).

Is not God prejudiced against the Jews, favoring the Gentiles?
Answer: Whoever calls upon the name of the Lord will be saved (v. 13).

If people cannot hear the truth, are they still responsible?
Answer: The ends of the earth have heard! (v. 18).

Is the witness of nature enough to make people responsible before God?
Answer: In nature people can see the power and divine nature of God so that they are without excuse (1:20).

Token intellectual assent that Jesus is Lord and that He rose from the dead is never sufficient for salvation. Paul explains, "For with the heart man believes, resulting in righteousness" (v. 10). Belief in the saving power of the risen Christ must come from the innermost part of a person's being. But more than that, Paul says, "With the mouth he confesses, resulting in salvation" (v. 10).

Confession with the mouth is evidence of genuine faith in the heart. It is not an addition to faith; it is the response of faith. Frequently both our Lord and the apostle Paul indicate the coordination of faith and a confession (cf. Luke 12:8; 1 Tim. 6:12). Confession with the mouth does not bring about genuineness of belief in the heart; rather, it is the natural response to the saving work of Christ and gives evidence to it like nothing else. The opportunity both to believe and confess is available to all.

The Basis for Personal Responsibility (10:11–15)

Having established opportunity, like a criminal lawyer Paul now moves on to establish responsibility. Saying, "For the Scripture says . . . ," is Paul's customary habit, as he appeals to Scripture to validate his teaching. Here he again alludes to Isaiah 28:16 when he says, "Whoever believes in Him will not be disappointed" (from *kataischunō,* literally meaning "to disgrace or be put to shame"). The key element in salvation is again seen to be faith. Salvation is not appropriated to the sinner's life until he or she has a heart-felt belief in the Lord Jesus. But just as the gospel is near to all—Jew and Gentile—likewise it is offered to all. The word "whoever" is used to indicate the universality of God's offer of salvation (v. 11): "for there is no distinction between Jew and Greek" (v. 12). The immediate purpose of the universal offer of salvation is to show Jews that it is possible for Gentiles to be saved. God's prerequisite to salvation is faith, not racial distinction. Therefore the call to salvation is to whoever will believe, whether Jew or Gentile. The reason is that "the same Lord is Lord of all, abounding in riches for all who call upon Him" (v. 12). How is God rich to all of us? He is rich to all in His mercy, grace, love, sovereignty, and all the other attributes of God that make Him God. He is rich to all of us by devising a plan for our rescue from sin even before the worlds were created, long before we sinned (Eph. 1:3–7). He is rich to all of us by giving opportunity for us to hear the gospel when we turned our backs on Him in disobedience because of our sin. The Lord God is rich in His attitude toward all sinners and ready to receive anyone who calls on Him for salvation. But the responsibility to call on the Lord in salvation is ours.

"Whoever will call upon the name of the Lord will be saved" (v. 13). Paul restates his belief that the gospel is offered to all by quoting the prophet Joel (Joel 2:32). The expression "call upon the name of the Lord" is a common Old Testament expression of worship to God (cf. Gen. 4:26; 12:8; 1 Kin. 18:24; Ps. 79:6; Is. 64:7). Paul's application of this formula to Christ is another example of his practice of taking Old Testament passages that refer to God the Father and, without any qualification whatever, applying them to Christ.

Thus, in the New Testament, sinners are advised to call upon the name of the Lord Jesus Christ for salvation (cf. Acts 9:14, 21; 22:16; 1 Cor. 1:2; 2 Tim. 2:22). As C. K. Barrett explains, "'Calling upon the name of the Lord' is far more than knowing how to use the right religious formula; it means trusting the one whose name you invoke, looking to him for salvation. But faith is a big thing, not to be exercised lightly; it can exist only in terms of personal relationship."[1] The basis for human responsibility in salvation arises out of the fact that the gospel is offered to all, irrespective of national heritage, and therefore all are responsible to respond to that offer. If we fail to respond to the offer, our failure is itself a response. Remember the words of Jesus:

> For God so loved the world, that He gave His only begotten Son, that whoever believes in Him shall not perish, but have eternal life. For God did not send the Son into the world to judge the world, but that the world should be saved through Him. He who believes in Him is not judged; he who does not believe has been judged already, because he has not believed in the name of the only begotten Son of God." (John 3:16–18)

Failure to believe in Jesus as Savior is an active choice not to believe in Him as Savior, and it automatically brings God's judgment.

Paul now gives a rationale for his responsibility to present the gospel worldwide. People are told that they must call upon the name of the Lord to be saved. However, they will not call on Him unless they have been moved to believe in Him, and they cannot believe in Him unless they have heard about Him. Furthermore, they cannot hear about Him unless the good news of the gospel has been brought to them. And the gospel message will not be taken to them until someone has been sent to them. Consequently, salvation begins with God's sending process. Isaiah was asked the double question, "Whom shall I send, and who will go for Us?" Isaiah's answer was classic: "Here am I. Send me!" (Is. 6:8). Isaiah was willing to go with the message, but he could not go until he was sent by God. But God has not been derelict in His sending duties. Jesus said to His disciples, "As the Father has sent Me, I also send you" (John 20:21). He told those gathered in Jerusalem on the Day of Pentecost, "You shall be My witnesses both in Jerusalem, and in all Judea and Samaria, and even to the remotest part of the earth" (Acts 1:8). The last command of Christ recorded in the Gospel of Matthew is, "Go therefore and make disciples of all the nations" (Matt. 28:19). The Lord's words are plain and irrefutable: "Go into all the world and preach the gospel to all creation" (Mark 16:15). God's sending part of the great commission is complete; now our going and discipling part needs to become complete. We must proclaim the gospel message in every nook and cranny of the globe because we are commissioned to do so, and, as Paul asks, "How shall they believe in Him whom they have not heard?" (v. 14).

Paul concludes this portion of his argument with a quote from Isaiah 52:7: "How beautiful are the feet of those who bring glad tidings[2] of good things!" (v. 15). Martin Luther explains:

> The word "beautiful" stands for purity, for they (that preach the gospel of peace and bring glad tidings of good things) do not proclaim the Gospel for their own advantage or on account of vain glory, as this happens here and there today. They preach solely from obedience to God and for the sake of the salvation of their hearers. But the Hebrew word means also what is lovely and pleasant. Therefore the meaning of the expression is: "For those who are under the Law, the message of the Gospel is lovely and desirable." The Law indeed reveals sin, makes the sinner guilty, and fills his conscience with fear; the Gospel, however proclaims to those who have been terrified the desired healing.[3]

These words were originally intended by the prophet to describe those who carried the good news home to Jerusalem that the days of Babylonian exile were passed. But in the context of the New Testament, these words indicate that the feet of a gospel messenger are beautiful to those who believe the message and place their faith in the Lord Jesus and become new creations in Christ Jesus (2 Cor. 5:17). This may happen to any man, woman, boy, or girl who hears the gospel and believes, but the responsibility for believing is clearly the individual's. God devised salvation's plan; Jesus brought it down to man; now the ball is in our court, so to speak, and we are responsible to respond to God's good news of salvation in Christ.

The Failure of Personal Responsibility (10:16–21)

Paul now comes to the crux of his argument concerning human responsibility and the righteousness of God. He claims that God takes the responsibility for Jewish unbelief and places it squarely on the shoulders of the Jews. The gospel has been near them, it has been offered to them, but it has not been believed by them. As proof of this, he again quotes from the Jews' own Scripture as recorded in Isaiah 53:1, "Lord, who has believed our report?" (v. 16). The report was Isaiah's message of the gospel concerning the Messiah. It was brought to the mouths of the Jews and offered to them, but that message was not received. So it was faith that was absent, not opportunity. It was faith the Jews lacked, not knowledge. "Faith comes from hearing, and hearing by the word of Christ" (v. 17).[4] The word translated "report" (Greek, *akoē*) in verse 16 is the same word in the original language as that translated "hearing" in verse 17. We must understand that hearing alone does not bring salvation, but faith in the message heard does. The immoral Gentile is not saved by looking at a tree and conceptualizing a god-form represented in that tree. The moral person is not saved by leading a moral lifestyle. Salvation comes when the message of the gospel is preached, believed, and then confessed. And that message is found in only one place—the Word of God. You may read the great works of literature and not be saved. You may read the Quran and remain in your sins. But when you read the Word of God, the Bible, and believe what it says about Jesus, that's when faith is credited to your account as righteousness.

In typical Pauline style, the apostle anticipates an objection from his Jewish readers. Is it not possible that some of his Jewish brethren have not heard the message of the gospel? (v. 19). Could it be that somehow the message didn't reach their ears? Paul first uses the language of Psalm 19 to remind them of the testimony of the stars and the heavens. "Their voice has gone out into all the earth, and their words to the ends of the world" (v. 18). There is not a place on this planet where the message of God's creation does not eloquently speak of Him. That was Paul's argument in the first chapter of this letter (1:19–20). Then he returns to the evidence of history by quoting Moses in Deuteronomy 32:21 to prove that the Gentiles believed what they saw of God in the universe and the witness of their own conscience. Why not the Jews? Finally, Paul very convincingly turns to the greatest of the Jewish prophets and quotes Isaiah 65:1: "Isaiah is very bold and says, 'I was found by those who sought me not, I became manifest to those who did not ask for Me'" (v. 20). The prophet's statement is very bold because he utterly rules out any merit or privilege on the part of the Jews and says that the Gentiles, who had been indifferent to God, would someday have the gospel preached to them and would come to a knowledge of God. Then, in a startling interpretation of history, Paul proclaims that this is that day, and the gospel is open to anyone who believes in Jesus Christ.

It's time for a conclusion. Has there been opportunity for the entire world to know something of God and be led to faith in Christ? Yes. Has that opportunity been true for the Jew? Yes, it has. And has the message gone out to the entire world so people could hear the words of the gospel, think about them, analyze them, and discuss them? Yes, the message has gone out. And has this been true for the Jew? Yes, it has. So if the message was heard, what's the problem? It has not been believed. Was this true of the Jew? Yes, it was imminently true of the Jew. So who is responsible that the message has not been believed? Certainly God is not responsible. The individual—Jew and Gentile—is responsible. Paul places the blame on men and women for lacking faith, not on God for denying them opportunity. He rests his case with a final quote from Isaiah 65:2: "All the day long I have stretched out My hands to a disobedient and obstinate people" (v. 21). The Lord God has patiently dealt with Israel throughout history ("all the day long"), but God's chosen people have been disobedient to His love. Each of us is responsible for the guilt we bear if we snub God's love and reject His Son as Savior. What's true for the Gentile is also true for the Jew. God has loved the Jewish people with an everlasting love (Jer. 31:3), but Israel is guilty of spurning that love and is therefore responsible for God's judgment in their future.

Study Questions

1. How is Christ the end of the law to everyone who believes?

2. What does the apostle have in mind when he writes, "Who will ascend into heaven? ... to bring Christ down"?

3. How many times does Paul mention the terms *faith* and *believe* in this chapter?

4. How does this chapter drive home human responsibility?

5. Is it possible to reconcile God's sovereignty with human responsibility? Give your own thoughts.

CHAPTER 22

The Purpose of God and Israel's Future
Romans 11:1–36

Preview:

Though the Jews do not believe in Christ, God still has a remnant who trust Him as Savior. And though the Jews are God's natural branches, they have only temporarily been broken off of the tree of blessing. Gentiles have been grafted into that tree but will someday be broken off and judged. When God has completed His work with the Gentiles, the Jews will again come into favor and receive Christ the Deliverer as their Savior. All things will work for the glory of God!

It would be hard to overstate Paul's concern that the Jewish believers of his day not believe that God had rejected His chosen people in favor of the Gentiles. This was especially true because Gentiles, at that moment in history, were coming to Christ in swarms. Paul belabors this point: Just because God has turned His loving attention to the Gentiles does not in any way mean He is no longer interested in the Jews. Not in the least. The theme of God's rejection of the Jews being only partial and not total is not new. In chapter 9 Paul demonstrated that God's rejection of His people was not complete: A remnant had received God's salvation. And in chapter 10 Paul demonstrated that God's rejection was not arbitrary: Every Jew had been given an opportunity to believe as much as every Gentile. But still the question lingers in the minds of many Jews: "Did God really cast away His people whom He loved with an everlasting love?" (see Jer. 31:3). Did Jehovah forsake His promise to His beloved?

John Calvin commented:

What he has hitherto said of the blindness and obstinacy of the Jews, might seem to import that Christ at his coming had transferred elsewhere the promises of God, and deprived the Jews of every hope of salvation. This objection is what he anticipates in the passage, and he so modifies what he had previously said respecting the repudiation of the Jews, that no one might think that the covenant formerly made with Abraham is now abrogated, or that God had so forgotten if that the Jews were now so entirely alienated from his kingdom, as the Gentiles were before the coming of Christ. All this he denies, and he will presently show that it is altogether false. But the question is not whether God had justly or unjustly rejected the people; for it was proved in the last chapter that when the people, through false zeal, had rejected the righteousness of God, they suffered a just punishment for their presumption, were deservedly blinded, and were at last cut off from the covenant.[1]

Israel's Rejection Leaves a Remnant (11:1-6)

To the question, "God has not rejected His people, has He?" (v. 1), comes Paul's now expected response, "May it never be!" The problem of the unbelief of Israel as a "disobedient and obstinate people" was prevalent in chapters 9 and 10. Paul now anticipates this theme will cause the Jews to wonder if God is finished with Israel as a nation. Thus he frames his question in Greek in such away as to require the answer "No" and then gives several lines of proof.

As exhibit A that God has not totally rejected His people, Paul offers himself. He says, "For I too am an Israelite, a descendant of Abraham, of the tribe of Benjamin" (v. 1). There are two views why Paul offers this biographical material, but the most probable one (which may boast exponents in Luther, Calvin, Hodge, Godet, and others) is that Paul is appealing to his own salvation as proof that God has not completely abandoned Israel. Paul was enjoying the promises of God, and as long as he did, he offered a living example of God's continuing relationship to Israel. As exhibit B, Paul now offers the faithfulness of God. "God has not rejected His people whom He foreknew" (v. 2). God's foreknowledge is the guarantee that He has not cast off His people. Had He done so, it would mean a revocation of God's promises to Abraham, Moses, David, and others that guaranteed to them an ultimate restoration of the seed of Abraham.

And as exhibit C, the apostle offers an Old Testament quotation. The reference is to 1 Kings 19:10, 14, where Elijah is the speaker, "Lord, they have killed Thy prophets, they have torn down Thine altars, and I alone am left, and they are seeking my life" (v. 3). Although Israel often fell into a state of apostasy, God always preserved a remnant of true believers. The Northern Kingdom in Elijah's day had grossly violated its covenant relationship with God and had slain His prophets. So bleak was the situation that Elijah felt he was the only believer left. Paul reminds his readers, "But what is the divine response to him?" (v. 4).

The Greek expression for "response" is *chrēmatismos*, which is used of a divine reply. To his question, Elijah received a divine and therefore certain response: "I have kept for Myself seven thousand men who have not bowed the knee to Baal" (v. 4). The presence of a remnant of believers in the Northern Kingdom meant that God would preserve that kingdom. He did so for another 130 years. Even after the Assyrian captivity, a few believing Israelites from the ten tribes returned to form the nucleus of the Hebrew population in Galilee.

Having presented three lines of evidence to support his answer to the question "God has not rejected His people, has He?" Paul now draws a conclusion. It is utterly ridiculous to think that the nation Israel has been entirely rejected by God, for even at the present time, there is a remnant according to the election of grace. This faithful remnant is not saved by their line of descent, nor by personal righteousness, but upon the same ground that Gentiles are saved—by the grace of God. No claim to special merit can be made even by this remnant (v. 5). "But if it is by grace, it is no longer on the basis of works, otherwise grace is no longer grace" (v. 6). A priori grace cannot include works. They are mutually exclusive. If works are to be added to grace, as the Jews thought, then grace is completely canceled out. Salvation is a free gift, and no payment at all can be made, or it would cease to be free.

The Spirit of Stupor (11:7–10)

Paul continues his questions and observations: "What then? That which Israel is seeking for, it has not obtained, but those who were chosen obtained it, and the rest were hardened" (v. 7). What was Israel seeking for? Righteousness. Chapter 10 indicates that while seeking to establish their own righteousness, the Jews did not recognize the divine method of imputed righteousness. It was their own fault that they did not receive what they were seeking, for they were seeking it by works and not by faith. The remnant, however, did obtain the righteousness of God through the grace of God. The rest of national Israel has become hardened, that is, spiritually blinded (v. 7). The Greek verb *pōroō*, which is used for "hardened," means "to render insensitive." Because they didn't seek the righteousness of God, the rest of Israel became insensitive to God. Such moral insensitivity was the judicial penalty inflicted on them for their refusal to heed God's word. Further, "God gave them a spirit of stupor" (v. 8). This quote from Deuteronomy 29:4 and Isaiah 29:10 gives reference to the unseeing eyes and unhearing ears of those who refuse to recognize the truth of God. Each of the gospel writers used this expression to indicate the Jews' failure to recognize Jesus as the Messiah (cf. Matt. 13:14; Mark 4:12; Luke 8:10; John 12:40). The spirit of stupor literally means the spirit of stinging. The word (Greek, *katanuxis*) is used of the numbness that is the result of a bite or poisonous sting. Israel had refused to seek righteousness in God's way and had attempted to establish their own righteousness in their own way. Thus God hardened them in a blinding stupor and poisoning insensitivity toward the truth of God. They have "eyes to see not and ears to hear not, down to this very day" (v. 8).

Paul adds one more Old Testament testimony before moving on. "And David says, 'Let their table become a snare and a trap, and a stumbling block and a retribution to them. Let their eyes be darkened to see not, and bend their backs forever'" (vv. 9–10). The words "snare," "stumbling block," and "retribution" are closely related. Their combination serves to enforce the turning of the table to its opposite intent. The table is indicative of the bountiful mercy and blessing of God to Israel. Israel has not eaten of the good things of God's table. The recurring motif of the unseeing eyes indicates the principle that the temporary "blindness" has overtaken all of Israel, with the exception of the believing remnant. Thus the application is clear. Those who seek their own righteousness must bend their backs to the bondage of sin. But those who seek the righteousness of Christ and receive it by grace become a part of the believing remnant of God.

Israel's Rejection Is Not Permanent (11:11–15)

But the apostle is not just the bearer of bad news; he has good news too. Again Paul introduces his thought with a question and his reply of abhorrence. "I say then, they did not stumble so as to fall, did they? May it never be!" (v. 11). And Paul is quick to continue, "But by their transgression salvation has come to the Gentiles, to make them jealous." One of the purposes of the fall of the Jewish nation, in the eyes of God, is that the Gentile nations may come to Him in salvation. In return this will provoke the Jews to jealousy, as was suggested in Romans 10:19 where Deuteronomy 32:21 was quoted. When the Jews see the Gentiles feasting on bread from the banquet table of God and enjoying the salvation that could have been theirs, they will be convinced of their apostasy and foolish rejection of Jesus as their Messiah. If, however, the fall of the Jews brings the riches of salvation to the world, how much more their fulfillment, or large-scale conversion, will bring riches to the Gentile nations and glory to God (v. 12). Thus Paul begins to lay the groundwork for the proof that Israel's rejection is not permanent. The Jews will be restored to God.

The apostle now addresses the Gentiles directly in response to the antici-pated question: "Paul, as the apostle to the Gentiles, why are you so con-cerned about the salvation of Jews?" Paul's answer reflects both his conviction concerning his divine calling and the compassion he has for his own people. He magnifies his office in that the salvation of the Gentiles will provoke the Jews to jealousy and bring them to salvation as well. The swelling of the ranks of true believers among Paul's own countrymen will cause the swelling of the ranks among the Gentiles, and the apostle's ministry will then be greater. "For if their rejection be the reconciliation of the world, what will their acceptance be but life from the dead?" (v. 15). The "acceptance" is being contrasted with the "rejection." The rejected Messiah of Israel was taken by them to the cross, and there He reconciled the world to Himself.

Question: If Israel's blindness brought salvation to the Gentile world, what will God's renewal of Israel's faith bring? Answer: The ultimate reception of a repentant Israel will bring revival on an unprecedented scale. We may expect to see a mighty evangelistic movement in the last days that will be char-acterized by large numbers of Jews coming to receive Jesus Christ as their Messiah and Savior.

The Wild Olive Branches (11:16–24)

Paul furthers his argument that God's rejection of His chosen people is not permanent by advancing a horticultural example. "If the root be holy, the branches are too. But if some of the branches were broken off, and you, being a wild olive, were grafted in among them . . ." (vv. 16–17). In preparing to warn the Gentiles, Paul introduces the principle of dedication of firstfruits to God (cf. Num. 15:20–21) and the organic relationship between the root of a tree and its branches. These two metaphors illustrate one central truth: Israel is not only the firstfruits in God's program of salvation, but also the nation in which that salvation is rooted. However, some of the branches of Israel have been broken off through unbelief. The Gentiles, being wild olive trees, have been grafted into the life of the Abrahamic root in place of those dead Jewish branches that have been discarded. Gentiles must remember, however, that not all branches of Israel were discarded. Only unrepentant Israel has been broken off. The life of the tree of Abraham has not been removed. The wild branches gain sustenance from the root, which still bears a remnant of Jewish believers. There is still hope for Israel as long as the root is healthy.

The History and Future of Israel[2]

Book of Romans	Old Testament	New Testament
Chosen by God to be His people (9:9–16)	Deut. 9:4–6; 10:15	2 Tim. 1:9
Blessed by God throughout their history (9:3–5)	Deut. 4:32–34; 1 Chr. 17:20–22; Is. 5:1–4; Hos. 11:1	Luke 1:54–55; Acts 13:26; Heb. 8:6–10
Disobedient to God and His Law (10:21)	Neh. 9:26–30; Is. 65:2–5	Matt. 23:34–37; Acts 7:51–60
Rejected Jesus their Messiah (9:31–32)	Ps. 118:22; Is. 8:14–15; 28:16	Luke 2:34; 1 Pet. 2:6–8
Righteous only by faith in Christ (4:13–25; 10:11–13)	Is. 53:5–6, 10–12; Jer. 23:5–6	Acts 5:30–31; 1 Cor. 15:3–4
Gentiles blessed by Israel's rejection (9:30; 10:20; 11:11)	Is. 55:4–5; Hos. 2:23	Eph. 2:12; 1 Pet. 2:10
Remnant still enjoys God's blessing (9:27; 11:5–8)	Is. 10:20–23	2 Cor. 3:13–14
Restored by God in the future (11:25–26)	Is. 66:12; Jer. 31:33; Zech. 14:9–21	Luke 21:24; 2 Cor. 3:14–16

The apostle issues a strong warning to the Gentiles about their attitude toward unbelieving Jews. "Do not be arrogant toward the branches; but if you are arrogant, remember that it is not you who supports the root, but the root supports you" (v. 18). Gentile believers must never forget that they are not natural descendants of Abraham, but have become members of God's family by grace. They have nothing of which to be arrogant and must especially be careful not to be critical of the Jews, God's chosen people, whom they have replaced in the family tree. The strong warning continues. If the Gentiles argue that the Jewish branches were broken off so the wild Gentile branches could be grafted into Abraham's tree, Paul has no argument. "Quite right," he says (v. 20). But these natural branches were broken off because they lacked the one ingredient that would bring them life—faith. "They were broken off for their unbelief" (v. 20). But if faith is the only thing that stands between the Gentiles and becoming castaway branches, they should not be conceited, for faith was God's gift to them just as an ancestral link to Abraham was God's gift to the Jews. The only difference is that faith justifies; ancestry does not. "For if God did not spare the natural branches, neither will He spare you" (v. 21).

The great lesson of this passage is certainly that just as the Jews of the Old Testament became proud, assuming they alone knew God, the same thing may happen to Gentiles in the New Testament era. Gentile believers must not yield to the temptation to disrespect the Jews. If it had not been for the grace of God, Gentiles never would have been grafted into the life of God the Jews enjoyed. The new life that enables them to produce fruit grows from the same root the old stock of Israel grows. New Testament believers must not assume they are better than the Jews because the Jews were cut off for their unbelief. The Gentile church must never forget its reliance on the divine grace of God, else its end will be the same as that of the old branches. The process of being grafted into the life of God finds its basis in the grace of God. We must never lord the grace of God over those who have been cut from the tree, for it is much easier to put the natural branches back than to graft different branches in their place. We therefore must rest totally on the grace of God for our salvation as the remnant does.

In verse 22 Paul unveils an oxymoron, a combination of contradictory or incongruous words, two things that don't appear to go together, like "genuine imitation," "strangely familiar," "small crowd" or "jumbo shrimp." "Behold then the kindness and severity of God." For those who continue in God's kindness, there is kindness. For those who do not, there is the severity of being cut off. What is Paul talking about? To properly understand, we must scrutinize the context. In the preceding verses, the apostle has been contrasting the disobedience and rejection of God's grace by the Jews (9:27, 31; 10:21; 11:7–10, 15) and consequently God's lopping off their branches from the chosen tree (11:17–21) and replacing them with the Gentile branches (11:11–12, 17–19) who were grafted into the tree in place of the Jews. In either case, God is the active agent. God rejects the disobedient Jews, and God saves the obedient Gentiles. God is both the "rejecter" and the "acceptor." That's the divine incongruity. The God who rejects one, accepts another, all based on the exercise of faith.

God's severity is directed against "those who fell," in this context speaking of the Jews who disobeyed Him and whose branches were cut out of God's tree. God's kindness is directed toward "you"; in this context Paul is addressing the Gentiles. The apostle never tires of reminding the Gentile believers that had it not been for God's strictness in meting out justice to those Jews who failed to have faith in the Savior, the door to the gospel would not have swung open for the Gentiles. However, Gentile believers must never take God's grace toward them for granted. It is not automatically theirs, and Paul warns them, "You also will be cut off," if they do not continue in the grace of God's kindness (v. 22). This is not a threat to losing their salvation; it is simply to contrast that God did not automatically save Jews because they were Jews, and He will not automatically save Gentiles because they are Gentiles. The condition is always faith. If they exercise faith in the finished work of Christ at Calvary's cross, they will be saved.

By nature, Gentiles are "a wild olive tree" (v. 24). Having Gentiles in the family of God was "contrary to nature," because God, for reasons of His own, chose the Hebrews to be His special people. "Grafting of trees (adding a shoot of one tree to another tree) is reported in both Jewish and Greco-Roman literature. Sometimes shoots from a wild olive tree would be grafted onto a domestic olive tree that was bearing little fruit in an attempt to strengthen or save the life of the tree. The unproductive original branches would be pruned off, and the new graft was considered 'contrary to nature.'"[3] But what is contrary to nature is not too difficult for faith, and it was by faith that the Gentiles became members of the larger family of God.

Israel's Restoration Is Certain (11:25)

The expression "For I do not want you, brethren, to be uninformed" (cf. Rom. 1:13; 1 Cor. 10:1; 12:1; 2 Cor. 1:8; 1 Thess. 4:13) indicates that what Paul is about to say is of extreme importance. He is in the process of revealing a mystery "lest you be wise in your own estimation" (v. 25). The Gentiles dare not fall into the trap, as those in Rome apparently had done, of disparaging the Jews as a nation lest they become self-complacent in their new-found position. Paul reveals to them a mystery, not in the sense of a secret, but in the sense of a divine truth previously unknown. The mystery is that "a partial hardening has happened to Israel until the fulness of the Gentiles has come in" (v. 25). The spiritual blindness or hardness of heart displayed by Israel is not only to be understood as partial and not total, but also as temporal and not eternal. This hardness has a grip on Israel until the "fulness of the Gentiles" has come. According to Acts 15:14, God is visiting the Gentiles today to call out a people for His name.

"The fulness of the Gentiles" describes the present age, during which God is predominantly saving Gentiles. While individual Jews (whom Paul refers to as "the remnant") are also being saved today, the present age is primarily a time when God is working in the hearts of Gentiles. At the so-called Council of Jerusalem, where it was first discussed whether or not Jehovah would be pleased to save Gentiles as well as Jews, the apostle James declared, "Simeon has related how God first concerned Himself about taking from among the Gentiles a people for His name. . . . Therefore it is my judgment that we do not trouble those who are turning to God from among the Gentiles" (Acts 15:14, 19). So what does this mean for the future? Eschatologically the nation of Israel will remain hardened to the gospel until God's Church is complete and New Testament saints are raptured to heaven at the close of this present age. Then, during the Tribulation period, God will again focus His attention on Israel in order to restore the Jewish people to a place of blessing.[4]

All Israel Will Be Saved (11:26)

Here at Romans 11:26 Paul makes his own somewhat puzzling statement when he concludes, "And thus all Israel will be saved." The Greek expression *kai houtōs* (translated "and so") shows the relationship of what has preceded to what follows and can be translated "and accordingly." Throughout this passage Israel has been taken to mean a nation in contradistinction to the Gentiles as nations. But also a remnant of Israel has been paired with elect Gentiles saved out of those nations. It must mean the same here. When the apostle said, "All Israel will be saved," he was not teaching the universal salvation of national Israel. Nowhere does the Bible teach the universal salvation of humankind; salvation is always based on faith, and that's true for Israel as much as for the Gentiles. Paul has repeatedly argued that Jews are not saved because they are Jews, but because they have faith in the God of Abraham, just as Abraham did (Gen. 15:6; Rom. 4:3). The German theologian Adolph Harnack attacked Paul for his "all Israel will be saved" (v. 26) statement, saying that he allowed his patriotism to override his logic. But Harnack misunderstood Paul. We must never understand his statement here as repudiating what he has so meticulously argued against throughout the rest of the epistle.

How then are we to understand this optimistic appraisal of Paul? Good people differ,[5] but two almost contradictory concepts must be maintained in any proper understanding of "all Israel." First, although the words cannot imply universal salvation for Israel, they must nevertheless refer only to Israel as a special entity. And second, the words must apply to particular individuals within that special entity (a future election of God's grace) as opposed to the group as a whole. The "all" (Greek, *pas*) in this verse should be taken to mean Israel as a whole and not every individual Israelite. This clearly is the way the Jews used the phrase "all Israel." The Mishnah tractate Sanhedrin X.I. says, "All Israel has a portion in the age to come," and then proceeds immediately to name the Israelites who have no portion in that age." And yet, even though "all Israel will be saved" does not mean every Jew will come to Christ, there will be a large evangelistic movement among the Jews in the future. Still, only elect Jews will come to faith during that evangelistic movement. That's the lesson of Romans 9. God has always been pleased to operate on the basis of personal choices. Just as there is an election of grace among Jews in this age (the remnant), there will be an election of grace in the days to come. The difference will be in the quantity of Jews who will be saved in the future, not in the method. Among the things to come is a day when God's focus will be on the Jews as opposed to His present focus on Gentiles. That shift in focus will come after the "fulness of the Gentiles," when God takes His Church home (1 Thess. 4:13–18) and Satan and his henchmen are then free to concentrate their evil efforts on Israel as the people of God.

Stephen A. Kreloff says:

> During the tribulation period Satan will attempt to destroy Israel (Rev. 12). Zechariah announced that two-thirds of the Jewish population will die during this time (Zech. 13:8). . . . While the Jewish population will be dramatically reduced during the tribulation period, God will protect and preserve a remnant. The prophet Zechariah declared that the remaining one-third of the Jewish people will go through a period of intense suffering that will result in their turning to the Lord. . . . The surviving remnant of Jewish people alive at the end of the tribulation will constitute the entire nation of Israel.[6]

It is then, at the coming of Jesus Christ to reign in power and glory, when He delivers the earth from the Antichrist's rule, that Messiah will restore Israel to be the apple of God's eye. Massive numbers of elect Jews will fall at the feet of Jesus, not only as King of Kings and Lord of Lords, but as their Messiah as well.

The Deliverer from Zion (11:26–30)

Paul seals the restoration of Israel with a prophecy from Isaiah 59:20. "The Deliverer will come from Zion" (v. 26). This reference is to a manifestation to Israel of her Redeemer and Messiah. When He comes, Israel will be restored to the Root of God. Paul continues the quotation of Isaiah 59:21 but then passes into the promise of Jeremiah 31:33—"He will remove ungodliness from Jacob. And this is My covenant with them, when I take away their sins" (vv. 26–27)—to indicate that God will not fail to keep His covenant with Israel. "From the standpoint of the gospel they are enemies for your sake, but . . . they are beloved for the sake of the fathers" (v. 28). The Jews have been alienated from God's favor and blessing and thus are said to be enemies concerning the gospel. At the same time, they are beloved as the elect of God. Israel is still God's chosen people, regardless of its present condition. This proves that "the gifts and the calling of God are irrevocable" (v. 29). Those privileges and prerogatives in 9:4–5 have never been abrogated. What God promises, He also performs. Israel will one day be restored to the favor and blessing of God. Her restoration is prophesied; it will happen.

The apostle is still addressing the Gentiles. Verse 30 is a repetition of what he stated in verses 11, 12, 15, and 28, that the Gentiles have received God's mercy by way of the unbelief of Israel. Verse 31 indicates the relationship the salvation of the Gentiles has to the restoration of Israel. Verse 32 shows the relationship of God's mercy to all. Jew and Gentile alike must realize that both are undeserving sinners, and the expression of the love of God on their behalf is an act of mercy and grace.

Israel's Restoration Evokes Praise (11:33–36)

In the first eleven chapters of this epistle, Paul shows that the human race is split into two segments: Jew and Gentile. The promises of God came to the Jews first, but they failed to receive those promises and crucified the Lord of Glory. This resulted in the extension of those promises to the Gentiles. The day is prophesied, however, when Israel will once again be restored to the Father, and God will have mercy on all, both Jews and Gentiles. This plan of God calls forth transcendent praise.

"Oh, the depth of the riches both of the wisdom and knowledge of God!" (v. 33). Paul exclaims in this final doxology that the wisdom and knowledge of God are much greater than that of humanity, for the human mind could never conceive of a solution to the problem of how God could punish sin and still justly save the sinner. God's wisdom provided that solution. "How unsearchable are His judgments and unfathomable His ways!" (v. 33). Paul employs two emphatic words in describing God's wisdom—"unsearchable" and "unfathomable" (cf. Eph. 3:8). So unfathomable are the wisdom and knowledge of God that people can never descend to the bottom of that wisdom to search it out, nor can they trace it through history, because it is beyond possibility to follow completely. "For who has known the mind of the Lord, or who became His counselor?" This expression speaks of the unsearchable depth of God's knowledge. No one can completely know it. It implies that God, without dependence on any creature for counsel, devised the plan for our salvation (Eph. 1:9–11).

The apostle continues to sing the praises of God, "Or who has first given to Him that it might be paid back to him again?" (v. 35). In echoing Job 41:11,

Paul cannot resist going back to the principle of grace. The salvation that both Jews and Gentiles enjoy is based, not on what God must give back to them for what they have first given to Him, but on the basis of the grace of God alone. "For from Him and through Him and to Him are all things" (v. 36). God is the very reason for our existence. Out of God all things have come: He is their origin. Through God all things exist: He is their sustainer. And to God all things repair: He is their goal. In the circle of eternity, past, present, and future, God is all, and to Him all the praise for salvation must go. "To Him be the glory forever. Amen."

God isn't finished with His people Israel. His plan is unfolding today and progressing toward that day when Israel's hardness will be softened through tribulation and the Jewish people will then turn to Christ Jesus in huge numbers. Gentile believers can only pray that God will hasten that day.

Study Questions

1. Is God through with the Jews, never to restore them to salvation?

2. On what basis was there a remnant in Paul's day?

3. What advantage came to the world because Israel was temporarily rejected from a place of favor with God?

4. What will cause the Gentiles to be broken off from the olive tree of blessing?

5. What does Paul mean by "until the fullness of the Gentiles has come in"?

6. Does God keep His promises? (See verses 28–32).

SECTION VI: APPLICATION

The Christian's Need for Biblical Living

Romans 12:1 – 16:27

We should study the Bible for the purpose of translating theology into activity. We aren't just to learn the theology of justification and sanctification, we are to live it too. Thus Paul concludes his letter to the Romans with a healthy dose of practical application on how to live the Christian life and greetings to particular individuals who are doing so.

CHAPTER 23

Living a Life of Sacrifice
Romans 12:1-8

Preview:

Here Paul wants believers to consider how they serve the Lord. Their minds must be transformed in order to carry out God's will. Furthermore, every child of God must practice humility and exercise sound judgment in serving Him. All believers have been given spiritual gifts and a measure of grace to serve the body of Christ.

In the preceding eleven chapters, Paul piloted his readers through quite heavy doctrine. But doctrine is never taught in the Bible as an end in itself. It is always taught in order that it may be translated into practice. In John 13:17 Jesus declares, "If you know these things, you are blessed if you do them." Consequently, it is the Pauline practice to follow a doctrinal section of Scripture with a practical section, and usually these two are linked together with the word *therefore* (cf. Eph. 4:1; Col. 3:5).

This section begins with the third and final "therefore" in the epistle to the Romans. Each of these "therefores" marks a great division in the book. "Therefore having been justified by faith, we have peace with God through our Lord Jesus Christ" (5:1). " There is therefore now no condemnation for those who are in Christ Jesus" (8:1). " I urge you therefore . . ." (12:1). It is now Paul's purpose to tie together all the doctrinal material he has presented and tell his Roman readers what it means for them in everyday terms. As Karl Barth reminds us, "Paul is not here turning his attention to practical religion, as though it were a second thing side by side with the theory of religion. On the contrary, the theory, with which we have hitherto been concerned, is the theory of the practice of religion."[1] Hence the rest of this epistle is as intensely practical as what has preceded was intensely doctrinal.

The Basis for a Life of Sacrifice (12:1)

Paul's relationship with the brothers and sisters of the church at Rome, both Jews and Gentiles, is strong enough that he may speak firmly to them. Still, in this practical portion of his letter, he does not flaunt his authority as an apostle. He does not demand compliance of the Roman Christians. He exhorts them, urges them, begs them even to present their bodies as "a living and holy sacrifice" to God (v. 1). Although exhortation is not completely absent from the first eleven chapters, the main content is exposition. Theology is important but is most significant as a framework for godly living.

What is the basis on which Paul urges us to live the sacrificed life? It is the "mercies of God" revealed in the foundational first eleven chapters. Shut your eyes and think about the many mercies God has shown believers. Charles Erdman says, "These 'mercies of God' point back to the statements that Christians have been justified by faith in Christ the Son, that they are being sanctified by the power of the Holy Spirit, and that they are to be glorified as heirs of God the Father."[2] But God's mercies are much more extensive than that. The word *mercies* (Greek, *oiktirmos*) means compassion or pity as well as mercy. Remember all the compassion God showered on people who deserved none of it. That's what the first eleven chapters have been all about. Now, based on that compassion, Paul urges his friends in Rome to reciprocate sacrifice for mercy.

Paul says, "Present your bodies a living and holy sacrifice" (v. 1). This request is eminently linked to his discussion of sanctification in chapters 6 and 7. In fact, the word rendered "present" here (Greek, *paristēmi*) is the same word translated "present" in 6:13, 19. Paul now deals in greater detail with what it means to present ourselves to God. The Lord God wants the sacrifice of our life, not our death. Consequently, the sacrifice we are to make of our bodies (representing our whole person) is a living sacrifice. This is in contrast to the Old Testament sacrifices that were put to death on an altar. Since we know that we have died with Christ Jesus, we are in a position to present Him with our lives that are hidden with Him. Not only is the presentation of our bodies a living sacrifice, but it is also a holy and acceptable sacrifice. Holiness is contrasted with the defilement that is the usual characteristic of sinful humans. When the sacrifice of ourselves to God is holy, it is inherently acceptable to God and well-pleasing to Him. More than this, says the apostle, the sacrifice of ourselves to

God is our "spiritual service of worship." *Service* (Greek, *latreia*) is a term used for the function of priests in the tabernacle. The adjective (Greek, *logikos*) that precedes it may be translated either "reasonable" (i.e., rational) or "spiritual." But our worshipful service can only be spiritual in the biblical sense when it is characterized by our conscious, intelligent, rational service to the Lord God. In Paul's theology, spirituality is not some mindless fluttering of the heart but is the presentation of an entire life to the Lord. This sacrifice is logical because it was preceded by the sacrifice of God's Son in our behalf. It is spiritual because it is done willingly, in the power of the Spirit, and is not obligatory, done because of the letter of the Law.

The Deterrent to a Life of Sacrifice (12:2)

Not only is the presentation of our bodies the subject of Paul's request, it is the pattern of our behavior as well. "And do not be conformed to this world" (v. 2) is Paul's caution to the believers in Rome not to be fashioned after the pattern of this world or the present age (Greek, *aiōn*). He is speaking about being squeezed by the thinking of the age into a lifestyle that, while perfectly acceptable to those around us, is perfectly unacceptable to God. The world system of this age is evil (Gal. 1:4) and is dominated by "the god of this world" (2 Cor. 4:4). The believer, as a new creation in Christ, is to live in such a way as to prove daily that "the old things passed away; behold, new things have come" (2 Cor. 5:17). Today we would say this means that our lives are not to be governed by postmodern thinking in which we tolerate everything, believe nothing, and care about no one. The Christian's life is a life of sacrifice to God and others. That is not a twenty-first-century pattern, but it is a godly pattern. We are therefore not to have our lives governed by the thought patterns and dictates of this evil world system.

But how can we prevent that? Paul answers, "Be transformed by the renewing of your mind" (v. 2). The only possible way for believers not to be fashioned (Greek, *suschēmatizō*) after this world is to have our thinking processes transformed so our living practices can be transformed. The word *transformed* (Greek, *metamorphoō*) reaches far deeper than conformity to the world. It implies a fundamental change in the Christian's inward nature and a subsequent pattern of character that corresponds to that new nature. Thus the mind (Greek, *nous*, the center of logical reasoning, ethical judgment, and moral awareness) must be completely changed if we are to live a life that is holy and acceptable to God. It's a bit like deleting old files from a computer, completely erasing any evidence of their presence, and in their place loading new files, files that are produced for us by the Spirit of God.

And there's a very good reason this change must take place: "that you may prove what the will of God is, that which is good and acceptable and perfect" (v. 2). To prove (Greek, *dokimazō*) something is to test, scrutinize, or examine it. When we put God's will to the test of actual experience, we will find that it is good, acceptable (Greek, *euarestos*), and, in fact, perfect (Greek, *teleios*). God's will is good in that, even when we cannot conceive it to be so, it is never mistaken. It is acceptable in that when we recognize it as good, we will heartily endorse it. It is perfect in that it achieves the desired end God has in mind. When the righteousness of Christ is placed on us like a cloak, a life of transformation is produced that always sees God's will in these ways, regardless of the outcome.

E Pluribus Unum (12:3–5)

The United States of America was built on the principle of *e pluribus unum*—out of many, one. Many people, from many ethnic backgrounds, living in many states are citizens of one great country. It's a great idea in theory; it's a bit harder in practice, as every American knows. But new life in Christ brings that same principle to bear on serving the Lord—out of many talents, gifts, and people come one Church. Paul draws on that principle in the next portion of his letter to the Romans.

"For through the grace given to me I say to every man among you not to think more highly of himself than he ought to think" (v. 3). Paul now expands the biblical idea of the transformed life. His authority to speak in the way he does comes from the grace that is given to him. That grace is the spiritual gift of apostleship (cf. 1:5; 15:15). From his authority as an apostle of Jesus Christ, Paul counsels the men and women in the church at Rome not to entertain too high an opinion of themselves, their contributions to the church at Rome, or their position with one another. This only leads to disunity. Instead, they are to have sound judgment about their own importance. That's hard for all of us; the mirror tells us one story; our friends tell us another. But the transformation that comes through imputed righteousness is first exhibited in humility. If it is not, it likely will not be exhibited at all. Believers must be careful of being "above-minded" (Greek, *huperphroneō*), having an attitude of superiority. Rather, we are to have a sober assessment of ourselves, an assessment properly based in Galatians 2:20, where we recognize that we have been crucified with Christ and He now lives through us. *– all glory goes to K*

Paul uses the metaphor of the body to indicate that the life of humility must be lived in relationship to other believers. Each of us must recognize that we possess a special "gift" (Greek, *charisma*) as a result of our salvation and the indwelling gift of the Holy Spirit. There are many members in the body of Christ, and each of us, regardless of how humble our station in life or how deficient our education may be, has a gift from God to contribute to the whole body. The body needs us and our gift, just as we need others and their gifts in the body. In His sovereignty, God has just the proper place for each of us, because He has made us "individually members one of another" (v. 5). This last phrase proves the mutuality of the members of Christ's body. We are all in this together. It "calls attention to the need of the various parts of the body for each other. None can work independently. Furthermore, each member profits from what the other members contribute to the whole." Ray C. Stedman remembers, "A number of years ago I fell and injured my wrist rather severely. It swelled up and became very painful. And the rest of my body felt so bad about it that it sat up all night to keep it company. That is what the body of Christ is to do when one member is hurt. We are tied to one another, and when one hurts, all hurt."[4]

The Gifts of the Life of Sacrifice (12:6–8)

To be mutually beneficial in living the sacrificed life, each disciple of Christ possesses at least one special gift (Greek, *charisma*) designed to be used in ministering to the body. Paul describes seven gifts, distributed among the individuals in the Church, that, when they are properly exercised, function as a huge benefit to the Church at large. That the gifts are different is evident from the chart below. Why they are different is twofold: (1) because the body needs more than one gift and (2) because gifts are meted out "according to the grace given to us" by the indwelling Holy Spirit. Elsewhere Paul informs us that these gifts are "grace-gifts" given with a corresponding measure of faith, just the right amount of faith to exercise the gift (1 Cor. 12:8–11; Eph. 4:7), that they are distributed to each believer according to God's sovereign will (1 Cor. 12:11) and for the profit of the entire church congregation (1 Cor. 12:7). It is because of the potential of pride in the gift received that the apostle reminds us that we did not choose our gift, and God gave specific gifts to specific people to accomplish specific tasks in the church. We must enjoy our gift(s), and use them to build up the church, both quantitatively and qualitatively (Eph. 4:7–16), but we must never boast or become pride-filled because of our gift. After all, if we could earn or in any way merit our spiritual gift, it would cease to be a gift.

The list of gifts presented in Romans is not a complete list. Somewhat similar lists are found in 1 Corinthians 12:8–10 (where nine gifts are mentioned), in 1 Corinthians 12:28 (where eight gifts are mentioned); and in Ephesians 4:11 (where four/five gifts are listed). The list of spiritual gifts or functions within the body presented in Romans is shown in the table that follows.

Spiritual Gifts in Romans[5]		
Prophesying	The ability to receive truth from God and communicate it to others	Rom. 12:6; 1 Cor. 12:28
Serving	The ability to minister to the needs of others in the congregation	Rom. 12:7; 1 Cor. 12:28
Teaching	The ability to explain God's truth to others to affect change in them	Rom. 12:7; 1 Cor. 12:28
Exhorting	The ability to encourage the faint-hearted and comfort the afflicted	Rom. 12:8; 1 Thess. 5:14
Giving	The ability to financially help others without ulterior motives	Rom. 12:8; 1 Tim. 6:17–18
Leading	The ability to govern others without "lording" leadership over them	Rom. 12:8; 1 Tim. 5:17
Showing Mercy	The ability to minister to the sick or needy with cheerfulness	Rom. 12:8; Luke 10:33–34

Each of these gifts has been listed in the gerund form as a verbal noun, because, while grace gifts are nouns, they are always actively used or they are of no value to the church.

What are believers to do with their gifts? Since the members of the body of Christ have different gifts, each of us is to use his or her gift as God intends. The first-century prophets spoke the words of God to the local church (Acts 13:1–2). While the revelation of God has ceased, the repetition of what was revealed has not. Today we communicate what God has revealed in harmony with that which has already been spoken by God. If serving is our gift (Greek, *diakonia*), we are to do the work of a deacon, helping out around the church wherever that help is needed. This denotes a very broad office that may cover almost any kind of service in the local church. If we have been gifted as a teacher—one who has the art of making the unchanging message of God understandable to the unlearned—we must not neglect to give attention to teaching. Or if exhortation is our gift, unlike the teacher who appeals to the mind, we will take our brother or sister in the Lord aside and appeal to his or her heart to console or encourage him or her. Exhortation (Greek, *paraklēsis*) is a specific and highly necessary ministry in the local church, especially in times like these.

Although most won't own up to it, many in the local congregation have the gift of giving. Each member of the church has the opportunity to give, but some have been especially financially blessed by God expressly for the purpose of helping out in the church. This is one of the least exercised spiritual gifts today. The term liberality (Greek, *haplotēs*) sometimes has that meaning (cf. 2 Cor. 8:2; 9:11–13) but most often means with singleness of heart or motive (cf. 2 Cor. 11:3; Eph. 6:5; Col. 3:22). Essentially when we give, whatever we give, we are to do it with all our heart and without any expectation of receiving anything in return. If our gift is leadership, let us lead with diligence. The exercise of leadership in the church is as much a spiritual gift as any of the others. He who presides (Greek, *proistēmi*) is not to do so sluggishly but responsibly and diligently. And finally, if God has blessed us with the gift of showing mercy (and we could use a lot more in the church exercising this gift), we are to show mercy mingled with cheerfulness. This is the Christian gift of engaging in practical deeds of kindness.

There is a place in the local church for those who cannot teach or preach. Many within the church go about their business in an unspectacular way doing a much needed work in showing kindness and helpfulness to their fellow believers. Each of these gifts is necessary for the proper functioning of the body of Christ. Since that is the case, one gift cannot be exalted over another, and therefore the sacrificed life exhibits humility in its relationship to others in the local church.

Study Questions

1. List and discuss the things Paul wants believers to do to present an acceptable sacrifice to God.

2. How does a child of God *prove* the will of God in his or her life?

3. What is the source of our gifts?

4. From these verses, what do you think is your gift(s)?

CHAPTER 24

Living a Life of Service
Romans 12:9–21

Preview:

True Christian love should not be hypercritical. Christians should be devoted to one another, give preference to one another, and be kind and thoughtful in little things. Believers should not be haughty or have a wrong estimation of themselves. Vengeance should be left to God. Evil must be countered and overcome with what is right and good.

The Christian's life of service takes on new meaning and desirability when we remember Jesus was a servant for us and calls us to be a servant for Him. Paul was a servant of Christ (Rom. 1:1; Titus 1:1), as were James (James 1:1), Peter (2 Pet. 1:1), Jude (Jude 1:1), and others in the New Testament church. They set examples for us to follow. Now it is our turn. Our life of service has a code of conduct, which Paul reflects on in Romans 12:9–21. The injunctions in this section are a practical outworking of Jesus' Sermon on the Mount. Believers are expected to live the servant life in behalf of other believers as well as the world. The twenty-eight servant actions that follow are representative of what Paul means by living the servant life.

Living a Life of Service with Loving Attitudes (12:9–10)

Love without hypocrisy (v. 9). Paul says the Christian's love must be genuine, without any show or hypocrisy (Greek, *anupokritos*). Why? God's love is like that. Paul wants the Roman believers to exhibit what he calls "brother-love"

(Greek, *philadelphia*). In the Bible, brother-love is an unhypocritical, unfeigned, sincere love, the kind of love the Father has for the Son and demonstrated toward us when He gave His Son to die for us (Rom. 5:8). This kind of love is for all members of the local assembly, regardless of their race, heritage, station in life, or financial status. Any other kind of love is hypocritical or insincere and unworthy of those who bear the name of Christ.

Hate everything evil (v. 9). *Hate* is a strong word (Greek, *apostugeō*), and in the original this particular word is used only here in the New Testament.[1] It means to abhor or have an absolute horror at something. It is used of anything we find despicable, anything that causes us to turn our head away in revulsion. Most Christians do not abhor evil. We dislike it, we do not condone it—but hate it? We don't often find what turns God's stomach turning ours. The kinds of first-century sins enumerated in Romans 1 are present in the twenty-first century too, but we tolerate them; we don't abhor them. There is no horror at sin anymore. We should not expect God to remove sin from us until we actually hate it and have rooted out of our lives of service any secret love we still hold for that which is evil.

Hold on to everything good (v. 9). The contrast to abhorring evil is loving good. Paul uses the familiar word *agape* to verbalize how we should hang on to everything that is good. Of course, love is not without its boundaries. We do not simply love for love's sake, but we do love everything that is good. Thus we embrace good literature, fine art, and superb music with the same gusto with which we embrace good theology, fine liturgy, and superb preaching. They may not have the same eternal value, but they have the same source— the creative God who loves us and gives us good things.

Be devoted in brotherly love (v. 10). Paul's admonition here is that the local assembly is to be characterized by believers wholly devoted to the welfare of one another in brotherly love.[2] Biblical brotherly love is tender, understanding, and forgiving. It implies a certain intimacy we do not have with friends or family outside the church. A devotion to one another exists between those within the family of Christ that does not exist between the members of Christ's family and Adam's family. It's the kind of devotion that causes us to hang in there when things at church aren't perfect or people in our small group aren't so easy to get along with. Biblical brotherly love understands the principle of eternal kinship and responds to Paul's advice in Galatians 6:10, "So then, while we have opportunity, let us do good to all men, and especially to those who are of the household of the faith."

Give preference to others (v. 10). We need a devalued opinion of our own worth before the Lord but a greatly inflated opinion of what He can do through a devalued person who is yielded to Him. That devalued person may have more value for a particular service than do we. That is why the apostle challenges us to know our gifts, our natural abilities, and ourselves and not to always assume we are the best person for the job. When opportunities and tasks arise that someone else in the body is better suited for, we must give preference to that person. This is true for the pastor, elders, deacons, and every member of the local church. When someone can do the job better than we can, we graciously give way and give our blessing with no hidden animosity.

Living a Life of Service in Living Action (12:11–13)

Be diligent (v. 11). Paul asks us not to lag behind in our diligence in serving the Lord through the church. The two Greek words *oknēros* (which KJV translates "slothful") and *spoudē* (which KJV translates "business") mean "sluggishness" and "earnestness." Paul's counsel is not to allow ourselves to become sluggish or lacking in earnestness in anything we do for the Lord. It's another way of saying, "Whatever your hand finds to do, . . . do it with all your might" (Eccl. 9:10). Given the fact, as missionary/statesman James Moffatt used to say, we have all eternity to enjoy our victories but only one short hour before the sunset to win them, we are wise to be diligent in living the servant life.

Be fervent (v. 11). Linked to the preceding admonition is the call to be fervent in spirit. The word *fervent* (Greek, *zeō*) means to boil with heat or to be hot. In the spiritual realm, it means to be spiritually blazing for God. Apollos was such a man. "This man had been instructed in the way of the Lord; and being fervent in spirit, he was speaking and teaching accurately the things concerning Jesus" (Acts. 18:25). "But that's not my personality," you object. Paul isn't speaking of personality; he is speaking of spirit. The fervent life of Christ's servant is lived more like Apollos and less like Casper Milquetoast.

Serve the Lord (v. 11). Paul was a superstar, the best known of the early Christian authors. He authored approximately 24 percent of the New Testament. He was a world traveler, a church planter, a man whose feet were on the ground (Acts 14:1–7) but whose head was in heaven (2 Cor. 12:2–4). Still, he said this of his service to the Lord: "You yourselves know, from the first day that I set foot in Asia, how I was with you the whole time, serving the Lord with all humility and with tears and with trials which came upon me through the plots of the Jews" (Acts 20:18–19). Serving the Lord is less with stars in our eyes and more with tears in our eyes.

Rejoice in hope (v. 12). Alexander Pope said, "Hope springs eternal in the human breast,"[3] but for some, the spring is getting weaker. Still, for those living the servant life, there is much to rejoice about in hope. Jesus Christ gives us living hope (1 Pet. 1:3), dying hope (1 Cor. 15:55–57), resurrection hope

(Rev. 20:6), the blessed hope (1 Cor. 15:51–52), and eternal hope (Titus 3:7). We rejoice in hope because we rejoice in Christ. Read the newspaper, watch the news on television, or talk to those around you, and you may fall prey to hopelessness. But Jesus Christ is the intersection of all the world's fears and God's hope. We rejoice in hope because we have Christ in us, "the hope of glory" (Col. 1:27).

Persevere in tribulation (v. 12). Who better knew about the trials and tribulations of living the servant life than the apostle Paul? Read in 2 Corinthians 11:23–28 the catalogue of tribulations he endured as an apostle. Still, Paul admits: "We are afflicted in every way, but not crushed; perplexed, but not despairing; persecuted, but not forsaken; struck down, but not destroyed" (2 Cor. 4:8–9). How did he do it? Perhaps Paul could put up with such tribulation because of the link between perseverance and prayer. Since no one can persevere in his or her own strength, Paul says we must be devoted to prayer. Those given to prayer are not given to despair.

Be committed to prayer (v. 12). Without constant, persistent, and meaningful prayer, no one could have the joy and endurance the apostle displayed in his many troubles. Perhaps the reason many twenty-first-century believers don't get as much out of prayer as Paul seems to have gotten is because our approach to prayer is much different. He knew how to get answers to his prayers because he knew that prayer was not primarily about getting answers. He was committed to prayer because he was committed to becoming more intimate with His heavenly Father. Often it was in a prison cell, the hold of a sinking ship, or on the bitter end of criticism that he prayed, but it was also then that he was reassured of how much God cared for him and would still use him in spite of his tribulations.

Contribute to the saints (v. 13). A destructive famine was plaguing Jerusalem. Paul could not travel directly to Rome as he desired. Rather, he had collected money from the saints in Macedonia to take to the poor Christians of Jerusalem (see 1 Cor. 16:1–2.; 2 Cor. 8:1–2.; Acts 24:17). The man who insisted on theological purity and personal piety also insisted on showing generosity in helping the poor and feeding the hungry. Speaking to the Corinthians about participating in the support of the saints, the apostle said, "But just as you abound in everything, in faith and utterance and knowledge and in all earnestness and in the love we inspired in you, see that you abound in this gracious work also" (2 Cor. 8:7).

Practice hospitality (v. 13). Hospitality is the lost art of Christianity. In the past, when a visiting Bible teacher, musician, evangelist, or youth team came to the church, homes would open for hospitality. Today, we make reservations at a local motel and bill the church. Hospitality is a casualty of modernity.

How can we practice hospitality today? How about inviting a different family in your church for lunch each Sunday, a family you know isn't doing as well financially as you are? How about giving a working mother a break by offering to watch her children one night? How about helping a single mom change the oil in her car? Finding ways to practice hospitality is just a matter of keeping your eyes open and looking for opportunities. We must practice hospitality willingly, gladly, not grudgingly or out of a sense of duty.

Living a Life of Service in Life's Difficulties (12:14–16)

Speak well of your persecutors (v. 14). In the original language, *bless* is a compound word (Greek, *eulogeō*, made up of the prefix *eu* ["well"] and the root *logos* ["word"]). It means to speak a good word. Our English word *eulogy* is derived from *eulogeō*. Simeon spoke a good word when he held the Christ child (Luke 2:28). So did the crowd when they shouted, "Hosanna to the Son of David; blessed is He who comes in the name of the Lord; hosanna in the highest!" (Matt. 21:9). To "bless" those who persecute us is to speak well of them when they speak evil of us. When a soldier asked General Robert E. Lee what he thought about a subordinate who had been particularly critical of the general, Lee replied that he thought the man was a good soldier. When asked if he knew what the officer had been saying about him and if that would change his opinion, General Lee replied, "You asked me what I thought of him, not what he thought of me."

Rejoice with those who rejoice (v. 15). Jesus had a full social life. He dined at the house of Simon the leper (Mark 14:3). He ate often at the home of His close friends Mary, Martha, and Lazarus (John 12:1–2). Jesus enjoyed eating and drinking in the way any godly person would. Did He rejoice when others rejoiced? Yes, he attended a wedding in Cana of Galilee where friends were being married (and it's a good thing He did). Jesus was not a monk, a hermit, or a social recluse. He knew how to enjoy the company of friends and strangers alike. He is a model for all of us.

Mourn with those who mourn (v. 15). Jesus also knew how to mourn. Once as Jesus approached Jerusalem, "He saw the city and wept over it" (Luke 19:41). And it's quite likely that He shed some tears as He lamented, "O Jerusalem, Jerusalem, who kills the prophets and stones those who are sent to her! How often I wanted to gather your children together, the way a hen gathers her chicks under her wings, and you were unwilling" (Matt. 23:37). And the shortest verse in the Bible, John 11:35, reminds us that He mourned with His friends: "Jesus wept." Like the venerable Job who asked, "Have I not wept for the one whose life is hard?" Jesus mourned with those who mourn. He proved His humanity by feeling pain with others and shedding tears for them.

Preserve harmony in the church (v. 16). "Be of the same mind toward one another" is another way of saying, "Live in harmony with one another." We may not always see eye to eye with other believers, but nothing is accomplished through disunity. If we cannot get along with the people in our local assembly, how can we storm the gates of hell together (Matt. 16:18)? If we do not have the same mind toward one another in the church, what attraction will there be to Christianity for those in the world? So many of our actions within the church are calculated to minister to those who are without (see Col. 4:5; 1 Thess. 4:12; 1 Tim. 3:7). Harmony in the body of Christ is as important as harmony in the human body. When there is disharmony in our physical bodies, with one group of cells devouring another group of cells, we call that cancer, and often surgery is the only answer.

Do not be huge-headed (v. 16). One of the ways to preserve harmony within the church is to check your spiritual hat size often. Paul was afraid huge-headedness was true in the Roman church. Often the writers of Scripture remind us that "whoever exalts himself shall be humbled; and whoever humbles himself shall be exalted" (Matt. 23:12); "God is opposed to the proud, but gives grace to the humble" (James 4:6); "Humble yourselves, therefore, under the mighty hand of God, that He may exalt you at the proper time" (1 Pet. 5:6). Still, surprisingly, many in the church prefer to be coddled, praised, and immortalized rather than do the work of the ministry. It's the Diotrephes complex—he "who loves to be first among them" in the church (3 John 1:9). If our ego needs to be fed by our service, then our ego is all the reward we will have (Matt. 6:2).

Befriend the unlikely (v. 16). The King James Version translates this verse, "Condescend to men of low estate." But that sounds so condescending! Better understood, this means to associate and fellowship with those whose social or financial standing hasn't reached yours as yet. Don't be snobbish, but readily associate with the humbler folks in the church. Immediately after Jesus said, "For everyone who exalts himself shall be humbled, and he who humbles himself shall be exalted" (Luke 14:11), He went on to give this example: "But when you give a reception, invite the poor, the crippled, the lame, the blind, and you will be blessed, since they do not have the means to repay you; for you will be repaid at the resurrection of the righteous" (vv. 13–14).

Be honest with yourself (v. 16). Paul knew the Old Testament well. Solomon said, "Do not be wise in your own eyes" (Prov. 3:7), and Paul simply quoted him. But what is the antidote to being wise in your own eyes, trusting your own heart? Solomon spoke to that as well in the preceding verses:

> Trust in the LORD with all your heart,
> And do not lean on your own understanding.
> In all your ways acknowledge Him,
> And He will make your paths straight. (Prov. 3:5–6)

The only way to be honest with ourselves with regard to our self-estimation and abilities is to submit everything to the careful scrutiny of God and trust His heart and mind instead of our own. The church will function much more smoothly when we all place our plans on His altar and seek only His understanding.

Living a Life of Service before Our Enemies (12:17–21)

Don't repay evil for evil (v. 17). Sanctified servants of God don't repay evil for evil. The Bible often addresses the issue of vindictiveness. "When we are reviled, we bless; when we are persecuted, we endure; when we are slandered, we try to conciliate" (1 Cor. 4:12–13). "See that no one repays another with evil for evil, but always seek after that which is good for one another and for all men" (1 Thess. 5:15). Unlike the Israelites living under the "eye for an eye" principle of the Old Testament, Christians are to be a blessing instead.

Respect what is right (v. 17). We are to live a life of service in such a way that our neighbors, coworkers, and family members will have no cause to question our Christianity. People expect Christians to behave a certain way; sometimes their expectations are correct, sometimes not. Regardless, we are to live with such consecration to God and dedication to our Lord Jesus Christ that anyone outside the church will have no cause to accuse us (1 Tim. 5:14), slander us (Rom. 14:16), or shame us (1 Pet. 3:16). Paul's concern is that we be honest with our neighbors. If we are not, we will place a stumbling block in their path and a roadblock in the way of their accepting the gospel (1 Cor. 10:32).

Live in peace with all (v. 18). Paul knows that a life of service ministers to cantankerous neighbors as much as it serves Christian brothers and sisters. This admonition is not without precedent. Hebrews 12:14 says, "Pursue peace with all men." Jesus said, "Blessed are the peacemakers, for they shall be called sons of God" (Matt. 5:9). But Paul is not pipe dreaming here. He makes two important qualifications: (1) "if possible," because making peace isn't always possible. The apostle isn't advocating "peace at any price." We cannot abandon right living or correct doctrine just to make peace (cf. Matt. 10:34–36; Luke 12:51–53). And (2) "so far as it depends on you," because it doesn't always depend on us. Sometimes a neighbor is just stubborn, unreasonable, or opposed to getting along. But, if it's possible and the ball is in our court, we must attempt to live in peace with all.

Never take personal revenge (v. 19). If this sounds like déjà vu, it is. This injunction is a repetition of verses 14, 17, and 21. It's the closest we get to a "theme" running through the code of conduct. We can't know for sure, but perhaps Paul was concerned that there was a potential problem for revenge between Jewish and Gentile factions of the church at Rome. Paul tempers this third appeal to refrain from retaliation by calling his readers "beloved."[4] How tender. How appropriate. If Paul cannot convince his Christian brothers and sisters at Rome to live in harmony with one another and refrain from vengeance, whom can he convince?

Allow God to make things right (v. 19). There is a second half to never taking personal revenge. We shouldn't take personal revenge because it's not our place; it's God's place. Proverbs 20:22 advises, "Do not say, 'I will repay evil'; wait for the LORD, and He will save you." So the flip side to "Never take your own revenge" is "Leave room for the wrath of God." In support of this, the apostle introduces the quotation from Deuteronomy 32:35, "Vengeance is Mine, and retribution, in due time their foot will slip." Paul paraphrases it, 'Vengeance is Mine, I will repay,' says the Lord." God doesn't often remit vengeance immediately. In fact, rarely does God repay retribution immediately. But there is a day of judgment coming and punishment to follow. Paul promises a day "when the Lord Jesus shall be revealed from heaven with His mighty angels in flaming fire, dealing out retribution to those who do not know God and to those who do not obey the gospel of our Lord Jesus. And these will pay the penalty of eternal destruction, away from the presence of the Lord and from the glory of His power" (2 Thess. 1:7–9).

Treat your enemy with respect (v. 20). In light of God's impending wrath, and quoting from Proverbs 25:21, we are to treat our enemy kindly and not vengefully. If he is hungry, we are to give him food; if he is thirsty, we are to give him drink. "For in so doing you will heap burning coals upon his head." What does this enigmatic expression mean? There are various interpretations. One is that this quotation from Proverbs 25:22 reflects an Egyptian ritual in which a man showed his repentance by carrying a pan of burning charcoal on his head. This was a dynamic symbol of his change of mind. An equally appropriate view is that heaping coals of fire on the head refers to the sense of shame, punishment, or remorse that is engendered in the mind of our enemy when we show kindness to him or her. Greek scholar Kenneth S. Wuest says:

> In Bible times an oriental needed to keep his hearth fire going all the time in order to insure fire for cooking and warmth. If it went out, he had to go to a neighbor for some live coals of fire. These he would carry on his head in a container, oriental fashion, back to his home. The person who would give him some live coals would be meeting his desperate need and showing him an outstanding kindness. If he would heap the container with coals, the man would be sure of getting some home still burning. The one injured would be returning kindness for injury, the only thing a Christian is allowed to give back to the one who has injured him.[5]

Do not be overpowered by evil (v. 21). Paul concludes his sampling of entries in the Christian's code of conduct with the double-edged sword, "Do not be overcome by evil, but overcome evil with good." The word translated "overcome" is *nikaō* in Greek, the language in which Paul wrote his letter. It means "to conquer," "to prevail or to carry off in victory." Thus Paul is cautioning his Roman readers not to be carried off in victory by that which is evil, not to let the enemy have the upper hand, not to cave in to the things he has just cautioned them about. He advises them to be on their guard, just as Peter warned in 1 Peter 5:8: "Be of sober spirit, be on the alert. Your adversary, the devil, prowls about like a roaring lion, seeking someone to devour." The difference between a life of victory and a life of defeat can be the outcome of just one battle. Therefore, "Put on the full armor of God, that you may be able to stand firm against the schemes of the devil" (Eph. 6:11).

Overpower evil with good (v. 21). Conversely, we are to prevail in our lifelong battle with Satan. We are to carry off on our shoulders the victory of what is good. We have been told that we are "more than conquerors" through Him who loved us (Rom. 8:37 KJV). The concept of *nikaō* is seen only twice in the Gospels (Luke 11:22; John 16:33) and twice in Romans (3:4; 12:21). But once you get to the epistle of John, the concept blooms (1 John 2:13, 14; 4:4; 5:4–5), and it absolutely explodes in the book of Revelation (Rev. 2:7, 11, 17, 26; 3:5, 12, 21; 5:5; 6:2; 11:7; 12:11; 13:7; 15:2; 17:14), with the final reference in 21:7 promising, "He who overcomes shall inherit these things, and I will be his God and he will be My son." The Bible virtually ends with the idea that when we live the life of sacrifice and the life of service, we overcome all things and inherit all that God has for His children. What an appropriate ending for Romans 12, the Christian's code of conduct!

Study Questions

1. Make a list of all the commands or imperatives in this section.

2. Is there an action or attitude that is more important than all the rest?

3. Is it always possible to be at peace with everyone? Why or why not?

4. Since people are so different, how is it possible to have the same mind toward one another?

5. Put in your own words how good can overcome evil.

CHAPTER 25

Living a Life of Submission
Romans 13:1-14

Preview:

Believers must live properly in the world, including obeying government authorities and rulers. Christians should practice good citizenship and receive praise from those who rule, because they do so as ministers of God for good. If believers disobey legitimate government, they will suffer as evildoers. Practicing love for one another fulfills the law; and this love will do no wrong! Christians should "behave properly," because the day of service is short. They must leave no room for the working of the flesh and its lusts.

First-century men and women were vitally interested in their position in the Roman Empire. Jesus was questioned in Mark 12 by the Jewish leaders concerning His attitude toward the Roman government. The Corinthian Jews dragged Paul before Gallio, the proconsul of Achaia, and charged him with propagating a religion that was illegal in the empire (Acts 18:12–13). Paul's opponents at Thessalonica went to the civil magistrates and accused the Christians of subversion to the state (Acts 17:6–7). The question of church versus state was very much on the minds of first-century believers. Still today, anyone who chooses to live the sacrificed and servant life must also choose to live a life of submission to those in authority. In this chapter Paul explains why.

The Principle of Willing Submission (13:1)

"Let every person be in subjection to the governing authorities." Even though governments generally function under the authority of nonbelievers, the teaching of the Lord Jesus (Mark 12:17), the teaching here of the apostle Paul, and the historic position of the church (cf. the Westminster Confession of Faith, Chapter 23, Section 4) has always been that the believer must live under the law, governed by a magistrate, and be respectful and responsive to that magistrate. This is often not easy. The first-century Christians were in an especially difficult situation, being persecuted, harassed and often killed for their faith. F. F. Bruce says:

> Yet the evidence shows how, in face of gross provocation, Christians maintained their proper loyalty to the state, not least in Rome itself. "The patience and faith of the saints" wore down the fury of persecution. When the decrees of the civil magistrate conflict with the commandments of God, then, say Christians, "we ought to obey God rather than men" (Acts 5:29); when Caesar claims divine honours, the Christians' answer must be "No." For then Caesar (whether he takes the form of a dictator or a democracy) is going beyond the authority delegated to him by God, and trespassing on territory which is not his. But Christians will voice their "No" to Caesar's unauthorized demands the more effectively if they have shown themselves ready to say "Yes" to all his authorized demands.[1]

The Reason for Willing Submission (13:1–2)

So why should a Christian submit to any government, whether that government is spiritually in tune with God or not? The answer: "For there is no authority except from God, and those which exist are established by God" (v. 1). No authority exists anywhere unless God says so. That means the pharaoh of the Exodus was God's man (Ex. 9:16); Pilate was God's man (John 19:10–11); Nebuchadnezzar was God's man (Jer. 25:9; 27:6; 43:10). It is God who establishes kings and dethrones kings (cf. Dan. 4; see also Prov. 21:1). He is sovereignly controlling the affairs of people so only those whom He chooses gain the seat of power. Having advanced the reason why we willingly submit to the authorities, Paul cautions his readers, "Therefore he who resists authority has opposed the ordinance of God" (v. 2). As a general rule, God condemns civil disobedience toward the lawfully existent government. Resistance to governmental authority is resistance to the ordinance of God. Those who would riot and rebel must know that opposition to government is opposition to God. Resisting government unlawfully and unethically brings the judgment of God on believers (v. 2). Nevertheless, the obedience Christians owe to the government is never absolute and must carefully be weighed in light of their subjection to God.

William Hendriksen asks:

Does this mean, then, that the apostle was urging unlimited compliance, a subjection so absolute that even when the command of the magistrate should be in direct conflict with God's revealed will, it must nevertheless be obeyed? Of course not! We should not forget that Paul was a Jew, well-versed in the Old Testament, as he proves again and again in his epistles. Therefore he also knew about, and heartily approved of, the courage shown by Daniel and/or his three friends when they disobeyed royal edicts and ordinances that were manifestly contrary to God's will as revealed in his law. See chapters 1, 3, and 6 of the book of Daniel. These chapters show that God rewards those who, in extremely difficult circumstances, remain faithful to himself, and who therefore deliberately disobey their earthy ruler.[2]

The Purpose of Government (13:3–4)

One of only three institutions established by God (the family and the church being the other two), government led by godly people was God's design for the state. But that ideal was never realized because of humankind's sin. Bad people oust good people from government routinely. For instance, the Taliban ruled Afghanistan ruthlessly, but the majority of the Afghan people did not want the Taliban to be their rulers. Since God's purpose in ordaining government in the days of Noah was to restrain wickedness and promote virtue, we are to be in submission to any government that fulfills this purpose. Government is for our good. Sometimes, however, even good government can go bad. The Declaration of Independence was composed to rebuke George III's government for punishing virtue while at the same time rewarding wickedness. As noted above, Christians need never blindly fall under subjection to injustice or a government that has gone bad. When a wicked government demands its citizens do what God demands they not do, Christians have both the right and the responsibility to make their voices heard.

If we are looking to live in peace under a government that is also looking for justice and peace, the solution is simple: "Do you want to have no fear of authority? Do what is good, and you will have praise from the same" (v. 3). Government is "a minister of God to you for good" (v. 4). The word *minister* is one with which we are familiar. It is *diakonos* in Greek, the same word used to describe the spiritual gift of service in Romans 12:7. It is not at all ironic that Paul chose the same word for the governor of the nation who seeks justice and the good of the people as he did for the servant of the church who seeks to advance the kingdom of God. Both are ordained of God and are chosen for their positions by God. Both are charged with doing what is best for the people. The lesson is clear. If we do not want government intrusion or retribution, we must do what is good and godly, and good government will praise us. But when we do what is good and godly and bad government persecutes us for it or prevents the free exercise of doing what is good and godly, then it is our responsibility to help change government, if we can, from within the process. We run for office or campaign for others. We sign petitions. We raise our voices. It is only when ungodly government cannot be changed from within that we have the right to respond with nonsubmission. Still, as William Barclay points out,

> Paul's main view of the state was that in his day, as he saw things, the Roman Empire was the divinely ordained instrument to save the world from chaos. Take away that Empire, as Paul saw it, and the world would disintegrate into flying fragments. It was in fact the *pax Romana*, the Roman peace, which gave the Christian missionary the chance to do his work. Ideally men should be bound together by Christian love; but they are not; and the cement that keeps them together is the state.[3]

The Physical Reason for Compliance (13:4)

Before deciding to rebel against good government, one must consider the consequences to noncompliance with the rule of law. Paul points out those consequences when he says, "But if you do what is evil, be afraid" (v. 4). Why would anyone fear good government? We think twice before breaking the laws of government because "it does not bear the sword for nothing." God did not create government the way we see much of it today. God created government with teeth. When a law was broken, consequences were swift and just. Good government wields a sword of justice. God granted human government the power of enforcing itself, and therefore this verse provides New Testament justification for capital punishment. The divine directive was established in Genesis 9:6, "Whoever sheds man's blood, by man his blood shall be shed." The hands of good government should never be so tied that they cannot execute good judgment and the wrath of God upon those who do evil. Government is to be "an avenger [Greek, *ekdikos*, one who exacts a penalty] who brings wrath upon the one who practices evil" (v. 4). When it is not, good government ceases to be good, and the physical reason for compliance is removed.

The Moral Reason for Compliance (13:5)

Paul now advances a second reason for compliance to the governing authorities: "Wherefore it is necessary to be in subjection, not only because of wrath, but also for conscience' sake" (v. 5). The Christian always lives in a tension between the two competing claims of obedience—the state and God. The state has a right to demand our respect and conformity. Thus we are to be in submission to those in authority over us, not only out of fear and respect, but also out of a good conscience before God. However, we dare not blindly bow to the state if our conscience is offended by the wickedness of the state. There may be times when we ought to "obey God rather than men" (Acts 5:29; cf. 4:19). Since the state and its magistrate are not infallible, the believer may at times have to conscientiously object to what the state requires that is in direct contradiction to the law of God.

We must respect the consciences of believers that lead them to opposite conclusions. In a similar vein, Reinhold Neibuhr was a pacifist during World War I. He not only felt that capital punishment was wrong, but that bearing arms to defend the government was wrong as well. But having seen what happens when good government gives way to bad government, by World War II Neibuhr changed his mind. He argued that it was impossible to avoid sin simply by refusing to take action to preserve justice and decency against injustice and tyranny. He said that if Christians fail to take action against injustice, the Christians themselves become involved in sin.[4] Paul was not living under ideal social conditions, but he recognized that his conscience was a powerful force to bring him to respect civil laws, even those of a corrupt government.

The Response of the Submissive Life (13:6–7)

If we are submissive to governing authorities for the sake of the law and conscience, what will be the result? Too often our submission is just theoretical, or if actual, it is grudging submission. We complain constantly about the government and political officials, for there seems to be so much to complain about. But what does the Bible say should be the response to government by one living a life of submission? "For because of this you also pay taxes" (v. 6). There it is—the "T word." *Taxes*. Here the antecedent for the word "this" appears to be "conscience" in the preceding verse. We pay taxes for our conscience's sake, the same reason we live a submissive life. Again Paul reminds us that when good government prevails, we pay taxes so the ruling authorities can devote themselves and their work to being true ministers of God, just as a pastor does. When bad government prevails, we attempt to change it, but we still pay our taxes in the meantime.

Paul now asserts his general principle: "Render to all what is due them: tax to whom tax is due; custom to whom custom; fear to whom fear; honor to whom honor" (v. 7). The apostle is arguing that Christians living a submissive life pay whatever they owe without complaint. To elucidate that principle even more, he enumerates four categories in which submissive Christians owe others. The first is *tax* (Greek, *phoros*), the tax levied on houses, land, property, or persons (Luke 20:22–25; 23:2). The second is *custom*, from the Greek *telos*, which literally means "end" (as in Rev. 22:13). It refers to a toll or custom paid on goods that have been received by the consumer (Matt. 17:25). The third is *fear* (Greek, *phobos*), which variously means "fear" (Matt. 28:8), "dread" (Matt. 28:4), "terror" (Luke 21:26) or "reverence" (Acts 2:43). And finally there is *honor* (Greek, *time*), which means "the price paid for something," "value," or alternatively "deference" or "the honor given by reason of rank or office" (1 Tim. 1:17). Why does Paul give this apparently unrelated grouping of examples of what we owe good government? Together these represent both our actions and attitudes if we are living a life of submission.

The Law and the Submissive Life (13:8–10)

Romans 13:8 is one of those verses that often has been taken out of context and been used to say something the apostle never intended. "Owe nothing to anyone except to love one another" seems to be an open and shut case for a prohibition against borrowing or lending anything for any reason at any time. Christian financial planners have used this verse to keep young couples out of debt. Staying out of debt is a good idea, for "the borrower becomes the lender's slave" (Prov. 22:7), but this verse has little or nothing to do with finances. Paul has moved on from paying taxes to another general principle. Living the submissive life is built on the cornerstone of love for one another. So Paul says the only debt we really ought to incur is the debt of love, so we can live a life of submission. Pay your taxes; pay your custom; pay your respects; but always be in debt to love. "For he who loves his neighbor has fulfilled the law" (v. 8). Isn't that what Jesus answered when asked what was the foremost commandment? "'You shall love the Lord your God with all your heart, and with all your soul, and with all your mind, and with all your strength.' The second is this, 'You shall love your neighbor as yourself.' There is no other commandment greater than these" (Mark 12:30–31). The debt of love we owe can never be fully repaid, and no one understands that better than the one who lives a submissive life.

In support of what the apostle has just said, he quotes from the Ten Commandments themselves. "You shall not commit adultery [#7], You shall not murder [#6], You shall not steal [#8], You shall not covet [#10]" (cf. Ex. 20:1–17). And then the apostle makes a summarizing statement of the rest: "And if there is any other commandment, it is summed up in this saying,

'You shall love your neighbor as yourself'" (v. 9). Paul is not just taking a shortcut to quoting the Ten Commandments. He is saying that the entire Decalogue, at least the second half of it, is to be understood in the context of loving your neighbor as yourself, living a submissive life. Notice that the first four commandments are not even mentioned, for they all reflect a person's relationship to God (e.g., "You shall have no other gods before Me"; "You shall not make for yourself an idol"; "You shall not take the name of the LORD your God in vain"; and "Remember the sabbath day, to keep it holy.") The commandments from the second tablet of Law omitted were #5 ("Honor your father and your mother") and #9 ("You shall not bear false witness against your neighbor"), and these are covered in Paul's summarizing statement.

The point is this: The commandments that relate humans to their fellow humans are all about living a submissive life. Honoring father and mother means submitting to their authority. Refraining from murder is submitting your hatred and wrath for your fellowman to the restraining grace of God. Not committing adultery is an act of love to your fellowman by not violating the sanctity of marriage. Not stealing means submitting your will to your means and not taking from another person when you can't afford something yourself. Not bearing false witness means resisting the temptation to better yourself by demeaning your neighbor. And not coveting means that you are bringing under submission your natural desires to want what belongs to your neighbor. Instead of being negative commands, the Ten Commandments are revealed to be very positive commands when viewed in the context of owing your neighbor nothing but your love. Paul concludes: "Love does no wrong to a neighbor; love therefore is the fulfillment of the law" (v. 10). When we live a submissive life, we place the needs of our neighbor above our own needs because we love our neighbor as we love ourselves (Gal. 5:14).

The Timetable of God and the Submissive Life (13:11–14)

Paul now moves toward a conclusion about the need for every Christian to live a life of submission. If we don't do it now, it may soon be too late. "This do, knowing the time, that it is already the hour for you to awaken from sleep" (v. 11). Paul constantly enjoined the duty of spiritual vigilance in relation to God's timetable (cf. 1 Thess. 5:4). The urgent nature of these endtime days necessitates that we Christians awake out of our lethargy and fervently begin to live a sacrificed life, a servant life, and a submissive life. It is time for believers to stand up and be counted and to make a mark for God. That mark will consist as much in how we live as in what we say. In these waning years before our Lord's return, people need to see Christians who know how to live in light of the theology they believe. That is what Paul is getting at in chapters 12—16 of his epistle. One thing is sure, "Now salvation is nearer to us than when we believed" (v. 11). This is another of Paul's irrefutable truisms. The salvation of which the apostle speaks is that for which our bodies now groan, "waiting eagerly for our adoption as sons, the redemption of our body" (8:23). We are now much closer to that day than the day we first believed. This adds urgency to living the submissive life we ought to live. Time is short. The sound of the trumpet is near (1 Thess. 4:16).

Armed with this knowledge, how should we then live? "Let us therefore lay aside the deeds of darkness and put on the armor of light" (v. 12). What does the apostle mean by the deeds of darkness? Verse 13 catalogues six vices that qualify for living in the darkness rather than living in the light. This list is obviously not exhaustive, but it is suggestive.

1. *Carousing* (Greek, *kōmos*). Reveling, engaging in an orgy, boisterous merrymaking. Bacchants, devotees of the god Bacchus, used to engage in nocturnal processions as half-drunken frolickers who would gorge themselves with food and wine and then take to the streets with torches singing the praises of their decadent god. This is the sort of thing Paul warns the Christians they must never do if they are to live a submissive life (see also Gal. 5:21; 1 Pet. 4:3).

2. *Drunkenness* (Greek, *methē*). Being in a drunken stupor, the result of drunken bouts where one drinks oneself senseless (see also Luke 21:34; Gal. 5:21).

3. *Sexual promiscuity* (Greek, *koitē*). The King James Version translates this as "chambering," and that's not far off the mark. The word means sleeping in a bed or cohabitation, with the clear connotation of sexual intercourse. This is jumping from bed to bed, hooking up, engaging in a series of meaningless sexual encounters outside of marriage (see also Heb. 13:4).

4. *Sensuality* (Greek, *aselgeia*). Unbridled lust, shamelessness, sexual debauchery. Our grandparents used to call this lasciviousness or licentiousness, but the best definition can be found at night on any premium cable channel (see also Mark 7:22; 2 Cor. 12:21; Gal. 5:19; Eph. 4:19; 1 Pet. 4:3; 2 Pet. 2:7; Jude 1:4).

5. *Strife* (Greek, *eris*). Debate, wrangling, contention, dissension. It's the kind of activity that is constant before a divorce or manslaughter (see also Rom. 1:29; 1 Cor. 1:11; 3:3; 2 Cor. 12:20; Gal. 5:20; Phil. 1:15; 1 Tim. 6:4; Titus 3:9).

6. *Jealousy* (Greek, *zēlos*). Depending on the context, it can mean zeal, enthusiasm, ardor, jealousy, or contentious rivalry. It refers to fervor of mind, the kind of ardor that pursues or defends something vociferously (see also John 2:17; Acts 5:17; 13:45; Rom. 10:2; 1 Cor. 3:3; 2 Cor. 7:7, 11; 9:2; 12:20; Gal. 5:20; Phil. 3:6; Col. 4:13; Heb. 10:27).

Jesus said it rightly: "Men loved the darkness rather than the light; for their deeds were evil" (John 3:19). The darkness is a place of spiritual dullness, depravity, debauchery, and despair. The only way out of the deeds of darkness is to come to the Light, Jesus Christ. Paul says it this way: "Put on the Lord Jesus Christ, and make no provision for the flesh in regard to its lusts" (v. 14). Having laid aside the clothes of our dark life, when we walk in the Light, we now are robed in Christ's righteousness so that the Father never sees what we were, but what we are in Christ. Now we don't feed the flesh. We don't take excursions back into the darkness. We don't love to lust. All who live a submissive life are clothed with the Lord Jesus Christ and do not feel ashamed to be His servant. We count it a privilege.

Study Questions

1. When is it necessary for believers in the Lord to disobey government authorities?

2. Does Paul have in mind obeying "good" laws as opposed to "evil" laws?

3. What services must Christians render to government? Discuss.

4. From verses 8–9, list the ways love is to be applied and lived out in the life of the child of God.

5. On what basis, and for what reason, is the believer in Christ to live a spiritual and moral life?

CHAPTER 26

Living a Life of Sensitivity
Romans 14:1–15:13

Preview:

Christians should always be considerate to believers who are weak in faith. We live unto the Lord and should not judge those who hold differing opinions. In no way should we become a stumbling block to fellow Christians; we should live by the principle of love. Whatever is done for our neighbors must be for their good. We need to follow Christ and accept others as He accepts us. Gentiles can now join the Jews in living praiseworthy lives unto the Lord.

Having addressed the need for all who have been justified by faith to live a submissive life in relation both to governing authorities and others, Paul now continues a similar theme in chapter 14. This time, however, he urges his readers to live a life sensitive to the faith differences among them.

The Principle of Acceptance (14:1)

As we have seen so often before, Paul begins with a general principle and then proceeds to specifics in his teaching. Anyone who chooses to live a life of sensitivity must "accept the one who is weak in faith" (v. 1). In every church there are going to be differences of opinion, variations of belief, as well as variations of spiritual maturity. What was the nature of the weakness of which the apostle speaks? Scholars differ dramatically on the root of the weakness in the lives of the Roman believers, but whatever the particular religious scruples were that caused differences between them, the basic problem was that some of the believers had not grasped the great truths Paul had just expounded in his epistle. A better translation of Paul's words would be, "But him being weak in the faith receive." Did you notice the often-forgotten word? It's the definite article *the*. Paul did not say, "Accept the one who is weak in faith" as if the problem here is that some Christians simply do not have sufficient faith and that's why they are weak. He said the weak are those who are weak in the faith. Paul uses the word *faith* here as that complete body of teaching that comprises New Testament theology.

Those who were weak in the faith were Christians who did not have full understanding that salvation is the free gift of God and that believers face no condemnation whatever because of the atonement of Christ. Paul enjoyed his Christian liberty to the fullest and was totally emancipated from foolish superstitions and unbiblical taboos. Some of the Romans, however, were still clinging to these taboos, for they did not fully accept the doctrine of justification by faith alone. In relation to this, Paul addressed both those living freely in Christ and those in Christ who were still bound by fleshly legalism. The strong who had internalized Bible doctrine were to receive the weak, those who did not fully rest in the grace of God. But they were not to argue with them over secondary points of difference.

So what is the responsibility of the strong to the weak? We are to encourage them, teach them, mentor them, and often put up with them. And we must do all that without being condescending in any way. The word *accept* (Greek, *proslambanō*) is made up of the prefix *pros,* meaning "to, near, with or toward," and the root word *lambanō,* meaning "to take," "to lay hold of and not let go," "admit," or "receive." When Apollos came to Ephesus and preached the Word but gave evidence of knowing only of the baptism of John, Priscilla and Aquila "took him aside *(proslambanō)* and explained to him the way of God more accurately" (Acts 18:26). Hence the meaning of Paul's instruction to the Romans in 14:1 is clear: Our responsibility to the weak is to take them into our friendship and fellowship; to take them to our heart as fellow strugglers; and not to criticize them, shun them, or ridicule them for their lack of maturity or knowledge.

The Example of Eating Meat (14:2–4)

Paul now proceeds to give a specific example of what it means to be weak in the faith. He addresses the controversy of eating meat that had once been offered to idols.

In His dealings with the Jews, Jehovah had issued certain rules, regulations, and requirements with respect to what the Jews were to consider clean or unclean animals. These regulations are recorded in Leviticus 11:1–47 and Deuteronomy 14:3–21.[1] The Jews were steeped in the belief that certain foods were taboo because they were judged unclean. Jesus, however, said, "There is nothing outside the man which going into him can defile him; but the things which proceed out of the man are what defile the man. . . . Do you not understand that whatever goes into the man from outside cannot defile him; because it does not go into his heart, but into his stomach, and is eliminated? . . . That which proceeds out of the man, that is what defiles the man. For from within, out of the heart of men, proceed the evil thoughts, fornications, thefts, murders, adulteries . . ." (Mark 7:15, 18–21).

This was the basis for the difference of opinion that crept often into the fledgling church (see Acts 15:29; 21:25; 1 Cor. 8). The weak in the faith believed that it was unlawful and unspiritual to eat meat, especially, as in the case at Corinth where the meat had once been offered to pagan idols but was now on sale in the agora or marketplace (1 Cor. 8).[2] They refused to buy and eat such meat because of their religious scruples. So "one man has faith that he may eat all things, but he who is weak eats vegetables only" (v. 2). The strong consisted of those who believed that the meat, especially meat offered to idols, was in no way violating the principles of Scripture. Even meat offered to idols was not physically or spiritually defiled, since idols of wood and stone were not real and could have no effect on the meat. These were the nonvegetarians. They freely shopped in the agora of ancient Rome, looking for the best bargains on meat, fruit, and vegetables. Likely these believers were of the Gentile group in the church. Their scruples were not as rigid as those of the weak. Paul says, "Let not him who eats regard with contempt him who does not eat" (v. 3). They were not to despise, ridicule, or humiliate those who were weak in the faith and held religiously to a vegetarian diet or refrained from eating meat offered to idols (1 Cor. 8:7).

But the weak had a responsibility to the strong as well. Says Paul, "Let not him who does not eat judge him who eats, for God has accepted him" (v. 3). Those who erroneously held to a vegetarian diet were often given to judgmental attitudes toward those who liked a steak now and then. Paul's point is that if God has received the weak in his weakness and the strong in his strength, shouldn't the weak and the strong accept each other? In fact, he asks, "Who are you to judge the servant of another? To his own master he stands or falls; and stand he will, for the Lord is able to make him stand" (v. 4). Bruce Corley and Curtis Vaughan remark:

> How often piddling opinions and trivial issues keep Christians apart! We might have expected Paul to take sides with the strong since he undoubtedly agreed with them (cf. 14:14), but Paul was so completely free from

spiritual bondage "that he was not even in bondage to his emancipation" (Bruce, p. 243). In areas of life that were open to question, Paul took the course of pleasing all, in order to preserve the unity of the church (cf. 1 Cor. 10:23–33). The apostle argues that the opinions which divide the strong and weak are not all that important. Why debate unessential matters and thereby rupture the community of faith?[3]

Essentially addressing the weak in faith, Paul draws a conclusion that is found many times in Scripture (cf. Matt. 7:1; Luke 6:37; 1 Cor. 4:3–5). Each Christian is the property of God, and no one is in a position to see the inner motives of others. God's jurisdiction over all believers is not to be infringed upon by either those who are weak or those who are strong. Christ alone is Judge.

The Example of Observing Days (14:5–6)

A second concrete example is now given of the differences between those who have laid hold of the truths of God's Word and those who tenaciously cling to some legalistic practice. The subject is the honoring of certain days over others. Paul writes, "One man regards one day above another, another regards every day alike" (v. 5). Those who are weak choose a certain day and proclaim it holy—holier than other days. Those who, like Paul, understand the liberty we have in Christ Jesus, do not observe days but rather serve and worship the Lord consistently seven days a week. Paul clearly aligns himself with those who are seven-day-a-week Christians.

It would be hard not to miss the implication here. Paul is speaking of Sabbath keeping. Even though the fourth commandment, "Remember the sabbath day, to keep it holy" (Ex. 20:8), is the only one of the ten not to be repeated in some form in the New Testament, there were still believers in the church at Rome who felt the Sabbath should be somehow observed. Paul identifies them as the weak in the faith, and he is probably again referring to the Jews who had become followers of Christ in Rome. They would meet with other members of the church in worship on the first day of the week (cf. Acts 20:7), but in the back of their minds, they still clung to the Sabbath as well. Perhaps they would refuse to shop on the Sabbath or would hold Jewish-only Sabbath prayer meetings. Maybe they had their own messianic congregation meeting on Saturday and then would join with the full church on Sunday. Paul isn't explicit in how they were regarding one day as special, just that they were.

But there may be more to Paul's concern than just Sabbath-keeping. Not only did the Ten Commandments issue a directive to honor the Sabbath, but Moses also prescribed the observance of other specific days of religious festivals. If the Jews of Rome were continuing to pay tribute to their culture by celebrating these religious festival days and excluding the Gentile believers, one can see how this would mar the living of a sensitive life. Perhaps the apostle was referring to special days, like fasting days, that were a part of the ingrained system of religion out of which these Jewish believers were saved (Luke 18:12).

Since we have no direct knowledge of how the Jewish believers in Rome were regarding one day above another, we have no reason to speculate further. We do have, however, Paul's response to the practice. He says, "Let each man be fully convinced in his own mind" (v. 5). William R. Newell comments:

> Paul's instruction is, Let each man be fully assured in his own mind. Moses never could have said a thing like that! There is a sense in which these words reveal our liberty in Christ as does no other single passage. The Law allowed no liberty of action in such things: its very spirit and essence was bondage to a letter. Conscience was judged beforehand by the letter of the Law; conduct was prescribed. When a man gathered sticks on the Sabbath, he was stoned! Not so, now! Not being under the Law, or the legal principle, but in the Risen Christ, under God's eternal favor, we have entered upon what the Spirit, in Chapter Twelve, calls our "intelligent service."[4]

Preliminary Conclusions (14:7–9)

The apostle concludes, "For not one of us lives for himself, and not one dies for himself" (v. 7). The adage "No man is an island unto himself" is the modern outgrowth of these verses, but that is not the central truth taught here. The basic teaching is that each Christian must live his or her life in full view of the Lord Jesus Christ. We do so as servant to master, and therefore our relationship to Him will affect our relationship with other Christians. We must interact with others in ways pleasing to the Lord and not in judging the strong or demeaning the weak. The ground of our actions toward one another is the absolute lordship of Christ Jesus as established in His death, burial, and resurrection. "For if we live, we live for the Lord, or if we die, we die for the Lord" (v. 8). From His authority as resurrected Lord, He bids us live in harmony with one another.

If the full import of the phrase "We are the Lord's" hits us head-on, it will change the way we live in relation to others. There will be no belittling, no judging. There will only be "Christ-living." "We are the Lord's" means that we are His purchased possession; we belong to Him. He owns us. Nobody I know likes that concept. But how we feel about it isn't the issue. It's biblical. "Do you not know that your body is a temple of the Holy Spirit who is in you, whom you have from God, and that you are not your own? For you have been bought with a price: therefore glorify God in your body" (1 Cor. 6:19–20). "You are not your own; you have been bought with a price" is biblical proof that Jesus is the Lord and Master and we are His slaves and servants. As servants we live as He requires, not as pleases us.

The Judgment Seat of God (14:10–12)

But there is an additional motivation for living a life of sensitivity toward one another. John G. Mitchell points out that there are two grounds for receiving the weaker brother.

> The first ground for receiving weaker brethren is that we have the same Lord, the same standing. We are going to glory together. We'll spend eternity together. This puts our receiving others on the unchanging absolute of our relationship to the Savior. We have no grounds for judging other Christians. . . . The second ground for receiving weaker brethren is because the Lord is the judge. He is not only the Lord over all believers, but He is the judge of all believers. And, remember, He is going to judge righteously. In the final analysis, friend, we have to stand before God.[5]

Paul asks, "But you, why do you judge your brother? Or you again, why do you regard your brother with contempt? For we shall all stand before the judgment seat of God" (v. 10). He is speaking both to the weak and the strong. Why do we engage in silly disputation when we must both stand before Jesus our Judge? Only He will be able to settle our petty church disputes, and we may be surprised at His disposition. Those who are looking down on their fellow Christian now will one day look up to Jesus. On the day when every knee bows before the Lord and every tongue gives praise to God (v. 11), we'll learn whether or not we have truly been engaged in living a life of sensitivity. When we judge one another, we are taking to ourselves a responsibility that belongs to Jesus Christ alone, "for not even the Father judges anyone, but He has given all judgment to the Son" (John 5:22). Ironic, isn't it, that we church members routinely do what even the Sovereign Father refuses to do.

Paul gives one final reminder to help the faithful get along when they have differences of opinion: "So then each one of us shall give account of himself to God" (v. 12). The weaker Christian does not have to defend the actions of the strong. The stronger Christian will not have to answer for the actions of those weak in the faith. I don't have to answer to the Judge for what you do, and you should be glad that you don't have to answer for what I do. We must give an account of our life and activities, individually, one-on-one, with the Lord of Glory. This responsibility naturally drives us to constantly take inventory of our religious scruples and convictions to make sure they are based in the infallible Word and not in the traditions or whims of humans.

A Principle to Live By (14:13)

Paul now advances a principle by which believers can get along in the church: "Therefore let us not judge one another anymore, but rather determine this— not to put an obstacle or a stumbling block in a brother's way" (v. 13). The two words Paul used to describe tripping up our brother are similar in meaning but not the same. The first derives from *proskoptō*, meaning "to strike against" (Matt. 4:6; 7:27; Luke 4:11; John 11:9–10; Rom. 9:32; 14:21; 1 Pet. 2:8) It is *proskomma* and means to deliberately place an obstacle in the path so someone will strike his or her foot on it and stumble. The second word is *skandalon* and means more of an offense rather than a stone. In ancient Greece this was the word used for the trigger on a trap. When you put a piece of cheese on a mousetrap and the mouse was caught, the trigger on the trap was called the *skandalon*. This makes Paul's admonition even clearer. In the local assembly, those who live a sensitive life are not only sensitive to the varying beliefs, idiosyncrasies, and foibles of other believers, but in "Christ-living" we never purposefully place anything in the path of fellow believers to cause them to stumble, nor do we place any bait on the trap hoping to make their lives difficult. Our job is to clear debris from our fellow believers' paths, not to contribute to their downfall.

Paul's conclusion is simple. Have strong opinions, but live so as not to cause those whose opinions differ from yours to be set back on the road to spiritual maturity. Don't flaunt your freedom; don't impose your feelings. Instead, live with one another in mind. Keep your fellow Christians in mind when you speak and act. Don't make a move without fixing your fellow believers in your eyes and your Savior in your mind.

A Warning to the Strong (14:14–19)

Martin Luther, who began his treatise *On the Freedom of a Christian Man* with the words, "A Christian man is a most free lord of all, subject to none," went on in the next sentence to say, "A Christian man is a most dutiful servant of all, subject to all." F. F. Bruce commented, "He was never a more faithful follower of Paul—and of Paul's Master and his—than in the juxtaposition of these two affirmations."[6] By this Luther meant that even though our liberty in Christ may permit us to engage in a certain activity, we nevertheless might not be wise in doing so. Paul casts his lot with the strong in faith who are not given to the legalism of the weak. "I know and am convinced in the Lord Jesus that nothing is unclean in itself" (v. 14). Paul is well aware, however, that he may become a "stumbling block" (Greek, *proskomma*) to the weaker believer, for the conscience of the weak will not allow him to engage in the activities of Paul (v. 14). Thus there is no virtue in flaunting Christian liberty. "For if because of food your brother is hurt, you are no longer walking according to love" (v. 15).

Ray Stedman says:

> We can compare this to crossing a swinging bridge over a mountain stream. Some people can run across a bridge like that even though it does not have any handrails. They are not concerned about the swaying of the bridge, or the danger of falling into the torrent below. But others are very uncertain on such a bridge. They shake and tremble; they inch along. They may even get down on their hands and knees and crawl across. But they will make it if you just give them time, if you let them set their own speed. After a few crossings they begin to pick up courage, and eventually they are able to run right across. It is like that with these moral questions. Some people cannot see themselves acting in a certain area that they have been brought up to think is wrong. As in the case of the swinging bridge, it would be cruel for someone who had the freedom to cross boldly to take the arm of someone who was timid and force him to run across. He might even lose his balance and fall off the bridge. This is what Paul is warning about in verse 15.[7]

As believers, we must not insist on our liberty in the presence of those whose consciences would be offended by that liberty. To do so is to fail to walk in love under the lordship of Christ. To the strong in the faith Paul admonishes, "Do not destroy with your food him for whom Christ died" (v. 15). No liberty is more important than our brother or sister in the Lord. If we are to live a life of consideration for our neighbor, then we must learn that even though there are things we feel we biblically may do, many of those same things, for the sake of others, we should not do.

"Therefore do not let what is for you a good thing be spoken of as evil" (v. 16). Paul reaffirms that the position of the strong is right and good but advises them not to let what is good become the object of misunderstanding. "For the kingdom of God is not eating and drinking, but righteousness and peace and joy in the Holy Spirit" (v. 17). The kingdom of God is not to be marked by eating or not eating certain things, or characterized by observing or not observing certain days as holier than others. Nor is any other secondary religious issue to be given precedent. The true character of God's kingdom is reflected in our righteousness (personal holiness in our daily walk), peace (perfect peace with God and a consistent attempt to be a peacemaker), and joy (perfect union and intimate love through the Holy Spirit). (See Matt. 5:3–11.) Hence Paul can conclude, "So then let us pursue the things which make for peace and the building up of one another" (v. 19). He cautions the Romans not to ride moral or theological hobby horses but to pursue issues that will build the common bond of faith between the weak and the strong. How much stronger our witness would be to a watching world if the basis of our Christian fellowship was not those peripheral matters that divide us but rather the common salvation that unites us.

Learning to Build Up, Not Tear Down (14:20–23)

In light of this, the apostle concludes, "Do not tear down the work of God for the sake of food" (v. 20). Convictions are necessary, says the apostle, but not at the expense of the work of God. The reason is simple: "All things indeed are clean, but they are evil for the man who eats and gives offense" (v. 20). Nothing is unclean of itself, but certain foods become unclean to those who eat them when their conscience tells them otherwise. So, for the sake of their conscience, people should avoid those foods. To the strong Paul advises, "It is good not to eat meat or to drink wine, or to do anything by which your brother stumbles" (v. 21). What a beautiful picture: a Christian who knows he is at liberty to do something but refuses to do so for the sake of another. That's living a life of sensitivity.

Paul began Romans 14 with a general principle: "Accept the one who is weak in faith" (v. 1). Throughout the chapter, Paul gave specific examples of that principle. Now he concludes with a general principle: "The faith which you have, have as your own conviction before God" (v. 22). "Faith" here means a firm conviction before God that what one believes is right. It is entirely proper for us to have and cherish certain convictions. We study the Word and mature as believers, and that maturing process results in coming to certain moral and ethical conclusions. We are convinced we have biblical reasons for what we believe, but the real measure of our maturity is not in what we believe; it is in how we act. We may have personal convictions based on the Word, but we may have to keep those convictions to ourselves to prevent a weaker believer from stumbling into sin. We must not force our convictions on others; nor should we flaunt them before our Christian brother or sister. That's learning to build up, not tear down.

Getting Along with Other Believers

What to do:

Accept the one who is weak.	Romans 14:1
Let each be convinced about what to eat.	Romans 14:5
Pursue what makes for peace.	Romans 14:19
Pursue what builds up one another.	Romans 14:19
Bear the weaknesses of those without strength.	Romans 15:1
Please the neighbor for his good.	Romans 15:2
Be of the same mind one with another.	Romans 15:5
Accept one another as Christ also accepted us.	Romans 15:7

What not to do:

Do not treat with contempt those who eat different foods.	Romans 14: 3
Do not judge.	Romans 14:4
Do not place a stumbling block before the brother.	Romans 14:13
Do not destroy the weak brother with what you eat.	Romans 14:15
Do not let what is good for you be spoken of as evil.	Romans 14:16
Do not tear down the work of God by what you eat.	Romans 14:20
Do not do anything that makes your brother stumble.	Romans 14:21
Do not simply please yourself.	Romans 15:1

One final comment by the apostle in this chapter: "But he who doubts is condemned if he eats, because his eating is not from faith; and whatever is not from faith is sin" (v. 23). If you are not convinced a certain activity you see your Christian friend engaged in is right, do not participate yourself simply at his or her urging. You must be convinced in your mind that the activity is legitimate, permitted by God in His Word. If you participate against what you believe, if you cave in to the pressure of the group, you have given in to what is sinful for you. If your actions do not arise from your convictions, they become sinful actions to you and are unacceptable to God. You must make up your own mind or be guilty of acting from peer pressure and not from faith.

That's why Paul concludes, "Whatever is not from faith is sin." When I was a boy growing up, my mother used to say, "If you're in doubt, don't." Maybe she was reading Romans 14.

Living with Christ as Our Example (15:1–3)

Paul's teaching on living a life of sensitivity spills over into chapter 15. It's unfortunate that those who placed the chapter breaks in the Bible did so at this point, for there is clearly no break in Paul's thought until Romans 15:13. The apostle presses on in his discussion of the strong in the faith helping the weak. He says, "Now we who are strong ought to bear the weaknesses of those without strength and not just please ourselves" (v. 1). Again, Paul casts himself as one of the strong, one who has grasped the principle of Christian liberty and freedom from man-made taboos. But note that he does not revel in his strength of understanding doctrine but rather uses his strength to assist the weak. His desire is that the strong bear with those whose scruples he regards as weaknesses or sicknesses (Greek, *asthenēma*). Paul can argue this because He has excellent precedent for such behavior. "For even Christ did not please Himself" (v. 3). As the prime example of one strong in the faith, living in light of those weak in the faith, the apostle proposes the Lord Himself. The Lord Jesus had every right to please Himself, for what He would do would of necessity be right. Yet He was willing to set aside His own desires and follow the Father's directives. The quote from Psalm 69:9, "The reproaches of those who reproached Thee fell upon Me" (v. 3), is applied to the life of the Lord in that He obeyed the will of the Father even when He Himself might have chosen an easier path (Matt. 26:39). He did not exercise His perfect freedom so that the ultimate task of salvation could be accomplished.

Learning from Christ's Example (15:4–12)

Paul's statement about those things in Scripture written earlier being for our instruction is akin to his word in 2 Timothy 3:16 about the profitableness of Scripture. An earnest study of the Word of God will not only make the weak strong but will enable us to bear the burdens and weaknesses of others. The instruction imparted by the Scriptures is directed toward perseverance and encouragement (v. 4). These culminate in hope, not some wistful desire that everything will turn out all right, but the confidence that all things indeed do work together for our good (Rom. 8:28). When we learn from Christ's example with regard to living a life of sensitivity, hope is the by-product of the learning process.

Christ Our Example
- He died for others (14:9).
- He did not please Himself (15:3).
- He bore the reproaches of others (15:3).
- He accepted us (15:7).
- He became a servant (15:8).

Assuming that his readers get the message, the apostle pronounces a benediction on his teaching with regard to getting along in the family of God. "Now may the God who gives perseverance and encouragement grant you to be of the same mind with one another according to Christ Jesus; that with one accord you may with one voice glorify the God and Father of our Lord Jesus Christ" (vv. 5–6). Paul appeals to the God who gives patience and consolation to bring the strong and weak together and advises, "Wherefore, accept one another, just as Christ also accepted us to the glory of God" (v. 7). Paul's point is that if the Lord can receive us with the great chasm that existed between Him and us, should we not also be able to accept one another even if there are minor differences between us?

Finally, Paul turns his apostolic guns squarely on Jew/Gentile acceptance of each other. With Christ as the example, the Jew must receive the Gentile and the Gentile the Jew in the same way and to the same extent that Christ received both Jew and Gentile. Jesus Christ came to be a servant of the circumcision, the Jews. The Greek word Paul uses to describe the Lord's relationship to the Jews is *diakonos*. Paul's assessment of the Lord's ministry squares with the Lord's own assessment. "For even the Son of Man did not come to be served, but to serve" (Greek, *diakoneō*, Mark 10:45). When we live with the beliefs and foibles of others in mind, even if we don't agree with them, we live as Christ lived for us. That's how the Lord Jesus expects us to get along in the church. That's what those things "written in earlier times" (v. 4) instruct us. When the Gentiles reflect on Jesus' service to the Jews, they break out in praise to God for His mercy to His people. Paul appeals to Psalm 18:49, where David includes Gentile nations in the heritage of God to Israel, to prove that what was written was now to be lived. "Therefore I will give praise to Thee among the Gentiles, and I will sing to Thy Name" (v. 9).

Not content with that, the apostle begins a series of quotations from the Old Testament to prove that it has always been God's intent for His people, Jews and Gentiles, to be one in Christ. First, he quotes from the Song of Moses, Deuteronomy 32:43, "Rejoice, O Gentiles, with His people" (v. 10). Then he quotes from Psalm 117:1, "Praise the Lord all you Gentiles, and let all the peoples praise Him" (v. 11). Isaiah 11:10 follows: "There shall come the root of Jesse, and He who arises to rule over the Gentiles, in Him shall the Gentiles hope" (v. 12). Paul's purpose is to indicate that Gentiles as well as Jews will be included in the family of God. The *goyim* (Hebrew for Gentiles) will put their trust in the Root of Jesse (the Lord Jesus) just as believing Jews will. And though there are (and will be) many differences between these two groups of believers, nevertheless, their common bond is faith in Christ. That commonality is much greater than their difference. As a result, Paul's ultimate prayer is, "Now may the God of hope fill you with all joy and peace in believing, that you may abound in hope by the power of the Holy Spirit" (v. 13).

This long portion of Paul's letter to the believers at Rome includes his final admonitions to them and reflects the need in the Roman church for acceptance of one another, warts and all, as brothers and sisters in Christ. It's a lesson the twenty-first-century church needs to heed carefully, for even today God is calling to Himself men and women, boys and girls from "every tribe and tongue and people and nation" (Rev. 5:9). The Christian tent is extremely big, and those who fellowship under it are extremely diverse. It's important that we learn to live together in harmony here, not forsaking our individual beliefs or doctrines, but submitting them all to the lordship of Christ. We can never claim to live a life of sensitivity to others if we do not.

Study Questions

1. What does the apostle Paul mean when he writes, "Let each man be fully convinced in his own mind" about what to eat or not eat?

2. Besides the eating or not eating of specific foods and the observing of certain days, what could we list today that may cause divisive opinions among Christians?

3. From this section of verses, list all of the imperatives and commands Paul gives Christians concerning being considerate to other believers.

4. What does Paul have in mind when he writes, "We who are strong ought to bear the weaknesses of those without strength"?

5. In verses 9–12, what is the apostle trying to get across when he quotes so extensively from the Old Testament?

CHAPTER 27

Paul's Future Plans
Romans 15:14–33

Preview:

The apostle Paul is a minister of the gospel, especially to the Gentiles. He can "boast" in the things that Christ has accomplished through him. His great desire is to preach the gospel where Christ is not known. He urges the Gentiles who have been blessed by the gospel to share with the suffering saints in Jerusalem. He also longs to visit the saints in Rome, to find rest and comfort in their presence.

The apostle Paul begins to conclude this letter long before he actually ends. The Romans' transition from learning doctrine to putting it into practice makes it difficult for him to say good-bye, for they were apparently weak in both areas. Paul has intense personal feelings for them even though he has never been to Rome. Since he has met many of them in other areas of the Mediterranean world, he also must express personal greetings. A lengthy list of final greetings is capped by a final note of praise to the Lord.

Explanation for Writing (15:14–16)

Paul assures his readers, "And concerning you, my brethren, I myself also am convinced that you yourselves are full of goodness, filled with all knowledge, and able also to admonish one another" (v. 14). After that lengthy segment of his letter on accepting one another, Paul did not want the Roman believers to think he considered them spiritually immature. Thus the admonitions he gives in this epistle are not to be received by them alone, but by every reader of the epistle to the Romans in every country in every age. Paul knew his readers; they were full of goodness and kindness but also "filled with all knowledge," practical discernment of every kind. He even credits them with independently being able to caution one another against specific faults. Today the word *counseling* is heard frequently, and innumerable counseling books and articles have been written. The apostle here reveals that in this respect "there is nothing new under the sun." There was mutual counseling already in his day, and it was of a high character. By and large the members of the Roman church were 'competent to admonish one another.'[1]

Nevertheless, the apostle has spoken boldly "on some points," a Greek idiom used to highlight the more pointed portions of the apostle's letter (see Rom. 6:12; 8:9; 11:18; 12:3; 13:3; 14:3, 10, 15). Clothed in the vocabulary of worship, Paul asserts that the reason for his writing the way he has is "because of the grace that was given me from God, to be a minister of Christ Jesus to the Gentiles, ministering as a priest the gospel of God" (vv. 15–16). God made the apostle an officiating priest (Greek, *leitourgos*) to preach the gospel as a priestly service (Greek, *hierourgeō*) that Paul might present the Gentiles as an acceptable thank offering (Greek, *prosphora*) to Him. They are sanctified, not by circumcision, but by something much better—the Holy Spirit. Paul wants to include the Gentiles of the church at Rome in that offering.

Vindication for Writing (15:17–21)

Having explained why he wrote this letter to the believers in Rome, Paul now vindicates that writing. "Therefore in Christ Jesus I have found reason for boasting in things pertaining to God" (v. 17). Paul justifiably feels he has a right to glory with respect to his work for God. After all, God has done a marvelous thing with the life of Saul of Tarsus and a marvelous thing through the life of Paul the apostle. But, says the apostle, "I will not presume to speak of anything except what Christ has accomplished through me" (v. 18). Paul was God's instrument to bring the Gentiles to faith. God even confirmed his message "in the power of signs and wonders" and "in the power of the Spirit" (v. 19).

> These "signs and wonders" were great in number and enormous in effect. . . . However, as Paul makes clear, many of the miracles that occurred during his lengthy pre-Romans ministry were the immediate results of preaching (note "by what I have said and done") applied to hearts and lives by the Holy Spirit. These successes were "gospel triumphs" (cf. 2 Cor. 2:14). In fact, in the book of Acts the emphasis is placed on these spiritual victories. See the following passages: Acts 13:42–44, 48–49; 16:5, 14–15, 32–34; 17:4, 11–12; 18:8, 27–28.[2]

It was in the power of the Holy Spirit, says Paul, that "from Jerusalem and round about as far as Illyricum I have fully preached the gospel of Christ" (v. 19).

What a marvelous, absolutely tireless love-laborer was this man Paul. Illyricum was the next province to Italy. Between Jerusalem and Illyricum lay the province of Syria, with its capital at Damascus, but its spiritual capital Antioch; and next to it Cilicia, with its great center Tarsus, Paul's own home, whither he had been sent by the brethren away from Jerusalem persecution (Acts 9:30); and whence Barnabas brought him to the work at Antioch (Acts 11:25–26); next province Pamphylia with Perga and Attalia; and above that Pisidia, centered at another Antioch; then Lycaonia, and above that the great and difficult Galatia with the churches Paul founded there; next proconsular Asia, centered at Ephesus, of course, and the mighty work there and the "fighting with beasts"; then at Troas across the Aegean came the call from Macedonia, and its cities Philippi, Berea and Thessalonica, the saints of which lay so close to the apostle's heart; then Achaia, centered at Corinth, whence he wrote this present letter to the Romans—vast city, vast wickedness, but much people for the Lord. And so we arrive at Illyricum. And through all these regions just traced, Paul has fulfilled the gospel of Christ; insomuch that verse 23 informs us that he had no more any place in these regions.[3]

So, Paul desired to preach the gospel where it had not yet been preached. He was a missionary pioneer, not a program producer. He wanted to labor where no seed had been sown, not reap what others had sown. His goal was not to "build upon another man's foundation" (v. 20), and thus he appeals to Isaiah 52:15, "They who had no news of Him shall see, and they who have not heard shall understand" as his motivating force (v. 21). Paul made it his ministerial ambition to break up fallow ground with the gospel, and in so doing the Lord drew him to various metropolitan centers such as Ephesus, Philippi, and Corinth. Each time Paul encountered first-time hearers of the message he bore. Nothing made Paul happier than blazing new trails, setting out for new territories. That's why Spain and what would become Western Europe weighed heavily in his passionate vision.

Paul's Plans Following the Writing (15:22–29)

While the pioneering spirit of Paul to spread the gospel where no man had done so had thus far hindered the apostle from coming to Rome (v. 22), nevertheless, years of desire were about to give way to an actual journey to Spain that would necessitate a stopover in the capital city of the empire (v. 24). Paul's activity in Spain would likewise be cultivating virgin soil, but before he made his way to the end of the known world, he desired to visit Rome for reasons already explained in the first chapter, verses 11 and 12.

Now Paul reiterates his desire: "For I hope to see you in passing, and to be helped on my way there by you, when I have first enjoyed your company for a while" (v. 24). He has spiritual benefit to impart to the Roman Christians as a teacher of the Word, and they have comfort, fellowship, and lodging to give to him. Reading between the lines, one can feel Paul's genuine love for these people. He is not just looking for funding for his journey to Spain, he sincerely wants to enjoy their company.

It is not certain that Paul ever reached Spain, but ancient tradition said he did. About A.D. 95 Clement of Rome said Paul's travels reached "to the bounds of the west" (*Epistle to the Corinthians* 5:7). The Greek behind the Muratorian Canon, a barbarous Latin translation of the eighth century, is believed to be of the second century, and it spoke of "the journey of Paul when he left Rome for Spain" (38–39). Lightfoot thought such a trip not improbable, but recent commentators are more cautious.[4]

Rome came before Spain, but Jerusalem came before Rome. "But now, I am going to Jerusalem serving the saints. For Macedonia and Achaia have been pleased to make a contribution for the poor among the saints in Jerusalem" (vv. 25–26). Paul was a natural to deliver to the poor saints an offering he had collected from the Christians of Macedonia and Achaia. After all, he had himself been impoverished again and again for the sake of the gospel (cf. 2 Cor. 11:27), and thus he had learned "how to get along with humble means" (Phil. 4:12). He not only sympathized with the poor of Jerusalem, his compassion drove him to do something about their plight. The Christians of Greece had not been affected by famine and affliction, and thus they became God's instruments of relief to those Christians who were. That's the way it ought to be. This was not only an act of Christian love, but a way of cementing the relationship between the Jewish and Gentile factions of the early Church, since the Christians of Macedonia and Achaia were predominantly Gentile. The contribution (Greek, *koinōnia*), or sharing of their wealth, was a voluntary gesture on the part of the Gentile churches, yet it also recognized the moral debt they owed to the mother church that had first disseminated the gospel (v. 27).

As soon as Paul had discharged his moral duty to the saints at Jerusalem, he was on his way to Rome and then Spain (v. 28). He was convinced that his coming to them would be more than a blessing. It would be "filled up to all the fulness of God" (see Eph. 3:19). At the time, Paul was unaware that when he finally arrived in Rome, he would be in chains. Nonetheless, his presence would mean the blessing of Christ. This proved to be the case, because it was during Paul's first visit to Rome that the Holy Spirit blessed us all by inspiring the apostle to pen the epistles to the Colossians, Ephesians, and Philippians, as well as a small personal letter to Philemon.

Paul's Plea for Prayers on His Behalf (15:30–33)

The tone of Paul's writing now speaks of closure. In drawing his letter to an end, he appeals for the support of Roman prayers in the face of the imminent dangers he must face before he comes to them. He asks them to "strive together with me in your prayers to God" (v. 30). As always, Paul's requests are specific: (1) that he may be delivered from those who are disobedient in Judea (v. 31); (2) that his service for Jerusalem may prove acceptable to the saints (v. 31); (3) that he may come to the Romans in joy by the will of God (v. 32); and (4) that he may find refreshing rest in their company (v. 32). Paul knows that dangers threaten him in Judea, for there are many who mark him as a traitor to the Jewish cause. He calls them "disobedient" because of their refusal to submit themselves to God's method of divinely imputed righteousness rather than self-initiated righteousness. Coupled with the hatred of unbelieving Jews is the danger that the church at Jerusalem might misread his intentions in bringing a monetary gift. Perhaps they might not receive it because it was given by the Gentiles. It shows how much the church needed the unity of which Paul often wrote. Also, Paul says he desires to come to Rome with joy by the will of God—that is, only if it be the will of God. And he wants to be refreshed both physically and spiritually while visiting his friends there. Since these requests are couched in the language of prayer, it is appropriate for him to close with a doxology. The beautiful benediction, addressed to the weak as well as the strong, to the Jew as well as the Gentile, is this: "Now the God of peace be with you all. Amen."

Paul has revealed his plans, and declared his intentions. Now he asks his Roman friends to pray that God will lead him directly and bless his plans. God does not lead us if we sit still and do not plan for the future, but neither does He automatically accept our plans as His own. We need to pray as well as plan if we are to receive the touch of God's blessing. Paul reflects that in Romans 15.

Study Questions

1. Summarize what Paul says concerning his ministry for the sake of the gospel.

2. From verse 19, how far had Paul preached the gospel, geographically speaking?

3. In what ways did the apostle want the Gentile converts to help the persecuted believers in Jerusalem?

4. From verses 22–33, what seemed to be driving Paul to travel so extensively around the Roman world?

5. From what the apostle Paul writes, what kind of relationship did he have with the Roman Christians?

CHAPTER 28

Paul's Personal Greetings
Romans 16:1-24

Preview:

The apostle Paul is careful to give praise and commendation to those who are laboring so intensely for the sake of Christ. He specifically acknowledges many by citing their name. He warns of those who would hinder the teaching of the truth, and he urges the believers to turn away from them. He is positive in that he knows the God of peace will someday crush Satan under the feet of those serving the Lord Jesus.

Some have questioned the appropriateness of chapter 16 after Paul's beautiful prayer concluding chapter 15. Was chapter 16 part of the original letter? Is it correctly placed in the text? Arguments have raged since the time of Marcion, and objections have been answered satisfactorily again and again. Therefore it is not necessary to repeat them here. Suffice it to say that Paul is having a difficult time saying good-bye to the believers in Rome. His efforts to do so extend much further here than in any of his other letters. In Romans 16, Paul greets twenty-six people by name and mentions others in less specific ways. It is evident that he had many friends who had settled in Rome and wished to bear greetings to them. Most of these people we know very little about, but the apostle knew them intimately. It is his letter; he greets his acquaintances, not ours.

The late Pastor Ray Stedman mused, "Something in all of us wants to see our names preserved. Years ago I visited the Natural Bridge of Virginia. There were hundreds of names and initials scratched on the rocks, but high up on the side of it, above almost every other name, was scratched 'George Washington.' Even the father of our country felt the urge to gain a kind of immortality by carving his name on the rock."[1] The people Paul acknowledges here in Romans 16 are etched in the Rock of Ages, carved in the book of eternity, which is forever settled in heaven (Ps. 119:89). They did not ask us to remember their names, but they will never be forgotten.

The Commendation of Phoebe (16:1–2)

Paul begins this concluding chapter with a recommendation for the woman to whom he is entrusting the letter for delivery: "I commend to you our sister Phoebe" (v. 1). Phoebe, whose name means "radiant," was apparently a businesswoman from the city of Cenchrea, the seaport city of Corinth on the Saronic Gulf (cf. Acts 18:18). She was a servant (Greek, *diakonos*) of the church in that city. Paul calls her "our sister" as a term of Christian endearment. Likewise, she is said to be a "helper" or befriender of many, including Paul. Apparently Phoebe was a widow, else she would not have been able to travel so freely in the Roman Empire. She was preparing for a business trip to Rome, and Paul seized that opportunity, since as a private citizen he was not permitted to use the official Roman postal system, to send his letter to Rome. Therefore he encourages the Roman Christians to "receive her in the Lord in a manner worthy of the saints" (v. 2). He asks them to "help her in whatever matter she may have need of you." Christians need to go out of their way to help other Christians. It is a token of the love we received when our Savior went out of His way to die for us at Calvary.

Greetings for Friends in Rome (16:3–16)

With verse 3 Paul begins to say hello to his friends in Rome. "Greet Prisca[2] and Aquila my fellow workers in Christ Jesus" (v. 3). This Jewish couple moved, under the dint of persecution and in their quest for souls, from Rome to Corinth, to Ephesus, and back to Rome again. They supplied lay leadership in various evangelistic endeavors. They were Christian heroes. Paul even says they "risked their own necks" for his life. Just when this heroism occurred we are not told, but their friendship with the apostle was so intense that he mentions them in the salutations of two other epistles (1 Cor. 16:19; 2 Tim. 4:19). Furthermore, verse 5 records Paul's greeting to "the church that is in their house."

> The Greek word for church *(ekklēsia)* has at least three meanings in the New Testament: (1) all the Christians in a house (v. 5), (2) all the Christians in a city (1 Cor. 1:2), and (3) all the Christians in the world

(Col. 1:24). The most frequent use is the second, as in "all the churches of the Gentiles" (v. 4), "all the churches of Christ" (v. 16) and "the whole church" (16:23). In each case they are the saints and brethren.[3]

"Greet Epaenetus, my beloved, who is the first convert to Christ from Asia" (v. 5). Since Priscilla and Aquila were heavily involved in missionary activity in Asia Minor,[4] it is appropriate for Paul to mention Asia Minor's first believer next. While Epaenetus's conversion is not mentioned in the book of Acts, it is here said to be the firstfruits, implying that there were many others to come. Perhaps it is coincidence that his name means "praiseworthy," but it is with this man that the floodgates of Asia Minor opened and praise was given to God for the conversion of multitudes of Gentiles.

"Greet Mary, who has worked hard for you" (v. 6). Mary is a Semitic name (Miriam) borne by at least six women in the New Testament. In what way Mary worked hard for the Romans is not known to us, but it is to God. It probably refers to her association with Priscilla and Aquila from the inception of the Roman church.

"Greet Andronicus and Junias, my kinsmen, and my fellow prisoners, who are outstanding among the apostles, who also were in Christ before me" (v. 7). It is impossible to know for sure if the second of the names is the feminine, Junia, or masculine, Junias. When Paul says they are his "kinsmen," he need not be referring to a close family relationship, for all Jews were his kinsmen (cf. Rom. 9:3). Since the apostle's imprisonments were many (cf. 2 Cor. 6:5; 11:23), it is difficult to say in which of these they shared as "fellow prisoners." They were, however, of note among the "apostles" (using this term in the general sense of "messenger," cf. 2 Cor. 8:23; Phil. 2:25) and came to know the Lord as Savior even before the apostle Paul.[5]

"Greet Ampliatus, my beloved in the Lord" (v. 8). Amplias is an abbreviated form of Ampliatus, a common name in the empire. William Barclay says that:

> Behind the name of Ampliatus there may well lie an interesting story. Ampliatus is a quite common slave name. Now in the cemetery of Domatilla, which is the earliest of the Christian catacombs, there is a decorated tomb with the single name Ampliatus carved on it in bold and decorative lettering. Now the fact that the single name Ampliatus alone is carved on the tomb—Romans who are citizens have three names, a nomen, a praenomen, and a cognomen—would indicate that Ampliatus was a slave, but the elaborate tomb and the bold lettering would indicate that he was a man of high rank in the Church. And from that it is plain to see that in the early days of the Church the distinctions of rank and place were so completely wiped out that it was possible for a man at one

and the same time to be a slave and a prince of the Church. Social distinctions did not exist. We have no means of knowing that Paul's Ampliatus is the Ampliatus of the tomb in the cemetery of Domatilla, but it is not impossible that he is.[6]

"Greet Urbanus, our fellow worker in Christ, and Stachys my beloved" (v. 9). Urbanus, or Urbane, by his very name, must have been a native of Rome. His Latin name means "urbane, elegant, polite." Apparently he was a man of some social standing. The fact that he is said to be "our fellow worker in Christ" and not, as Priscilla and Aquila, "my fellow workers," has led to speculation that he was not as close to the apostle as they were. Still, being a "fellow worker in Christ" with the apostle Paul is not bad company to be in. Stachys, a Greek name meaning "ear" (of grain), is not a common name and occurs with no further amplification other than "my beloved" (see vv. 5, 8, 12.)

"Greet Apelles, the approved in Christ" (v. 10). Apelles is a Greek name that is also borne by Jews. He is distinguished as "approved in Christ," (see 2 Tim. 2:15), but we are not left with a clue as to why. His is a common name found in Roman inscriptions, sometimes related to the imperial household.

"Greet those who are of the household of Aristobulus" (v. 10). Although it cannot be said with certainty, J. B. Lightfoot has suggested that this Aristobulus was the grandson of Herod the Great and the brother of Herod Agrippa I. If so, he lived in Rome as a private citizen and enjoyed a close friendship with Emperor Claudius. He is not greeted himself, but Paul greets the slaves of his household as Christians.

"Greet Herodion, my kinsman" (v. 11). This name, and the context of the preceding verse, would suggest that this man was one of Herod's household. He was a kinsman of Paul and therefore Jewish.

"Greet those of the household of Narcissus, who are in the Lord" (v. 11). It may be possible to identify this man with Tiberius Claudius Narcissus, a wealthy freedman of the Emperor Tiberius. Narcissus was executed by order of Agrippina, Nero's mother, shortly after her son's accession to the throne in A.D. 54. If his possessions were at this time confiscated, his slaves would have become imperial property and would have been known as the *Narcissiani*, or household of Narcissus. Paul does not greet Narcissus, but his slaves, and not all of his slaves, but only those "who are in the Lord."

"Greet Tryphaena and Tryphosa, workers in the Lord" (v. 12). Tryphaena and Tryphosa were probably sisters and possibly even twins. It was a common practice to name twins by using the same root word for both names. The name means "those who live voluptuously." Although their names stem from a pagan, Anatolian root, Paul nevertheless associates them with other workers for the Lord and gives them Christian greetings.

"Greet Persis the beloved, who has worked hard in the Lord" (v. 12). Persis, meaning "Persian woman," is said to be "the beloved," but with a woman Paul delicately avoids using the phrase "my beloved." Her name appears on Greek and Latin inscriptions as that of a slave or freedwoman.

Now we come to one of the more obscure and yet most interesting of all the people Paul greets. "Greet Rufus, a choice man in the Lord, also his mother and mine" (v. 13). It may be possible to make an identification between this Rufus and the man of the same name who Mark records was the son of Simon of Cyrene (cf. Mark 15:21). Mark says, "And they pressed into service a passer-by coming from the country, Simon of Cyrene (the father of Alexander and Rufus), to bear His cross." That Simon was identifiable by the name of his son Rufus must mean that the son was a man of some renown. F. F. Bruce, in addressing how Rufus's mother could act as mother to Paul, hazards the guess that when Barnabas brought Paul from Tarsus to become his missionary colleague, one of the teachers of the church at Antioch permitted Paul to lodge with him, a certain Simon surnamed Niger, "the dark-skinned," cf. Acts 13:1 (whom Bruce identifies with Simon of Cyrene). In the course of Paul's lodging there, Simon's mother cared for, or "mothered," the apostle. Although interesting, this plausible explanation is still speculation.[7]

"Greet Asyncritus, Phlegon, Hermes, Patrobas, Hermas and the brethren with them" (v. 14). Little is known of these believers other than that they were apparently of one community and were all men. Hermes was the name of the god of good luck and became a common slave name. Patrobas was abbreviated from Patrobius. Hermas is an abbreviation of some names, such as Hermogenes or Hermodorus and is very common (cf. *The Shepherd of Hermas* in apocryphal literature). "The brethren with them" probably refers to other members of the same house church.

"Greet Philologus and Julia, Nereus and his sister, and Olympas, and all the saints who are with them" (v. 15). Philologus and Julia were perhaps husband and wife. Both names occur several times in connection with the imperial household of Rome. Nereus, according to a tradition that goes back to the fourth century, is associated with Flavia Domitilla, a Christian woman who was banished to the Island of Pandateria by her uncle, Emperor Domitian, in A.D. 95. She was released after his death the following year.[8] Olympas is an abbreviated form of Olympiodorus. These all appear to have been a community of faith.

"Greet one another with an holy kiss" (v. 16). The holy kiss was a common feature of Christian greeting (cf. 1 Cor. 16:20; 2 Cor. 13:12; 1 Thess. 5:26; 1 Pet. 5:14). Justin Martyr mentions that it was a common feature in early Christian worship (*First Apology*, 66). It was "holy" as opposed to that in the question, "Judas, are you betraying the Son of Man with a kiss?" (Luke 22:48). Although a feature in the liturgy of the Eastern Church to this day, the holy kiss is noticeably absent in the Western Church.

Paul completes his extensive list of personal greetings to friends in Rome with the summary statement, "All the churches of Christ greet you" (v. 16). By that he means that every church to which the apostles ministered, every city to which he traveled and planted a local assembly, was vibrantly linked in the bonds of Christ, and therefore he bears greetings from each of them to the saints who are in the Roman church.

Warnings to Friends in Rome (16:17–20)

Ever the concerned apostle, Paul could not complete his letter without some personal admonitions. Like a parent who dearly loves his children and their friends, he gives them sage preemptory advice. "Now I urge you, brethren, keep your eye on those who cause dissensions and hindrances contrary to the teaching which you learned, and turn away from them" (v. 17). Paul's admonition and warning to his friends at Rome concern those who would cause divisions among the believers there. He commands two things: (1) Keep your eye on them, or mark them (Greek, *skopeō*), and (2) Turn away from, or avoid, them (Greek, *ekklinō*). "The proper treatment of such deviates from the truth is to lean away from them or 'avoid' them so as to have no dealings with them," says Gleason Archer. "This does not necessarily mean excommunication, but certainly involves a rebuke of that carnal type of tolerance which insists on maintaining friendly relations with offenders in such a way as to appear to condone their sin."[9]

Those who cause divisions may have been Antinomians who pushed their liberty in Christ to the limit. They may have been the ubiquitous Judaizers who seemed to incessantly plague Paul. Or they may have been prima donas who wished to be in the church's limelight (every church has them, cf. Diotrephes in 3 John 1:9–10). Whoever they were, Paul characterizes them as people who cause dissension and hindrance contrary to the doctrine the Romans had received in this letter. He further adds, "For such men are slaves, not of our Lord Christ but of their own appetites; and by their smooth and flattering speech they deceive the hearts of the unsuspecting" (v. 18). These smooth-talking teachers have ensnared innocent and unsuspecting believers in their doctrinal trap. Thank God, however, that the Romans have been obedient to the true gospel and have demonstrated that they are "wise in what is good, and innocent in what is evil" (v. 19). In Matthew 10:16 we are counseled to be "shrewd as serpents, and innocent as doves." The Greek adjectives *sophos* and *akeraios* are used both in Matthew and here. Paul cautions the Roman Christians to be alert and discerning in relation to false doctrine (cf. 1 Cor. 14:20). And what is the result of such vigilance? "The God of peace will soon crush Satan under your feet" (v. 20). In echoing Genesis 3:15, Paul reminds the believers at Rome that God has promised ultimate victory to His church, and shortly, despite Satan's crafty attacks, the enemy will be defeated. God will crush Satan, and the kingdoms of the world will become the kingdom of our Lord and of His Christ, and He will reign forever (Rev. 11:15).

Greetings from Friends with Paul (16:21–23)

"Timothy my fellow worker greets you, and so do Lucius and Jason and Sosipater, my kinsmen" (v. 21). Timothy, Paul's convert from Lystra and subsequent colleague, was particularly dear to Paul. Of him Paul said to the church at Philippi, "For I have no one else of kindred spirit who will genuinely be concerned for your welfare. . . . But you know of his proven worth that he served with me in the furtherance of the gospel like a child serving his father" (Phil. 2:20, 22). Lucius, Jason, and Sosipater are mentioned as Paul's kinsmen and therefore as Jewish Christians. Jason may have been Paul's host on his first visit to Thessalonica (Acts 17:6, 7, 9). Sosipater is probably Sopater of Berea, the son of Pyrrhus, according to Acts 20:4.

And then follows a tender insertion by Tertius. "I, Tertius, who write this letter, greet you in the Lord" (v. 22). Tertius, probably a native Italian, was the stenographer or amanuensis of the apostle.

> The name indicates that he was a slave, because his name means "third." In slave families they did not bother to think up names; they just numbered the children. First, Second, Third, Fourth, Fifth, and so on. Here are Third and Fourth of a family of slaves (his brother Quartus, Fourth, is mentioned in verse 23). They are educated slaves who became Christians. These men can read and write, and are part of this group in Corinth.[10]

Paul's practice of using an amanuensis is well attested. Apparently Tertius interjects his own greeting into Paul's narration because he too knows and loves the believers at Rome.

More greetings from friends follow. "Gaius, host to me and to the whole church, greets you. Erastus, the city treasurer greets you, and Quartus, the brother" (v. 23). Gaius is to be identified with the man whom Paul baptized at Corinth (1 Cor. 1:14) and may be identified as well with Titius Justus of Acts 18:7, who offered the use of his house to Paul when the fledgling church of Corinth was expelled from the synagogue next door. The Roman system of naming a citizen was by the use of three names (praenomen, nomen, and cog-nomen), and Gaius was a common praenomen (first name). His full name would then have been Gaius Titus Justus. Erastus was the city treasurer of Corinth and a believer. Quartus, of whom we know nothing, is simply men-tioned as "the brother."

Study Questions

1. From what Paul specifically makes note of, list the ways these beloved servants of Christ were serving.

2. From what the apostle says, where were the churches holding their meetings and assemblies?

3. What did Paul mean by "holy kiss"?

4. Some have accused the apostle of being harsh and aloof in his personal relations with other believers. What impression does the reader get from these verses that would confirm or deny this claim? Explain.

5. What does Paul seem to be saying in verse 20?

CHAPTER 29

Doxology
Romans 16:25-27

Preview:

Paul wants to establish the Roman Christians by the power of the gospel that was unknown and kept secret for long ages past. Now it is revealed through the Scriptures by the commandment of the eternal God. This knowledge is going to the nations, and it will lead to the obedience of faith. The only wise God, through His Son Jesus Christ, must receive the glory forever for what is happening.

Paul has already shown his penchant for benedictions in this letter, but now he must really sign off and send the letter on its way to Rome. Thus he concludes with a meaningful, reverent, and powerful doxology, praising the character of the God who loved him, saved him on the road to Damascus, and sustained him through the best of times and worst of times.

All Hail to the Powerful God (16:25)

Paul begins his hymn of praise with the words, "Now to Him who is able to establish you according to my gospel and the preaching of Jesus Christ" (v. 25). Paul's readers are commended to the only God who has the power to establish them securely by His election of grace and keep them from falling by His sovereign power. When Paul says "my gospel" (cf. 2:16), he is referring to the gospel of Christ he preaches. It is not his in that he originated it; it is his in that he has served it from the day of his conversion. Equivalent to that is the preaching of Jesus Christ, for that was the apostle's calling. This gospel came "according to the revelation of the mystery which has been kept secret for long ages past." The preaching of Christ was not a new innovation in the plan of God, but was the fulfillment of the Old Testament prophecies. This mystery was hidden for long ages prior to the birth of Christ. Now it has been demonstrated in the world by the sacrifice of Christ. And it is in accordance with the command of the eternal God. Only an all-powerful God could make the gospel plan happen.

All Hail to the Eternal God (16:26)

But Paul continues, "And by the Scriptures of the prophets, according to the commandment of the eternal God, has been made known to all the nations, leading to obedience of faith" (v. 26). This gospel that Paul preached was a mystery because the Old Testament prophets did not fully understand the new life we have in Christ. How could they? They had the promises of God, but we have the proof of those promises, the fulfillment of the Old Testament prophecies concerning the messiahship of Christ (cf. Is. 9:6; 53:1–2; Jer. 23; Mic. 5; et al.). The purpose of manifesting God's plan in Christ Jesus was that He may be discovered by people from all nations who are obedient in faith. The preaching of the gospel is not just for intellectual acceptance, but that people around the world may come to place their faith in the Christ of the gospel.

All Hail to the Wise God (16:27)

We have reached the grand finale: "To the only wise God, through Jesus Christ, be the glory forever. Amen" (v. 27). This great hymn of praise ends with the glory for people's salvation being directed toward God, exactly where it belongs. Inherent to Paul's theme throughout the epistle is that it is through Jesus Christ that praise and glory are channeled toward God. Therefore one cannot adequately or acceptably praise the Father unless he or she exercises faith in the Son. The all-wise God has placed just one door of entry to Himself and heaven. Jesus said, "I am the door; if anyone enters through Me, he shall be saved, and shall go in and out, and find pasture" (John 10:9). For the wisdom of creating the sinless, perfect Door to God and making that Door accessible to us all, the apostle thankfully gives praise "to the only wise God, through Jesus Christ." Amen.

George Vanderlip makes an astute observation about how Paul begins and ends this beloved letter to the Romans:

Key themes that we found expressed in the opening five verses are repeated. In our study of the first chapter of the letter we said that the essence of Paul's thought was expressed in the following four affirmations:

1. Paul has a message that is related to promises from the Old Testament (1:2).

2. His message is rooted in the risen Christ (1:4).

3. It is a message that is designed to bring about obedience of faith unto life (1:5).

4. It is a message that is for all the world (1:5).

When we compare the above four aspects of Paul's message with what he says in his concluding doxology we discover the following correspondence:

1. Paul's message is rooted in the "prophetic writings" (16:26).

2. His task is "the preaching of Jesus Christ" (16:25).

3. The goal for which he strives is "to bring about obedience to the faith" (16:26).

4. What he has to share is for "all nations" (16:26).[1]

That's what Romans is all about—the righteousness of God. Humans need it. God supplies it. And when we have faith in Jesus Christ as Savior, we receive it. Thanks be to God!

Study Questions

1. How will the Lord establish the Christians in Rome?

2. What is the revelation of the mystery?

3. What specifically do you think was the commandment of the eternal God?

Letter Writing in the Bible

Preview:

Not many things bring a smile to our faces or a lump to our throats more than receiving a letter or e-mail from friends or family. Getting news from home or from a friend in a distant land warms our hearts. Letters have always been an important means of communication.

Since Paul's letter to the Romans is the first of a series of letters found in the New Testament, it is appropriate here to give some attention to the practice of letter writing in the Bible.

Writing Materials

In ancient history, letters were written on just about anything people of those days had at hand—animal skins, stone, parchments, papyrus, wood, linen, and even potsherds (broken pieces of pottery). The earliest writing materials were clay tablets or stone (Ex. 32:16; Job 19:23–24). Men and women would use a chisel or other engraving tool to write on hard surfaces (Is. 8:1); and they would use a pen made from reeds (3 John 1:13) or a brush of sorts on softer surfaces (Job 19:24; Jer. 17:1).

By New Testament times, the writing paper of choice was papyrus. This is what Paul undoubtedly used to write the letter to the Romans. A contemporary of the apostle was Roman naturalist Pliny the Elder (A.D. 23–79). Pliny wrote in his encyclopedic book *Natural History* that "the process of making paper from papyrus is to split it with a knife into very thin strips made as broad as possible." These strips were then soaked in water, and the product was a kind of natural glue that held the strips together when they were laid up and down and back and forth to form a lattice look. The papyrus was then pressed dry and the edges trimmed.

Letters Found in the Bible	
King of Syria's letter to the king of Israel	2 Kings 5:5–7
Isaiah's letter to King Hezekiah	2 Kings 19:20–28
Hezekiah's letter of invitation to the Passover	2 Chronicles 30:6–9
Letter requesting that work on the temple stop	Ezra 4:7–24
King Artaxerxes' letter to Ezra	Ezra 7:11–26
Jeremiah's first letter to exiles in Babylon	Jeremiah 29:1–23
Jeremiah's second letter to exiles in Babylon	Jeremiah 29:24–29
King Darius's letter to his subjects	Daniel 6:25–27
Jerusalem Council's letter to Gentile believers	Acts 15:23–29
Commander Claudius Lysias's letter to Governor Felix	Acts 23:25–30
Letters to the seven churches in Asia Minor	Revelation 2–3

Letter-Writing Style

When Paul wrote to the believers in Rome, he had no computer, but often he did have a secretary or amanuensis who wrote down what he said on papyrus (see Rom. 16:22). Other times he simply wrote the letters himself (Gal. 6:11). Regardless, Paul's letter-writing style was typical for a citizen of the first-century Roman Empire.

The letter in Acts 23:25–30 from the Roman commander to the Roman governor is a perfect example of the style of a Roman letter. Claudius Lysias was the commander in charge of protection for Paul while he awaited trial in Jerusalem. Paul's nephew overheard a plot to kill the apostle and related what he heard to Lysias. The commander immediately prepared two centurions with two hundred soldiers, seventy cavalrymen and two hundred spearmen to escort Paul to Governor Felix in Caesarea. He sent a letter to Felix with the troops, beginning in the typical Roman style: "Claudius Lysias, to the most excellent governor Felix, greetings" (Acts 23:26).

All proper letters of the Roman period began, not with the name of the one receiving the letter, but with the name of the sender. The first words of Lysias's letter were "Claudius Lysias." We, of course, do it the other way around, but I think the Roman method is better. That way we know before we begin reading who sent the letter.

Do you know what the first word of all thirteen recognized Pauline epistles is? It's "Paul." The apostle never violates the Roman method; he begins every letter with his own name. Beyond this, Paul often identifies himself in a way that positions him for writing the letter. This positioning varies from letter to letter. For instance, he calls himself a bond-servant of Christ Jesus (Rom. 1:1; Phil. 1:1), a prisoner of Christ Jesus (Philem. 1:1); an apostle of Jesus Christ (1 Cor. 1:1; 2 Cor. 1:1; Gal. 1:1; Eph. 1:1; Col. 1:1; 1 Tim. 1:1; 2 Tim. 1:1), and a bond-servant and an apostle (Tit. 1:1). He makes no identifying statement in the Thessalonian epistles.

Then Paul adds something to Roman letter writing—an expression of thanks for those to whom he writes. You will find expressions like "I thank my God through Jesus Christ for your all" (Rom. 1:8) or "We give thanks to God always for all of you" (1 Thess. 1:2) in most of his letters (see Rom. 1:8; 1 Cor. 1:4; Eph. 1:16; Phil 1:3; Col. 1:3; 1 Thess. 1:2; 2 Thess. 1:3; 2 Tim. 1:3; and Philem. 1:4). It is evident that even though Paul often had to reprimand or exhort the churches to which he wrote letters, he was truly their friend and was thankful for them.

The epistolary form Paul uses is thoroughly consistent with other authors of the New Testament era. He begins each of his epistles with his own name, gives his salutation, adds a note of thanksgiving for his readers (Galatians is the only exception), and then, in epistles dealing with theological problems, he launches into a doctrinal section followed by a practical section. Finally, he concludes with personal greetings and an autograph. This basic form does not essentially vary from epistle to epistle.

BIBLIOGRAPHY

Barrett, C. K. *Reading Through Romans.* Philadelphia: Fortress Press, 1977.

Bruce, F. F. *The Epistle of Paul to the Romans.* Tyndale New Testament Commentaries. Grand Rapids: Eerdmans, 1963.

Calvin, John. *Commentaries on the Epistle of Paul the Apostle to the Romans.* (Published 1539.) Translated and edited by John Owen. Grand Rapids: Eerdmans, 1947.

Cranfield, C. E. *Romans: A Shorter Commentary.* Grand Rapids: Eerdmans, 1985.

Denny, James. *St. Paul's Epistle to the Romans.* Expositor's Greek New Testament. Grand Rapids: Eerdmans, reprint, n.d.

Godet, Frederic. *Commentary on St. Paul's Epistle to the Romans.* Grand Rapids: Zondervan, n.d.

Haldane, Robert. *Exposition of the Epistle of the Romans.* London: Banner of Truth Trust, 1966.

Hendriksen, William. *Exposition of Paul's Epistle to the Romans.* New Testament Commentary. Grand Rapids: Baker Book House, 1981.

Hodge, Charles. *Commentary on the Epistle to the Romans.* Grand Rapids: Eerdmans, reprint, 1950.

Luther, Martin. *Commentary on Romans.* Grand Rapids: Kregel, 1976.

Morris, Leon. *The Epistle to the Romans.* Grand Rapids: Eerdmans, 1988.

Moule, H. G. C. *Romans.* The Expositor's Bible. Grand Rapids: Zondervan, n.d.

Mounce, Robert. *Romans.* New American Commentary. Nashville: Broadman & Holman, 1995.

Murray, John. *The Epistle to the Romans.* New International Commentary. Grand Rapids: Eerdmans, 1965.

Shedd, W. G. T. *A Critical and Doctrinal Commentary on the Epistle of St. Paul to the Romans.* Grand Rapids: Zondervan, 1967.

Stott, John. *Romans: God's Good News for the World.* Downers Grove, IL: InterVarsity Press, 1994.

NOTES

Introduction

1. Jack Finegan, *Light from the Ancient Past* (Princeton, NJ: Princeton University Press, 1946), 288.

2. Sir William Ramsay, *St. Paul the Traveller and the Roman Citizen* (Grand Rapids: Kregel, 2001), 1–10.

3. Theodor Zahn, *Introduction to the New Testament* (Minneapolis: Klock and Klock Christian Publishers, 1977), 422.

4. John Murray, *The Epistle to the Romans*, New International Commentary (Grand Rapids: Eerdmans, 1965), xv.

5. Adam W. Miller, *An Introduction to the New Testament* (Anderson, IN: Warner Press, 1972), 209.

6. Augustine, Confessions viii. 29.

7. Martin Luther, *Luther's Works*, Weimar edition, vol. 54 (Philadelphia: n.p., 1961), 179ff.

8. John Wesley, *Works*, vol. 1 (1872), 103.

9. James I. Packer, *Fundamentalism and the Word of God* (Grand Rapids: Eerdmans, 1984), 106ff.

Section I: Prologue (title page)

1. Fredric Godet, *Commentary on Romans* (Grand Rapids: Kregel, 1977), 1.

Chapter 1—Greetings to the Roman Christians

1. F. F. Bruce, *The Epistle of Paul to the Romans* (Grand Rapids: Eerdmans, 1963), 75.

Chapter 2—Paul's Desire to Visit Rome

1. Rome was heir to Greek culture and learning. Most people viewed Rome as a militarized extension of the Grecian empire. This is not to say that the Romans had no culture of their own, but that it was successfully synthesized with the Grecian so as to form a new culture, the Graeco-Roman. The Roman orator-author Cicero (106–43 b.c.) places Greece and Rome in the same category in his treatise *De Finis* (On Ends). He says, ". . . not only Greece and Italy, but also every foreign country." Therefore, Paul can readily say to the Romans that he is debtor both to the Greeks (Greek, *Hellenes*), including the Romans, and to the less civilized barbarians (Greek, *barbaroi*).

Chapter 3—Theme of the Letter: The Righteous Shall Live by Faith

1. Martin Luther, *Commentary on Romans* (Grand Rapids: Kregel, 1976), 41.

2. John A. Witmer, *Romans,* In the Bible Knowledge Commentary (Wheaton, IL: Victor Books, 1983), 441.

3. Charles C. Ryrie, *Balancing the Christian Life* (Chicago: Moody Press, 1994), 65.

Chapter 4—Immoral People Are Condemned

1. Paul minces no words about how God perceives human theories that discount the existence of God. He calls them "a lie." Literally, the expression is "the lie." Atheism is not an alternative belief system; it is "the lie." Secularism is not a simple elevation of man's world over God's world; it is "the lie." Humanism is not just dethroning God and enthroning man; it is "the lie." Evolution is not the scientific explanation of origins as opposed to creationism; God calls it "the lie."

2. Set your political correctness aside. Lay down your defenses, your secular education, and your "scientific" studies about homosexuality. Just read what God says. Read it carefully with an open mind. Look at the words. "Abandoned." "Natural function." "Burned in their desire." "Indecent acts." "Error." Is any of this unclear? Can any theological or politically correct sleight of hand change the evident meaning of these words? Although today the world seeks to popularize and legitimize homosexuality and illicit heterosexuality, both remain despicable to God and are always, without exception, condemned by Him.

Chapter 5—Moral People Are Condemned

1. William Hendriksen, *New Testament Commentary,* Exposition of Paul's Epistle to the Romans (Grand Rapids: Baker, 1981), 97.

Chapter 6—Jewish People Are Condemned

1. This is true of Christians today. People own Bibles (Barna Research says the average American owns at least three versions), and take them to church, but they are little impacted by them because they don't often read them. In an article in *Christianity Today*, Wheaton College professor Gary Burge confessed that half the freshman students entering this bastion of evangelical thought could not sequence Moses in Egypt, Isaac's birth, Saul's death, and Judah's exile ("The Greatest Story Never Read," *Christianity Today*, 9 August 1999, 45–49). George Gallup Jr. is right when he says, "Americans revere the Bible—but, by and large, they don't read it. And because they don't read it, they have become a nation of biblical illiterates" (George Gallup Jr. and Jim Castelli, *The People's Religion* (New York: Macmillan, 1989), 60). George Barna concludes, "This lack of Bible reading explains why Americans know so little about the Bible that is the basis of the faith of most of them" (*http.//www.barna.org*). For a full discussion of Bible illiteracy among Christians today, see Woodrow Kroll, *Back to the Bible* (Sisters, OR: Multnomah, 2000).

Chapter 7—All People Are Condemned

1. Webster's Ninth *New Collegiate Dictionary*, ed. Frederick C. Mish (Springfield, MA: Merriam-Webster, 1991), 614.

2. William Hendriksen, *Exposition of Paul's Epistle to the Romans*, New Testament Commentary (Grand Rapids: Baker, 1981), 125.

Chapter 8—Justification by Faith Explained

1. Alva J. McClain, *Romans: The Gospel of God's Grace* (Chicago: Moody Press, 1973), 107.

2. Karl Barth, *The Epistle to the Romans* (London: Oxford University Press, 1977), 99–100.

3. John Calvin, *Romans–Galatians, Calvin's Commentaries* (Wilmington, DE: Associated Publishers and Authors, n.d.), 1376.

Chapter 9—Justification by Faith Illustrated

1. With the statistics on record, it would be difficult to argue that the world has not been blessed by the Jewish people.
See *http://www.us-israel.org/jsource/Judaism/nobels.html*.

2. Robert Haldane, *Romans* (London: Banner of Truth Trust, 1966), 181.

Chapter 10–Justification by Faith Experienced

1. Robert Haldane, *Romans* (London: Banner of Truth Trust, 1966), 186.

2. Gerhard Kittel, ed., *Theological Dictionary of the New Testament*, vol. 3 (Grand Rapids: Eerdmans, 1965), 645–49.

3. William Barclay, *The Letter to the Romans* (Philadelphia: Westminster, 1957), 72.

4. Woodrow Kroll and George D. Miller III, *Hope Grows in Winter* (Grand Rapids: Kregel, 2000), 14, 15.

5. Notice the change from "justified by faith" to "justified by His blood." We should not make too much of this; there is really no difference in thought, only in expression. The demands of God's justice had to be satisfied, or we could not be declared righteous (see Is. 1:27; 53:4–6). Our justification required Christ's death (Luke 24:26, 27). Thus, while Christ's blood is the basis for our salvation, the exercise of faith is the means that brings that salvation. On the distinction, see Woodrow Kroll, *Seven Secrets to Spiritual Success* (Sisters, OR: Multnomah, 2000), 171–79.

6. C. S. Lewis, *Surprised by Joy*, as cited in *The Quotable Lewis*, Wayne Martindale and Jerry Root, ed. (Wheaton, IL: Tyndale House, 1989), 357.

Chapter 11–Justification by Faith Imputed

1. On the various interpretations of the imputation of Adam's sin, see John Murray, *The Imputation of Adam's Sin* (Phillipsburg, NJ: Presbyterian and Reformed, 1992).

2. Charles Hodge, *Commentary on the Epistle to the Romans* (Grand Rapids: Eerdmans, 1977), 174.

Chapter 12–Sanctification Explained in Principle

1. F. F. Bruce, *The Epistle of Paul to the Romans* (Grand Rapids: Eerdmans, 1963), 138.

2. Ibid., 139.

3. William Barclay, *The Letter to the Romans* (Philadelphia: Westminster, 1957), 87.

Chapter 13–Sanctification Explained in Practice

1. D. Martyn Lloyd-Jones, *Romans: The New Man* (Grand Rapids: Zondervan, 1973), 245.

2. William Barclay, *The Letter to the Romans* (Philadelphia: Westminster, 1957), 93.

3. Warren W. Wiersbe, *The Bible Exposition Commentary*, vol. 1 (Wheaton, IL: Victor, 1989), 533–34.

Chapter 14—Sanctification and the Demands of the Law

1. Charles Hodge, *Commentary on the Epistle to the Romans* (Grand Rapids: Eerdmans, 1977), 216.

2. Karl Barth, *The Epistle to the Romans* (London: Oxford University Press, 1977), 232.

3. David N. Steele and Curtis C. Thomas, *Romans: An Interpretive Outline* (Grand Rapids: Baker, 1963), 113.

Chapter 15—Sanctification and the Battle Within

1. John Calvin, *Romans–Galatians*, Calvin's Commentaries (Wilmington, DE: Associated Publishers and Authors, n.d.), 264.

2. D. Martyn Lloyd-Jones, *Romans: The New Man* (Grand Rapids: Zondervan, 1973), 1–13.

3. William Hendriksen, *Exposition of Paul's Epistle to the Romans*, New Testament Commentary (Grand Rapids: Baker, 1981), 228.

4. Theodore H. Epp, *How God Makes Bad Men Good* (Lincoln, NE: Back to the Bible, 1986), 195–96.

5. F. F. Bruce, *The Epistle of Paul to the Romans* (Grand Rapids: Eerdmans, 1963), 148.

6. Hendriksen, *Romans*, 221.

In his reference Bible, C. I. Scofield offers this plausible explanation of Paul's comments:

Paul's religious experience was three strongly marked phases: (1) He was a godly Jew under the law. That the passage does not refer to that period is clear from his own explicit statements elsewhere. At that time he held himself to be "blameless" as concerned the law (Phil. 3:6). He had "lived in all good conscience" (Acts 23:1). (2) With his conversion came new light upon the law itself. He now perceived it to be "spiritual" (v. 14). He now saw that, so far from having kept it, he was condemned by it. He had supposed himself to be "alive," but now the commandment really "came" (v. 9) and he "died." Just when the apostle passed through the experience of Rom. 7:7–25 we are not told. Perhaps it was during the days of physical blindness at Damascus (Acts 9:9); perhaps in Arabia (Gal. 1:17). It is the experience of a renewed man, under the law, and still ignorant of the delivering power of the Holy Spirit (cf. Rom. 8:2). (3) With the great revelations afterward embodied in Galatians and Romans, the apostle's experience entered its third phase. He now knew himself to be "dead to the law by the body of Christ," and, in the power of the indwelling Spirit, "free from the law of sin and death" (8:2); while "the righteousness of the law" was wrought in him (not by him) while he walked after the Spirit (8:4). Romans 7 is the record of past conflicts and defeats experienced as a renewed man under law. (*Oxford NIV Scofield Study Bible* [New York: Oxford University Press, 1967], 1184)

8. F. F. Bruce, *The Epistle of Paul to the Romans* (Grand Rapids: Eerdmans, 1963), 43–44.

9. Gleason L. Archer Jr., *The Epistle to the Romans* (Grand Rapids: Baker, 1974), 43.

Chapter 16—Sanctification and Freedom from Sin's Power

1. F. F. Bruce, *The Epistle of Paul to the Romans* (Grand Rapids: Eerdmans, 1963), 159.

2. James A. Stifler, *The Epistle to the Romans* (Chicago: Moody Press, 1974), 135–36.

Chapter 17—Sanctification and the Benefits of Sonship

1. William Barclay, *The Letter to the Romans* (Philadelphia: Westminster, 1957), 109–11.

2. Gleason L. Archer Jr. *The Epistle to the Romans* (Grand Rapids: Baker Book, 1974), 48.

3. For a complete explanation of what the Christian can expect as a result of the Judgment Seat of Christ, see Woodrow Kroll, *Tested by Fire* (Neptune, NJ: Loizeaux, 1977) and Paul Benware, *The Believer's Payday* (Chattanooga, TN: AMG Publishers, 2002).

Chapter 18—Sanctification and the Prospects for the Future

1. William Hendriksen, *Exposition of Paul's Epistle to the Romans*, New Testament Commentary (Grand Rapids: Baker, 1981), 47.

2. Martin Luther, *Lectures on Romans*, Luther's Works Weimar edition, vol. 26 (Philadelphia: n.p., 1961), 3–4.

Chapter 19—Sanctification and the Power of God

1. William Hendriksen, *Exposition of Paul's Epistle to the Romans*, New Testament Commentary (Grand Rapids: Baker, 1981), 291.

Chapter 20—The Sovereignty of God and Israel's Past

Primogenitureship is
the idea that the firstborn in any generation in a human family has leadership in the family for that generation. The right of primogeniture is assumed throughout the Old Testament text, even when at times because of God's special purposes the birthright is sold or otherwise transferred to a younger person (Gen. 25:27–34; 35:23; 38:27–30; 49:3–4; Deut. 21:15–17; 1 Chr. 5:1–2). The 'birthright' belongs to the firstborn son and is his unless special circumstances intervene to change that fact. (Wayne Grudem, *Systematic Theology* [Grand Rapids: Zondervan, 1994], 461).

2. See Kenneth S. Wuest, *Romans,* Wuest's Word Studies (Grand Rapids: Eerdmans, 1976), 160.

3. John Murray, *The Epistle to the Romans,* New International Commentary (Grand Rapids: Eerdmans, 1965), 22.

Chapter 21—The Responsibility of Man and Israel's Present

1. C. K. Barrett, *Reading Through Romans* (Philadelphia: Fortress Press, 1977), 56.

2. Here the King James Version reads, "How beautiful are the feet of them that preach the gospel of peace, and bring glad tidings of good things!" The difference arises from the fact that the KJV was translated from the Textus Receptus and the NASB, NIV, and others were translated from another family of manuscripts.

3. Martin Luther, *Commentary on Romans* (Grand Rapids: Kregel, 1976), 150–51.

4. Some manuscripts here say, "word of God," using the Greek *Theos.* Theologically there is no difference.

Chapter 22—The Purpose of God and Israel's Future

1. John Calvin, *Romans–Galatians,* Calvin's Commentaries (Wilmington, DE: Associated Publishers and Authors, n.d.), 1473.

2. Chart created by Warren Baker. Used by permission.

3. Craig S. Keener, *The IVP Bible Background Commentary: New Testament* (Downers Grove, IL: InterVarsity Press, 1993), 437.

4. Theodore Epp explains:
The Church, or Body of Christ, came into existence when the nation Israel rejected Jesus Christ as its Messiah. Because of this rejection, God temporarily set aside His program for Israel and turned to the Gentiles to "take out of them a people for his name" (Acts 15:14). . . . . It is clear from Acts 15 that after

God is through with His program for the Church, He will then complete His program for Israel: "And to this agree the words of the prophets; as it is written, After this I will return, and will build again in the tabernacle of David, which is fallen down; and I will build again the ruins thereof, and I will set it up" (vv. 15–16). So after the Church is taken out of the earth God will finish His program for Israel. . . . During the Tribulation God will be dealing with Israel for refusing the Kinsman-Redeemer He provided. Because the nation Israel rejected Christ as its Messiah, it will pass through the Tribulation and will be broken and sifted by God. Then the nation will be saved and finally reestablished in its land. (Theodore H. Epp, *Practical Studies in Revelation* [Lincoln, NE: Back to the Bible, 1970], 89–90).

5. A sample of the diversity in opinion as to the meaning of "all Israel will be saved" is as follows. Charles Erdman says, "He is pointing to a time when Gentile kingdoms and the people of Israel shall be united in the blessings of a redeemed world" (Charles R. Erdman, *The Epistle of Paul to the Romans* [Philadelphia: Westminster Press, 1975], 127–28). Gleason Archer: "In the end there shall be a wonderful re-gathering of the whole family of God, comprising all of Israel, both the physical posterity who have become converted to Christianity and those Gentiles who have by conversion become Abraham's spiritual posterity" (Gleason L. Archer, Jr., *The Epistle to the Romans* [Grand Rapids: Baker Book House, 1959], 73). Kenneth Wuest: "By all Israel being saved, Paul means the individual salvation of each member of the nation Israel living at the time of the second Advent" (Kenneth S. Wuest, *Romans in the Greek New Testament* [Grand Rapids: Eerdmans, 1955], 199–200). Warren Wiersbe: "'All Israel shall be saved' does not mean that every Jew who has ever lived will be converted, but that the Jews living when the Redeemer returns will see Him, receive Him, and be saved" (Warren W. Wiersbe, *The Bible Exposition Commentary*, Vol. 1 [Wheaton, Illinois: Victor Books, 1994], 552–53). Steele and Thomas: "The day will come when God will bring all Israel (the physical nation) into the blessings of the New Covenant by bringing the individual members of the nation living at the time to faith in Christ, and thus 'all Israel will be saved'" (David N. Steele and Curtis C. Thomas, *Romans: An Interpretive Outline* [Grand Rapids: Baker Book House, 1963], 98). James Stifler: "The illogical notion that 'Israel' here is the spiritual Israel is no longer held. It is the fallen, rejected, natural Israel, the only nation in this age that has the promise of salvation as a whole. It will not be merely Christianized, but Christian" (James A. Stifler, *The Epistle to the Romans* [Chicage: Moody Press, 1974], 196). W. H. Griffith Thomas: "The word 'all' in this verse refers to Jew and Gentile viewed in the mass, and not individually. It is necessary to keep in mind the fact that 'all' in some passages means 'all without exception,' and in others 'all without distinction.' It has the latter meaning here" (W. H. Griffith Thomas, *St. Paul's Epistle to the Romans* [Grand Rapids: Eerdmans, 1946], 305). John Calvin: "Many understand this of the

Jewish people . . . but I extend the word Israel to all the people of God. . . . Paul intended here to set forth the completion of the kingdom of Christ, which is by no means to be confined to the Jews, but is to include the whole world" (John Calvin, *Calvin's Commentaries, Romans—Galatians* [Wilmington, Delaware: Associated Publishers and Authors, n.d.], 1484). Martin Luther at first believed in the final conversion of all Jews but then modified his belief to emphasize that only the elect of Israel will be saved, an expression that corresponds to the expression "the fulness of the Gentiles" (Martin Luther, *Commentary on Romans* [Grand Rapids: Kregel Publications, 1976], 162).

6. Steven A. Kreloff, *God's Plan for Israel* (Neptune, NJ.: Loizeaux, 1995), 93.

Chapter 23—Living a Life of Sacrifice

1. Karl Barth, *The Epistle to the Romans* (London: Oxford University Press, 1977), 427.

2. Charles R. Erdman, *The Epistle of Paul to the Romans* (Philadelphia: Westminster, 1925), 131.

3. Kenneth L. Barker and John Kohlenberger III, *Zondervan NIV Bible Commentary*, vol. 2 (Grand Rapids: Zondervan, 1994), 583.

4. Ray C. Stedman, *Expository Studies in Romans 9–16* in From Guilt to Glory, vol. 2 (Waco, TX: Word, 1978), 100.

5. Prophesying, in the biblical sense, doesn't resemble much of what is pawned off in the church today as prophetic utterance. Biblical prophesying was not at all akin to the ecstatic utterance of the Greek mystery religions. Nor was it the ability to predict future events. The prophet was enabled by God to receive divine revelation and to speak or write what God revealed (Eph. 2:20; 3:5: 4:11, 20–21; 1 Cor. 14:3, 26, 30). The prophet ministered to the spiritual needs of the congregation (1 Cor. 14:3), not by explaining God's Word and making application—that's the task of the preacher—but by revealing truth that had previously been unknown. Charles Hodge comments, "The gift of which Paul here speaks, is not, therefore, the faculty of predicting future events, but that of immediate occasional inspiration, leading the recipient to deliver, as the mouth of God, the particular communication which he had received, whether designed for instruction, exhortation, or comfort" (Charles Hodge, *Commentary on the Epistle to the Romans* [Grand Rapids: Eerdmans, 1977], 390).

The ministry of those first-century believers who had the gift of prophecy is preserved for us in the New Testament. There are no prophetic additions today to that of these inspired prophets. Christian doctrine today is not to be based on "prophetic utterances," "words from God," or any other claims to be speaking for God, because we have received the body of faith once for all delivered to the saints (Jude 1:3).

Chapter 24—Living a Life of Service

1. In Romans 9:13, Paul chooses a different word for "hate." There it is *miseō*. See the discussion on 9:13 for both the active or proactive meaning of hatred and the passive or comparative meaning of the word.

2. The concept of agape indicates that believers are to have God's benevolent love for one another. Paul uses this word no fewer than eighty times in his epistles, most of which refer to the Christian's mutual love. In Romans the word occurs only nine times and does not have the same high percentage of meaning "brother-love."

3. Alexander Pope, *An Essay on Man* (1734) (Menston, England: The Scholar Press Limited, 1969), 11.

4. Paul has an uncanny way of sensing points of tension in his writing. Every time the potential comes up for stress or disagreement, Paul adds the affectionate appellative "beloved." He also uses the term when he wants to highlight the worthy quality of an individual. Notice his pattern in Rom. 1:7; 16:5, 8, 9, 12; 1 Cor. 4:14, 17; 10:14; 15:58; 2 Cor. 7:1; 12:19; Eph. 5:1; 6:21; Phil. 2:12; 4:1; Col. 1:7; 4:7, 9, 14; 1 Thess. 1:4; 2:8; 2 Thess. 2:13; 1 Tim. 6:2; 2 Tim. 1:2; and Philem. 1:1, 2, 16.

5. Kenneth S. Wuest, *Romans,* Wuest's Word Studies (Grand Rapids: Eerdmans, 1976), 220.

Chapter 25—Living a Life of Submission

1. F. F. Bruce, *The Epistle of Paul to the Romans* (Grand Rapids: Eerdmans, 1963) 234.

2. William Hendriksen, *Exposition of Paul's Epistle to the Romans,* New Testament Commentary (Grand Rapids: Baker, 1981), 433.

3. William Barclay, *The Letter to the Romans* (Philadelphia: Westminster, 1957), 189.

4. Charles W. Kegley and Robert W. Bretall, *Reinhold Niebuhr: His Religious, Social, and Political Thought* (New York: Macmillan, 1956), 69–70.

Chapter 26—Living a Life of Sensitivity

1. Also see Daniel 1:8–16; the noncanonical books of Tobit 1:101–2; 1 Maccabees 1:62; 2 Maccabees 7; and the Jewish historian Josephus, Antiquities IV.vi.8.

F. F. Bruce writes:

The buying of butcher-meat in pagan cities such as Corinth and Rome presented some Christians with a conscientious problem. Much of the flesh exposed for sale in the market came from animals that had originally been sacrificed to a pagan deity. The pagan deity received his token portion; the rest of the flesh might be sold by the temple authorities to the retail merchants, and many pagan purchasers might be willing to pay a little more for their meat because it had been "consecrated" to some deity. Among the Christians there were some with a robust conscience who knew that the meat was neither better nor worse for its association with the pagan deity, and were quite happy to eat it; others were not so happy about it, and felt that somehow the meat had become "infected" by its idolatrous associations. (F. F. Bruce, *The Epistle of Paul to the Romans* [Grand Rapids: Eerdmans, 1963], 249).

3. Bruce Corley and Curtis Vaughan, *Romans: A Study Guide Commentary* (Grand Rapids: Zondervan, 1976), 151.

4. William R. Newell, *Romans Verse by Verse* (Chicago: Moody Press, 1948), 506.

5. John G. Mitchell, *Right with God: A Devotional Study of the Epistle to the Romans* (Portland, OR: Multnomah, 1990), 255–56. For a complete study of the Judgment Seat of Christ—where, when, who is the Judge, who are judged, what are the criteria, what are the rewards?—see Woodrow Kroll, *Tested By Fire* (Neptune, NJ: Loizeaux, 1977) and Paul Benware, *The Believer's Payday* (Chattanooga, TN: AMG Publishers, 2002).

6. F. F. Bruce, *The Epistle of Paul to the Romans* (Grand Rapids: Eerdmans, 1963), 246.

7. Ray C. Stedman, *Expository Studies in Romans 9—16*, cited in From Guilt to Glory, vol. 2 (Waco, TX: Word, 1978), 152.

Chapter 27—Paul's Future Plans

1. William Hendriksen, *Exposition of Paul's Epistle to the Romans*, New Testament Commentary (Grand Rapids: Baker, 1981), 484.

2. Hendriksen, *Romans*, 487.

3. William R. Newell, *Romans Verse by Verse* (Chicago: Moody Press, 1948), 539.

4. Dale Moody, *Romans*, Broadman Bible Commentary, vol. 10 (Nashville: Broadman Press, 1970), 227.

Chapter 28—Paul's Personal Greetings

1. Ray C. Stedman, *Expository Studies in Romans 9—16*, cited in From Guilt to Glory, vol. 2 (Waco, TX: Word, 1978), 182.

2. Prisca is a diminutive of Priscilla. She is the same woman frequently mentioned engaged in Christian work with her husband. See Acts 18:2, 18, 26; Rom. 16:3; 1 Cor. 16:19; 2 Tim. 4:19.

3. Dale Moody, *Romans, Broadman Bible Commentary,* vol. 10 (Nashville:

Broadman Press, 1970), 280.

4. "Asia" in the New Testament is always a designation for Asia Minor, modern Turkey.

Theodor Zahn notes:

The Roman Church did not have a founder in the same sense as did the Church in Ephesus or Corinth. . . . If so, Paul could not have remained entirely silent regarding such a person when speaking of the teaching to which the readers owed their conversion (6:17; 15:17). The first trace that we have of the presence of Christianity in Rome is the vague statement of Suetonius regarding the banishment of the Jews from Rome by the emperor Claudius, which occurred probably in or shortly before the year 52. Since the Jews were banished by this decree only from Rome, not from Italy, many may have remained in the vicinity of the city. Others, like Aquila, left the country altogether, not, however, before they had at least heard of Christ. Soon after the death of Claudius (Oct. 54) the Jews returned again to Rome in large numbers, and under Nero regained their old rights. . . . Among the Jews who during the three years prior to the composition of Romans returned to Rome or migrated thither were Christians from Palestine. Andronicus and Junias, Rufus and his mother, were not the only ones of this kind. . . . Andronicus and Junias became Christians even before Paul. (Theodor Zahn, *Introduction to the New Testament*, vol. 1 [Minneapolis: Klock and Klock, 1977], 427).

6. William Barclay, *The Letter to the Romans* (Philadelphia: Westminster, 1957), 232.

F. F. Bruce, *The Epistle of Paul to the Romans* (Grand Rapids: Eerdmans, 1963), 274–75. William Barclay also relates the possibility suggested by Bruce.

There is one of the great hidden romances of the New Testament behind the name of Rufus and of his mother, who was also a mother to Paul. It is obvious that Rufus is a choice spirit and a man well-known for work and saintliness in the Roman Church; and it is equally obvious that Paul felt that he owed a deep debt of gratitude to the mother of Rufus for the kindness that he had received from her. Who was this Rufus? Turn back to Mark 15:21. There we read of one Simon a Cyrenian who was compelled to carry the Cross of Jesus on the road to Calvary; and this Simon is described as the father of Alexander and Rufus. Now if a man is identified by the names of his sons, it means that, although he himself may not be personally known to the community to whom the story is being told, the sons are. To what church did Mark write his gospel? Almost certainly he wrote it for the church of Rome, and he knew that the church would know who Alexander and Rufus were. And again almost certainly here we find Rufus again. He was the son of that Simon who carried the Cross of Jesus. . . . We can weave all kinds of speculations about this. It was men from Cyprus and Cyrene who came to Antioch and who first preached the gospel to the Gentile world (Acts 11:20). Was Simon one of the men from Cyrene? Was Rufus with him? Was it they who took the first tremendous step to make Christianity the faith of a whole world? Was it they who helped the Church to burst the bonds of Judaism in which it might have been fettered? Can it be that in some sense we today owe the fact that we are Christians to the strange episode when a man from Cyrene was compelled to carry a cross on the road to Calvary? Turn to Ephesus when there is a riot raised by the people who served Diana of the Ephesians and when the crowd would have lynched Paul if they could have got at him. Who stands out to look that mob in the face? A man called Alexander (Acts 19:33). Is this the other brother facing things out with Paul? And as for their mother—surely she in some hour of need must have brought to Paul the help and the comfort and the love, which his own family refused him when he became a Christian. It may be guesswork, for the names Alexander and Rufus are common names; but maybe it is true and maybe the most amazing things happened form that chance encounter on the way to Calvary. (William Barclay, *The Letter to the Romans* [Philadelphia: Westminster, 1957], 235–36).

William Barclay relates:

There remains one other name that may have a perhaps even more amazing story behind it—the name of Nereus. In a.d. 95 there happened an event that shocked Rome. Two of the most distinguished people in Rome were condemned for being Christians. They were husband and wife. The husband was Flavius Clemens. He had been consul of Rome. The wife was Domatilla and she was of royal blood. She was the granddaughter of Vespasian, a former Emperor, and the niece of Domitian the reigning Emperor. In fact the two sons of Flavius Clemens and Domatilla had been designated Domitian's successors in the imperial power. Flavius was executed and Domatilla was banished to the island of Pontia where years afterwards Paula saw the cave where "she drew out a long martyrdom for the Christian name." And now the point—the name of the chamberlain of Flavius and Domatilla was Nereus. Is it possible that Nereus the slave had something to do with the making into Christians of Flavius Clemens the ex-consul and Domatilla the princess of the royal blood? Again maybe it is an idle speculation, for Nereus is a common name, but again, maybe it is true. (William Barclay, *The Letter to the Romans* [Philadelphia: Westminster, 1957], 237).

9. Gleason L. Archer Jr. *The Epistle to the Romans* (Grand Rapids: Baker, 1974), 101.

10. Ray C. Stedman, *Expository Studies in Romans 9—16*, cited in From Guilt to Glory, vol. 2 (Waco, TX: Word, 1978), 193.

Chapter 29—Doxology

1. George Vanderlip, *Paul and Romans* (Valley Forge, PA.: Judson Press, 1967), 111.

About the Author

Dr. **Woodrow Kroll** is president and senior Bible teacher of Back to the Bible. He is best known for his teaching on the *Back to the Bible* broadcast, heard or translated daily on more than nine hundred radio stations around the world. This broadcast, in one of twenty-five languages, can be heard by fifty percent of the world's population every day. He is also the speaker on the daily radio short feature *The Bible Minute* and the weekly television program also called *Back to the Bible*.

Dr. Kroll has written more than three dozen books, including *Seven Secrets to Spiritual Success, The Vanishing Ministry in the Twenty-First Century,* and *Surviving the Prodigals in Your Life: Stories of Courage and Hope.* Dr. Kroll's clear, incisive, and practical teaching of the Bible is widely appreciated throughout the world. "My greatest privilege," says Woodrow Kroll, "is preaching the Word of God." He and his wife, Linda, reside in Ashland, Nebraska, near the international headquarters of Back to the Bible.

Dr. **Mal Couch** is founder and president of Tyndale Theological Seminary and Biblical Institute in Fort Worth, Texas. He previously taught at Philadelphia College of the Bible, Moody Bible Institute, and Dallas Theological Seminary. His other publications include *The Hope of Christ's Return: A Premillennial Commentary on 1 and 2 Thessalonians, A Bible Handbook to Revelation,* and *Dictionary of Premillennial Theology.*

Dr. **Edward Hindson** is assistant chancellor, professor of religion, and dean of the Institute of Biblical Studies at Liberty University in Lynchburg, Virginia. He has authored more than twenty books, served as coeditor of several Bible projects, and was one of the translators for the New King James Version of the Bible. Dr. Hindson has served as a visiting lecturer at both Oxford University and Harvard Divinity School as well as numerous evangelical seminaries. He has taught more than fifty thousand students in the past twenty-five years.